TALKING TO A STRANGER

FOUR TELEVISION PLAYS BY
JOHN HOPKINS

PENGUIN BOOKS

Penguin Books Ltd, Harmondsworth, Middlesex, England
Penguin Books Inc., 3300 Clipper Mill Road, Baltimore, Md 21211, U.S.A.
Penguin Books Australia Ltd., Ringwood, Victoria, Australia

—

First published 1967

—

Copyright © John Hopkins 1967

—

Made and printed in Great Britain by
Hazell Watson & Viney Ltd
Aylesbury, Bucks
Set in Monotype Baskerville

All rights whatsoever in these plays are strictly reserved
and all inquiries concerning performance or readings
throughout the world should be made in advance to
Terence Baker, Richard Hatton Ltd, 17A Curzon Street,
London W1.

Each of these plays is self-contained as well as being a part of the complete work, *Talking to a Stranger*. Casts of each play and details of first transmissions immediately precede each of the four plays.

CONTENTS

PART ONE

ANY TIME YOU'RE READY, I'LL SPARKLE

First transmitted by Theatre 625 on B.B.C.-2 on 2 October 1966 with the following cast:

TERRY	Judi Dench
MOTHER	Margery Mason
FATHER	Maurice Denham
ALAN	Michael Bryant
JESS	Pinkie Johnstone
GORDON	Emrys James
LAWRENCE	Timothy Carlton
LEONARD	Calvin Lockhart
CHILD'S VOICE	Gaynor Jones
WAITER	Ricki Patterson
BARMAN	Bill Richards
COUPLE AT TABLE	Ron Gregory
	Elaine Jenks
TWO MEN IN CLUB	Richard Baker
	Colin Daily
LADY IN CLUB	Dian Anthony
MAN IN LAUNDERETTE	Michael Stephens

Story Editor	James Brabazon
Designer	Richard Wilmot
Produced by	Michael Bakewell
Directed by	Christopher Morahan

FADE IN *Terry Stephens' bedroom in a basement flat in London.*
[*Looking up into* TERRY'S *face.*

   *She is lying on her side in the bed, with the bedclothes
pulled up under her chin. Her eyes are wide open and she is
staring blankly at the wall beside the bed. She is huddled
into the corner of the bed, with her knees pulled up against
her stomach.*

   *The curtains are drawn across the window and the room
is shadowy, half-dark.*]

CUT TO FILM: *Looking down the side slopes of Whipsnade Zoo,
out across the countryside below, showing through the heat haze.*
   The sound of children laughing.

CUT TO *Terry's bedroom.*
   [*Looking close into* TERRY'S *eyes.*
      The sound of children laughing.]
CHILD'S VOICE [*rhythmically*]: I'll swing so high, I'll kick
the sky.

CUT TO FILM: *Looking through the wild and scrambling activity
of a children's playground.*
   *Children, between the ages of one and four, run, dig in the sandpit,
push the roundabout, climb the metal climbing frame, slide and
swing.*
   The sound of children laughing.
CHILD'S VOICE: I'll kick the sky and make it cry.

CUT TO *Terry's bedroom.*
   [*High shot, looking down at the double bed, framing it
exactly with* TERRY *in the top right-hand corner.*
      The sound of children laughing.
      The bedroom door creaks slightly as JESS *pushes it open
and looks into the room.*

11

Cut to TERRY'*s face in close-up as her eyes click shut and the sound of children laughing stops, abruptly.*
Silence.]

JESS [*quietly*]: Terry?

[*Silence.*]

Terry, love – are you . . .

TERRY [*briskly*]: Yes, I am.

[*Pull back as* TERRY *opens her eyes again, throws back the bedclothes, swings her legs out of bed and looks over her shoulder at* JESS.]

JESS: I didn't mean . . .

TERRY: 'S all right. [*Automatically,* TERRY *reaches for her transistor radio, which she keeps on the bedside table, a small whitewood table, unpainted. The radio is not there.*] Damn!

[*Dramatically,* TERRY *slumps and thinks.*

TERRY *is thirty years old. She is attractive, but not beautiful. She has black hair, a slight heaviness in the chin, a full mouth and brown eyes, which open shafts of darkness into her face.*]

SUPERIMPOSE TITLE: *Any time you're ready, I'll sparkle*

FADE TITLE.

TERRY [*suddenly*]: Yes, of course!

[TERRY *stands up and walks round the end of the bed towards the bedroom door and* JESS. TERRY *is wearing a nightdress.*

JESS *is wearing a dressing gown over pyjamas. She is twenty-three years old, small and mid-brown; hair, face, complexion and manner.*]

'Scuse me. [TERRY *touches* JESS *lightly on the shoulder as she walks past her and smiles.* TERRY *walks across the hall to the bathroom door and goes in. The transistor radio is standing on the edge of the bath.* TERRY *walks along the side of the bath and bends to pick it up. As she straightens up again, the room spins and* TERRY *lurches sideways, reaching for the wall.*]

[*Quietly*] Wheee!

[*She shakes her head abruptly and pushes away from the wall, turning towards the door.*

JESS *is standing in the doorway.*]

[*Grinning*] Must take more water with it. [TERRY *switches on the transistor radio, tuning it to the Light Programme.*] When I came in last night – just remembered – I had a bath. [*She walks back along the side of the bath.*] Needed a bath! Grubby hands – well, it's a grubby world. But dirt – actual dirt! – under his finger nails. Eeech! [*She acts a shudder, standing in the doorway, facing* JESS.]

[*Camp*] You just don't know where they've been! Oh, now – Jess! Don't look at me like that. I mean ... [*She lifts her hands up in front of her face, supplicating.*]

[*Tragic*] Is it my fault? Misguided – too young to know. Mistaken – too proud to listen. Misled – careless of danger! Misunderstood – misjudged – misbegotten! [TERRY *presses one hand against the wall beside her.*] If we're going to spend a lot of time in here, it might be an idea to have the wall taken out. Anyway ... [*She pats* JESS *gently on the cheek.*] You love me really. You know you do.

[JESS *steps back into the hall, as* TERRY *bursts out of the bathroom, the radio swinging in one hand, playing full blast.*]

TERRY: What's the time?

JESS: Ten o'clock, I think. Just gone.

TERRY: The exact time!

JESS: I don't know.

[TERRY *walks quickly into the bedroom and round the bed.*]

TERRY: Busy day today. Lots of things to do. Must know the time.

[JESS *follows* TERRY *as far as the doorway.*]

JESS: Sunday. It's Sunday, you know.

TERRY: Yes, love. Yes, I know it's Sunday. What I don't know ... [*She turns and looks across the room at* JESS.]

JESS [*mumbling*]: I didn't put my watch on. Sorry.

[JESS *turns and walks quickly away to her own bedroom.*
    TERRY *puts the transistor radio down on the bedside*

table, shifting an empty cup across its saucer, nearly knocking it on to the floor. She steadies herself, lifts the radio and puts it down behind the cup.]

CUT TO *close-up of a tea cup. Looking straight down at the tea leaves in an empty cup.*

MOTHER'S VOICE: There you are! You see. Those leaves – there – on the left.

Zoom down into the centre of the empty tea cup.

TERRY'S VOICE: Yes, I see them.

MOTHER'S VOICE [*triumphantly*]: A tall dark stranger.

The sound of Terry laughing.

CUT TO *Terry's bedroom.*

    [*Long shot across the width of the bedroom, holding* TERRY *small against the neutral wall behind her.*]

JESS'S VOICE: It's twelve minutes past.

TERRY [*laughing*]: One thing about my mother!

JESS'S VOICE: Exactly!

    [*Push forward towards* TERRY *as she walks away from the wall.*]

TERRY: Past ten?

JESS'S VOICE: What about your mother?

    [TERRY *turns her head and looks at* JESS.]

TERRY [*irritably*]: Twelve minutes past ten?

JESS: Yes.

    [TERRY *turns and looks at the bed.*]

What about your mother?

TERRY: She's a dab hand with tea leaves. Something to do with her gipsy blood.

JESS: Is she?

TERRY: What?

JESS: Your mother. Is she a gipsy?

TERRY: No. [TERRY *reaches down and scoops up the blankets. She drags them up across the bed.*] Too late to worry about you.

JESS: I thought you said . . .

TERRY: I did. Yes. It'd be fun, wouldn't it? Sitting round the fires – smoke – and evening skies. Sleeping in a cara-

van – all those fantastic colours! Blues and reds – yellows
– gold! [*She drops down on to her knees beside the bed.*]

JESS: All right if it doesn't rain.

TERRY: I look like a gipsy. Don't you think? [*She scrambles
under the bed, searching for her handbag.*]

JESS: I suppose – I never thought about it – but – well, yes,
you're dark.

TERRY [*quickly*]: But I can pass! [TERRY *pulls her handbag
out and sits back against the bed.*]

JESS: What d'you say?

TERRY: Funny – gipsies – you know? They're like the
Wandering Jew.

JESS: What?

[TERRY *looks in her handbag for her compact.*]

TERRY: Didn't you know that?

JESS: I haven't got the faintest idea . . .

TERRY: Jesus was on his way to Calvary – right?

JESS [*grinning*]: Yes? [JESS *sits on the end of the bed.*]

TERRY: With his cross – the whole bit – and he was tired.
He wanted a bit of a rest. But this bloke – er . . . [*She
lifts her head and looks at* JESS *silently for a moment.*]

JESS: I don't know . . .

TERRY: Ahasueras.

JESS: Oh.

TERRY: He said – no – Jesus couldn't rest there. Not outside
his house. 'Shove off' he said. And Jesus said – what is it?
'Truly I go away, and that quickly, but tarry thou till I
come.'

[*Silence.*]

So – there he is – waiting. [TERRY *looks at her face in the
mirror of her compact.*]

JESS [*hesitantly*]: Ahasueras?

TERRY: Eeech! This is one of my really ugly days! [*She
shuts her compact with a snap and drops it back into her handbag.*]
Sometimes – good days – I look at myself and I think –
you could go a long way and not find a pair of eyes . . .
[*She shakes her head bitterly.*] Then I look at the skin round
my eyes – d'you see? [*She turns her head and looks up at*

JESS.] All stretched – and the lines! I mean – yes, all right – laugh lines – but who needs them!

JESS: I think you're beautiful.

TERRY: Did I ever tell you about the girl – oh, really! What was her name? It's got so if I don't write it down ... [TERRY *snaps her fingers*.] Sarah. She used to work in the office. Don't know where she is now. Running her own nursery school if half the stories were true. She said – you won't believe this. We were having lunch – cup of coffee and a wimpy – without the bun. [TERRY *holds up her hands in horror*.] Buns are fattening! They're not the only thing. She said – 'Terry, do you know what it's like to be nearly beautiful?'

JESS: I don't believe it.

TERRY: Oh, she was a virus infection, that one! 'Nearly beautiful'! She had the most perfect face you ever saw – but – the most perfect! Made you sick. Like she never got spots. [TERRY *stands up and puts her handbag down on the bed*.] There's another story says it was a man called Kartophilos.

JESS: Who – was?

TERRY: He worked for Pontius Pilate. Told Jesus to get a move on – and Jesus said ... [TERRY *stretches and runs her hands through her hair*.] Oh – much the same thing. Where was I last night?

JESS: I was wondering.

TERRY: My hair! [TERRY *looks at her fingers and then rubs the tips together, wearing an expression of deep distaste*.] Maybe I was tarred and feathered. Was I, Jess – tarred and feathered?

JESS: I don't know. I was asleep when you came in.

TERRY: You're a lot of good. Feels like tar. Probably that new lacquer. 'Lets your natural colour show through.' I wish I didn't believe absolutely everything absolutely everyone tells me! I suppose I could wash it.

JESS: Looks perfectly all right.

TERRY: Oh, you're joking! I could go back to bed. I feel like going back to bed.

JESS: What's to stop you?

[*Silence.*]

TERRY [*abruptly*]: Things to do, love. Bustle, bustle, bustle!

JESS: I'm sorry I disturbed you.

TERRY: Just as well you did.

JESS: I didn't mean you should get up.

TERRY: What are you doing today?

JESS: Nothing. Well, I thought ... [JESS *shrugs and grins.*] Nothing.

TERRY: Go and see my mother?

JESS: What?

TERRY: Tell her I would've come myself – I was going to – then I decided to spend the day in bed.

JESS: Are you serious?

TERRY: She'll believe you. Tell her that, love – she'll believe you.

JESS: I don't know your mother.

TERRY: She'll love you.

[*Silence.*]

'I am going, but thou shalt tarry till I come again.' That's what he said.

JESS: You're going to see your mother today?

TERRY: That's right. [TERRY *rubs a hand across her stomach.*] Shall we go on a diet? I will, if you will?

JESS: Well, I don't know. Should you?

TERRY [*abruptly*]: What d'you mean?

JESS: You're not – fat – overweight. Not so I can see.

TERRY: You must be blind. [TERRY *pushes and pulls at her body, arms, thighs and waist.*]

JESS: If you don't need to – what's the point ...

TERRY [*plaintively*]: If any of it was in any of the right places! [TERRY *slaps herself on the bottom.*] Look at it! Honestly, there's enough there for two reasonably sized human beings.

JESS: Nonsense.

TERRY: It's all right for you. You look at you in the mornings. I have to look at me. Eeech!

[TERRY *shambles across to the door of the bedroom and* JESS *stands up.*]

[*Abruptly*] What d'you think you're going to do?

JESS [*guilty*]: Oh. Well, I thought . . .

TERRY: Leave it.

JESS: It won't take a moment.

TERRY [*cold*]: Leave it.

JESS: While you're in the bathroom.

TERRY [*hard*]: Don't make my bed.

JESS: All right.

TERRY: What are you doing in my room?

> [*Silence.*]

Did I ask you to come in?

JESS: No.

TERRY: You know the rules. You do know the rules?

JESS: Yes.

TERRY: By invitation – only.

JESS: Sorry.

> [*Silence*].

TERRY: Anyway, if you waste time making my bed, who's going to make my breakfast?

CUT TO *the kitchen of Mr and Mrs Stephens' house in the London suburbs.*

> [*Close shot of frying-pan and the egg in it, frying.*]

MOTHER'S VOICE: One egg or two?

TERRY'S VOICE: Two. What? Oh, no, make – one. I don't know.

> [*Pull back to include* MOTHER *as she turns to look at* TERRY. *She is several years younger than in the previous scene.*]

MOTHER: Make up your mind.

TERRY: Since when have I had any choice!

> [TERRY *is sitting at the kitchen table with a bowl of cornflakes in front of her, untouched.*]

MOTHER: It's a long time since you've been home, Terry. I hardly know you any more.

TERRY: It's a long time since I've been here. Home – that's another place altogether.

MOTHER: This will always be your home.

TERRY: Your home.

MOTHER: One egg or two?

TERRY: I haven't – look I haven't 'come home'.

MOTHER: You're here.

TERRY: Somewhere. I had to go somewhere. I couldn't stay – there.

MOTHER: No.

TERRY: Yes. Oh, yes! 'I told you so.'

[MOTHER *looks at* TERRY *and shakes her head, reproachfully.*]

You don't have to say it.

MOTHER: I wouldn't say it.

TERRY [*harshly*]: You don't have to.

MOTHER: Eat your cornflakes.

TERRY: I don't eat cornflakes for breakfast. Not any more. [TERRY *pushes the bowl of cornflakes to one side.*] As you said – it's been a long time.

[MOTHER *puts the plate with the egg and the rasher of bacon on it, down in front of* TERRY.]

MOTHER: Did he do that?

[*Automatically,* TERRY *puts her hand up to her face, half covering her left eye, which is slightly bruised.*]

TERRY: No, I banged – walked – into a door. I wasn't looking where . . .

[*Silence.*]

Yes, he did.

MOTHER: You can stay as long as you like. You know that. [MOTHER *straightens up and turns back to the gas stove.*]

TERRY: Yes, I know that.

MOTHER: Your father's pleased as Punch.

TERRY: I thought he loved me.

MOTHER: Your father misses you, Terry. He's always talking about you.

TERRY: I loved him.

MOTHER: 'Where's Terry? When is she coming to see us?'

TERRY: And then – I don't know – I mean, what happened?

MOTHER: You know how he goes on.

TERRY: Do you miss me?

[MOTHER *turns and looks at* TERRY.]

MOTHER: Oh, Terry – really! Now you've let it get cold. What is the good of making you a hot breakfast . . .
          [*Push in towards* TERRY.]
   . . . going to all that trouble – if you just sit there and let it get cold!

JESS'S VOICE: They'll be surprised to see you.

CUT TO *the kitchen of the basement flat.*
          [JESS *is standing at the kitchen table pouring a cup of tea for* TERRY.]

JESS: When was the last time you went to visit them?

TERRY: A remedy against sin. Did you know that? [TERRY *reaches across and takes the cup clumsily.*]

JESS: Careful!

TERRY: A remedy against – ha! I didn't know what sin was. Sin! You know? Till it was part of life. I mean, you fancy a bit – and if it isn't the bit you're supposed to fancy! Toast?

JESS: It's all gone.

TERRY: Shall we make some more? Shall we? [TERRY *picks up the milk jug and looks into it.*] Sin! 'Such persons as have not the gift of continence.' One or two of them, I can tell you – most of them married. No milk.

JESS: It's in the fridge.

TERRY: I have to fetch it myself!

JESS: Yes.

TERRY: It's all go. [TERRY *stands up and walks round the corner of the table towards the refrigerator.*] Toast?

JESS: Bread is very fattening.

TERRY: Yes, I know.

JESS: You don't want to get fat.

TERRY: That was before. Doesn't look so bad now. [*Desperately*] Does it?

JESS: Perfect it looks.

TERRY: You're such a comfort. [TERRY *opens the refrigerator and takes out a half-pint bottle of milk.*] I think they should change it.

JESS: Has it gone sour?

TERRY: 'Incitement to sin' – that's what they should say.

JESS: Oh.

> [TERRY *pours some milk into her cup of tea.*]

TERRY: The dolly man I was out with last night. 'Would you like to see my hand-tooled-leather-bound edition of *Playboy*? My wife's away . . .'

JESS: Who was that?

> [TERRY *puts down the bottle of milk on the table.*]

TERRY: You don't know him. Unfortunately, he knows me. Large wink at the audience, which means – etc., etc., etc.!

JESS: Put it back in the fridge.

TERRY: Funny – that's just what I said to him.

> [JESS *looks at* TERRY.]

Yes, I know. Such a nice girl, too! One time I was home – ouch! I said – I don't know – something like that. My mother . . . [TERRY *puts the bottle of milk back into the refrigerator.*] I didn't think she'd know what I was talking about. Just shows!

> [JESS *turns the toast and puts it back under the grill.*]

You have the gift of continence, haven't you?

JESS: I've never really thought about it.

TERRY [*laughing*]: Oh, come on!

JESS: No, Terry – I mean . . .

TERRY: I know what you mean! [TERRY *puts an arm round* JESS'S *shoulders.*] Exactly – what you mean. You – have never thought about it – like that. Just – the end of the evening – he takes you home – and he respects you. A kiss – to show he would, if he didn't respect you – everyone's pride is satisfied. A gentle caress. [TERRY *kisses* JESS *on the cheek.*] What does it feel like?

> [*Without dislodging* TERRY'S *arm from her own shoulder,* JESS *turns to face* TERRY.]

My own fault, of course. All – my own fault! 'He won't respect you.' Ooops! [TERRY *pulls the toast out from under the grill.*]

JESS: Oh!

TERRY: Lightly – just lightly – thanks.

    [JESS *takes the toast.*]

JESS: Sorry.

TERRY: No harm done. [TERRY *helps herself to one of the pieces of toast.*] Not – you understand – that my mother – heavens! mentioned the possibility. It never entered her head – the eventuality – right? Nice girls – and her daughter just naturally had to be a nice girl! Have you noticed how much I talk about her? [TERRY *starts to spread butter on the piece of toast.*] Funny, isn't it? No, I suppose it isn't. She's the only one I've got. God rest her. Or something like that. I never finished the gipsy bit, did I? We'll have to get some more marmalade. [TERRY *scrapes the marmalade jar and gets the last out of it.*] Gipsies – 'cause they come from Egypt – short for Egyptians. Clever? On the move all the time – 'cause they wouldn't help the Virgin Mary. Same deal – she was on her way to Egypt – you know? They wouldn't put her up for the night and – pow! Off on their travels. Makes a good story, doesn't it? You have the other piece. This'll do for me.

JESS: Okay. [JESS *is still standing at the sink, leaning back against it.*]

TERRY: One way or the other – it's a connection. I mean, it's pretty rough on them – all the same, they were there. Right? They were around, when he was. [TERRY *sits sideways on* JESS's *chair.*] I've always thought I'd make a great Christian. When they were feeding them to the lions – you know? One or two other things they did to them I wouldn't fancy too much – still – being there – part of it. Hiding about – and all the secret signs. Praying – and maybe he heard – or Peter – Paul . . .

    [*Silence.*]

    [*Quietly*] Matthew, Mark, Luke and John, bless the bed that I lie on. If I die before I wake, I pray the Lord my soul to take. [TERRY *laughs suddenly and takes a bite of her piece of toast.*] One thing – living with you – almost as good as living on my own. Talk, talk, talk – don't you ever get bored, listening to me – chattering on at you?

[JESS *shakes her head and smiles.*]

I'd soon tell me to shut up.

[*Silence.*]

I've always thought I'd be great with the suffering bit, if I knew – really – knew what it was all about.

[*The telephone rings.*]

I'll take it. [TERRY *stands up and walks out of the kitchen, taking the piece of toast with her.*]

CUT TO *the sitting room.*

[*Looking across the telephone at* TERRY, *as she walks into the room. She leans forward across the chair and picks up the receiver.*]

TERRY: Hello? ... Oh, hello, sweetie. How are you? ... Fine – I'm fine – just fine. Late – but otherwise ... [TERRY *takes the telephone on to the floor beside her and kneels over it.*] Yes, I was. How did you know? ... Where were you? I didn't see you ... He's rather dolly, isn't he? Who bought you for the night?

[TERRY *glances over her shoulder, when she hears* JESS *walk into the room behind her and gestures with her free hand, wearily.*]

Oh sweetie – no! Not him. He's death – with fifteen hands. How did you get on? ... You were lucky. I can tell you stories about that one – make your hair curl nothing! ... What? Oh no – some girl – at the office. I've never been out with him myself.

[TERRY *pats her mouth with her hand.* JESS *nods and walks out of the room again.*]

I can't remember exactly. She was always talking about ... I didn't believe one half ... [TERRY *closes her eyes tight in a desperate grimace.*] Yes, he looks very dolly ... No, I didn't see you last night. But I've seen him ... Tonight? I'm busy tonight. No, no – I'm going home. Annual visit ... Couldn't be more draggy – but – you know – parents! [TERRY *mouths* 'Shut up, shut up, shut up' *silently.*] Maybe next week. Look, I'll phone you ... Yes, I know I always say ... Yes, I know ... Yes!

[JESS *walks back into the room, carrying a packet of cigarettes and a box of matches.* TERRY *looks up at her, mouth open, eyes begging.* JESS *grins and puts a cigarette into her mouth.*]

Oh, yes – I do. I think you're absolutely right.

[JESS *strikes the match and lights the cigarette.*]

I'm sure he will. [TERRY *chokes and coughs violently.*] No, no – cigarette – smoke – wrong way! ... Yes – right. Next week. 'Bye now. [*Still coughing,* TERRY *puts the receiver down.*] Stupid cow!

JESS: Jocelyn?

TERRY: Jocelyn. [TERRY *stands up and sings.*] 'I'm in love, I'm in love, I'm in love, I'm in love ...' [TERRY *opens her arms wide.*] 'I'm in love with a wonderful guy.'

[JESS *applauds and* TERRY *bows.*]

The last time I was out with 'wonderful guy' – eeech! And I paid my own taxi fare home. He wouldn't give daylight. Thanks for the fag.

JESS: You should give it up.

TERRY: Yes, love. I know.

JESS: Seriously!

TERRY: Seriously – I should give it up. [TERRY *draws on the cigarette.*] Unlike you, however, I am not serious. I shall continue to smoke – until finally, and very suitably, I burst into flames! Did I tell you about the film I saw last night?

[TERRY *walks across the room to* JESS *and, as she reaches her, links arms with her and leads her back into the kitchen. They separate as they reach the table, and make for their chairs.*]

Not a lot to it, really. Certainly nothing you could cal' original – and I wasn't paying too much attention. [TERRY *picks up her cup of tea and cradles it in front of her face.*] I had enough to do dealing with my dolly gentleman. He wasn't paying too much attention either, to the film. Other things on his mind! [TERRY *drinks some of the tea.*] Let's have a warm cup of tea, love. Doesn't have to be hot – just warm?

JESS: It was hot when I poured it out.

TERRY: I treat you so badly. I don't know why you stay with me.

JESS: Shall I make a fresh cup?

[TERRY *points violently across the table at* JESS.]

TERRY: Brilliant. Brilliant! I don't know how you do it. [TERRY *looks down at her empty plate.*] What happened to my piece of toast?

JESS: Somebody must've eaten it.

TERRY: A likely story. [TERRY *reaches across the table and takes the piece of toast off* JESS'S *plate.*] D'you want your piece?

JESS: No.

TERRY: Pity to see it go to waste. [TERRY *laughs and rubs her hand across her stomach.*] Which is, of course – precisely where it is going. What was I talking about?

JESS: The film?

TERRY: They hanged these three men. The film was all about whether they would – should – you know? In the end, they did. Put them up on some horses, ropes round their necks and then – whipped the horses out from under them.

[*Silence.*]

I wasn't too interested. It was a bit draggy. Only – when the horses went and the men . . . [TERRY *gestures with the piece of toast.*] A girl – somewhere in the cinema – sort of cried out – sobbed – difficult to say exactly – made a noise. My dolly gentleman had one hand well inside my blouse and the other halfway up my skirt – but I heard – and I thought – why? [TERRY *spreads some butter on the piece of toast.*] End – finis – like they say – 'That's all, folks!'

JESS: What had they done?

TERRY: I don't know. I was watching the screen most of the time . . . [TERRY *shrugs and reaches for the jar of marmalade.*] Didn't take it in. I'm not sure they'd done anything, matter of fact. I think that's what the film was about. They hanged them anyway.

JESS: We must get some more marmalade.

TERRY: Hello! Mind-reading? I was just ...

JESS: Going to say that? Yes. You already have.

TERRY: You're getting at me. [TERRY *points the knife at* JESS.]

JESS: What was it called?

TERRY: I don't know. Can't remember. Heavy necking going on about then. He's very sweet, my dolly gentleman, but he does have one or two rather childish notions. [TERRY *stands up, biting at the piece of toast and moving round the table.*] Back row – and holding hands – starts holding hands. 'Bout the time the main film starts – funny thing – somehow you've got a dirty old man sitting next to you. Think I'll have a bath. [TERRY *shambles across to the door.*]

JESS: Didn't you say – I thought – you had a bath?

TERRY: Last night – yes. This – is the gay and glorious morning. I feel ... [TERRY *hunches her shoulders and pulls at her dressing gown.*] Oh, I don't know. Just – I need a bath. Warm, nice – warm bath – splosh!

JESS: I'll run it for you. [JESS *pushes away from the sink.*]

TERRY [*irritably*]: Sweetie, look ...

    [*Silence.*

      TERRY *stares grimly at* JESS, *who stands motionless, frozen in the middle of the kitchen.*]

Er – don't trail after me – hmm? Sunday or no Sunday – find something to do with yourself? Read the papers?

JESS: All right. Yes. I'll – er ... [JESS *gestures vaguely around the kitchen*] clear up in here.

TERRY: Do that. [TERRY *bites into the piece of toast savagely and turns away.*]

CUT TO *the hall.*

    [*Looking along the length of the hall to the kitchen doorway at the far end, as* TERRY *walks out into the hall, turns and walks forward, towards the camera, heading for her bedroom. She puts a hand up to her head as she walks and then, suddenly, she lurches sideways towards the wall.*

She presses her hand flat against the wall and steadies herself, her head back, staring up, mouth open.]

JESS'S VOICE [*irritably*]: Do you want this cup of tea?

[*Silence.*]

Terry?

TERRY: No. No, thanks.

[TERRY *presses her hand hard against the wall, straightens her arm and levers herself upright. She stands for a moment in the centre of the hall, between the two walls. She turns her head and looks at the walls left and then right. She takes a deep breath and walks on towards her bedroom.*

JESS *steps into the hall behind her and watches as* TERRY *walks into her bedroom.*]

CUT TO *Terry's bedroom.*

[*Looking across the telephone and the width of the bed at* TERRY, *as she shuts the bedroom door behind her. She walks steadily, with concentration, towards the bed. She supports her legs against the bed as she walks round it and then sits down, close to the telephone, looking at it.*

TERRY *reaches out to pick up the receiver and then pulls her hand back abruptly. She slumps, drops her hands into her lap and shuts her eyes.*

Silence.

TERRY *straightens up and bends forward, looking on the floor for her handbag. She leans over and looks under the bedside table. She pulls at the bedcover and looks under the bed. She sits up angrily. Her head swims and she sags sideways, pressing a hand against her temples.*]

TERRY [*shouting*]: Where the hell is my handbag?

[*Silence.*]

Jess! What have you done . . .

[*The bedroom door opens.*]

Don't come in.

JESS: On the bed.

TERRY: Just tell me – what?

JESS: I left it . . .

[TERRY *leans back and looks behind her. The handbag is resting against the pillows.*]

When I got . . .

TERRY: Oh.

JESS: . . . your cigarettes.

TERRY: Yes, all right.

JESS: I left it . . .

TERRY: Thanks.

[*Silence.*]

JESS [*diffidently*]: Are you feeling all right?

TERRY [*coldly*]: Perfectly. Yes. Perfectly – all right. [TERRY *turns her head and looks over her shoulder at* JESS.] Back to your chores.

JESS: Yes. [JESS *hesitates and then turns and walks out of the room.*]

TERRY: Shut the door.

[JESS *pulls the door shut behind her.*]

[*Quietly*] Thanks.

[TERRY *picks up her handbag and opens it. She looks for a small bottle of pills and cannot find them. As she searches, the telephone starts to ring.*

TERRY *turns the handbag upside down on the bed and rummages through the contents. She finds the pills, tranquillizers, on prescription.*

The telephone goes on ringing.]

JESS'S VOICE [*calling*]: Shall I take it?

TERRY [*violently*]: No!

[TERRY *opens the bottle of pills and tips two or three into her hand. She moistens her lips and then lifts her hand to her mouth. She throws the pills into her open mouth and, with an effort, swallows them dry.*

The telephone goes on ringing.]

JESS'S VOICE: Terry.

TERRY [*choking*]: Let it ring!

[TERRY *sits motionless for a moment and then reaches out to pick up the telephone receiver.*

It stops ringing.

Silence.

[TERRY *grins, turns and starts putting the contents of her handbag back into it.*

There is a quiet knock at the bedroom door.]

Yes, all right. Come on, Jess. Come in!

[*The door opens and* JESS *looks in.*]

JESS: Oh. You didn't answer it.

TERRY: No.

[*Silence.*]

JESS: Who was it?

TERRY [*patiently*]: If I didn't answer it, how would I know who it was? [TERRY *shuts the handbag with a snap.*]

JESS: I thought that was why – I mean, you were expecting someone ...

TERRY: No.

JESS [*grinning*]: I hate to let a telephone ring.

TERRY: Yes, love – I know. You get to feel sorry for it. All that ringing – and no one taking any notice!

JESS: If someone wants to speak to you ...

TERRY [*viciously*]: Suppose – just suppose – unlikely as it may seem – I don't want to talk to them?

JESS [*reasonably*]: If you don't know ...

TERRY: Anyone. Speak to anyone. Suppose!

JESS: Well ...

TERRY: It rings. You don't ask it to ring. You don't want it to ring. It rings. You pick it up and – pow! He's there – she's there – you're talking – and ...

[*The telephone starts to ring again.*]

[*Desperately*] Oh!

JESS [*briskly*]: I'll answer it.

TERRY: No you won't.

[*Silence.*

TERRY *reaches out and picks up the receiver. She holds it in her hand for a moment and then puts it up to her ear.*]

Hello ... Oh, hello, sweetie. How are you? ... Fine – I'm fine – just fine. Late – but otherwise ...

[TERRY *turns her head and looks at* JESS. *She nods at the door.*

JESS *turns, without speaking, and walks out of the room, shutting the door.*]

Parents, sweetie. Looking in on my parents today.
Annual visit – you know? Draggy – but it has to be done.
Dutiful daughter bit ... Did you? When was that? ...
You must've dialled the wrong number. One of your
other ladies ... Oh. [TERRY *stands up, picking up the
telephone as she does so.*] Tonight? Well, no – as a matter
of fact ... [*Abruptly*] I'm not busy. Just – I don't want to
go out with you. Not tonight – not tomorrow night – not
– well, you know what I mean. [TERRY *pulls on the telephone lead and walks restlessly between the bed and the wall.*] I
had a dolly time, Chris. You were very sweet – and all
that! You'll make someone a very nice – whatever the
word is – husband? ... I know that's not the idea, but
it's what you're cut out for. Ask your wife. [TERRY *rubs
a hand across her forehead.*] Oh, sweetie – let's not be
difficult – hmm? ... [*Harshly*] It's the only way I know
to talk. What d'you think? I put it on? Is that what you
think? ... [*Wearily*] No, there's no one else. I wouldn't
tell you if there was – but there isn't. [*Irritably*] Anyway,
what the hell has it got to do with you, if there is? ...
That's nice. Makes all the difference. If you didn't love
me – say you love me – whatever that means! ... It's so
much easier being flip. Haven't you noticed? I'm known
for it. All my friends tell me ... Stop talking to me, if it
makes you angry ... Oh, come on! What's so special?
Thirty-six, twenty-three, thirty-seven – maybe thirty-
eight. You'll find a substitute soon enough. I can name a
dozen. Come the dark and you won't even notice. Come
the dark ... [TERRY *giggles and sits down on the bed.*] ...
won't any of us notice ... That isn't what its about?
You could've fooled me. Last night in particular. Go
away, Chris. Leave it, please. Go away ... I can't hang
up. You know I can't ... No, I won't think about it
anymore. I've made up my mind ... No ... Chris, I will
hang up. I'll break all my rules – lifelong rules – if you
won't – God help me – if you don't ... Please ... I can't
listen.

[TERRY *puts the receiver down. She sits motionless for a*

moment and then reaches forward with the telephone to put it back on the bedside table. She slumps forward on to her knees on the floor, in front of the table, her arms resting on it.
> *Silence.*
> *There is a quiet knock at the door.* TERRY *does not react, staring at the telephone.*
> *The door opens and* JESS *looks in. She sees* TERRY *and pushes the door wide open. She walks quickly across the room to* TERRY.]

JESS [*urgently*]: Terry.

> [TERRY *lifts her head, turns and looks up at* JESS.]

TERRY: Well, well! Look who's here.

JESS: What happened?

TERRY: The telephone rang.

JESS: Who was it?

TERRY: My ex-dolly gentleman.

JESS: What did he say?

TERRY: What did I say.

JESS: What?

TERRY [*dramatically*]: 'Go, poor devil . . .' [TERRY *pushes herself up from the floor and declaims.*] '. . . get thee gone, why should I hurt thee? This world surely . . .' [TERRY *breaks off abruptly and laughs.*] The things I remember – half-remember! Sign of my misspent childhood, reading – when I should have been watching the telly. [TERRY *points fiercely at* JESS.]

> [*Triumphantly*] 'This world surely is wide enough to hold both . . .' [TERRY *presses her hands against her cheeks.*] I know how he feels. Oh, God – I do know.

> [JESS *takes a hesitant step towards* TERRY *and then stops.* TERRY *looks at her and nods.* JESS *steps close to her and puts her arms round her.* TERRY *slumps against her.*]

I do.

> [*Silence.*]

JESS: If you – I mean . . .

TERRY [*quietly*]: Love him? Yes, I do.

JESS: Then – why . . .

TERRY: What's that got to do with anything? I love – oh, a

lot of people. I love my mummy. God bless mummy and make her good. God bless daddy and make him strong. God bless Alan – my brother – Alan. You haven't met him. God bless Alan and make him love me. Make everyone love me. God . . .

[*Silence.*]

I know how he feels, Jess.

JESS: What did you say to him?

TERRY: Simple. The shortest distance between any two right-angles . . . [TERRY *laughs and holds tightly on to* JESS.] Thank you and good night. That's what I told him. Go away, sweetie. It's been fun – now – it's all over.

JESS [*simply*]: Why?

TERRY: It is – all over.

[*The telephone rings and* TERRY *starts to shake.*]

JESS: I'll answer.

TERRY: Hmm.

[JESS *starts to walk away towards the telephone, but* TERRY *cannot let go of her.* JESS *keeps one arm round her shoulders and leads her to the bed.*]

JESS: You sit down.

[TERRY *sits on the edge of the bed and watches* JESS *pick up the receiver.*]

Freemantle 9978 . . . Oh, hello, Laura.

[TERRY *straightens up.*]

Yes, Terry's here. But she's rather – busy – I don't think . . .

[TERRY *holds out her hand.*]

Just a minute, Laura. [JESS *covers the mouthpiece with her hand.*] You don't have to talk to her.

TERRY: Give it to me, love.

[JESS *hesitates and then, reluctantly, gives the receiver to* TERRY.]

Hello, sweetie. How are you? . . . I'm fine – fine – just fine. Late, but otherwise . . .

JESS: Cigarette?

[TERRY *nods enthusiastically and* JESS *walks across the room towards the door, looking furious.*]

TERRY: My parents are expecting me. You know what parents are like – standing on the doorstep with a stopwatch ... Yes, I've got parents. Certainly, I've got parents. What d'you think – spontaneous combustion? ... He's well. How's your little bit of sunshine? ... Not again? He's always in – where did you say? ... Leeds! For pity's sake! ... Just for the weekend? Don't you think that's a bit suspicious? Perhaps he's meeting his wife secretly ... Oh, that's right. He's the exception, isn't he – proving the rule! ... Party? Tonight? Sounds fun. If I get back in time, I'd love to.

[JESS *walks back into the room with the packet of cigarettes.*]

Well, you know – they sort of expect you to stay to tea – and tea means telly – and when you start watching ...

[TERRY *takes a cigarette from* JESS *and then points past her at the door.* JESS *looks puzzled, until* TERRY *points at the receiver and then at herself.* JESS *nods and walks back to the doorway.*]

Bring a friend! Sweetie, you know I haven't got a friend in the world. I might dig up an old enemy for you and we can swop.

JESS [*calling*]: Terry. Come here a minute, will you? I need some help.

TERRY [*calling*]: Yes, all right, Jess. I'm just coming. [*Into the phone*] Sorry, Laura – sounds like I'm needed ... Could be anything. You know Jess – mice or murder – a regiment of Guards – it's all one to her. See you tonight. 'Bye, now. [TERRY *puts the receiver down and looks at* JESS.] You're getting really quite good at that, aren't you? Almost had me convinced that time.

[*Silence.*]

I know it's stupid, but I had to talk to her.

JESS [*coldly*]: Your bath's ready.

[TERRY *lights her cigarette.*]

TERRY: You know what she's like. You know how she talks.

JESS: Does it matter?

TERRY: Yes. It matters. Yes, it does.

> [TERRY *stares at* JESS *silently, angrily.*
> *Silence.*]

No. No, you're right. It doesn't. I'm sorry.

JESS: Makes no difference to me. It's your bath.

TERRY: What?

JESS: If you want a cold bath?

TERRY: Have you run my bath for me?

JESS: Yes – and it's getting cold.

TERRY: Thanks. I can just fancy ... [TERRY *starts to shake again.*]

JESS: Terry – love!

TERRY: All right. No – it's ... [TERRY *wraps her arms round herself, grins at* JESS *and holds on tight.*] Hmm. Shakes. Nothing important. Geese – and all that – graves. Hate graves. They're going to burn me – and burn the ashes – burn them and burn them – till there's nothing left – I mean, really – nothing. [TERRY *stands up and shakes herself.*] Always supposing I go that far. Natural-type death. Myself – I put a lot of faith in the third world war ... [TERRY *laughs.*] ... and no four-minute warning.

ALAN'S VOICE: Pull yourself together, Terry.

TERRY: Pow! [TERRY *slaps her hands together.*]

ALAN'S VOICE: For goodness' sake.

CUT TO *the hall of Alan's house in the suburbs. Late at night.*

ALAN: You can't sit there.

> [*Close shot of* ALAN *as he shuts the front door and reaches up to bolt it. He is wearing pyjamas and a dressing gown.*
> ALAN *is thirty-five years old, just above average height, with fair hair slightly thinning across his forehead.*]

TERRY'S VOICE: Don't switch on the light.

ALAN: What?

> [*Swing with* ALAN *as he walks away from the front door, along the hall, towards the stairs. Look down at* TERRY, *who is sitting on the three bottom steps, leaning sideways against the banisters. Her face hides in the shadows.*]

34

TERRY [*deliberately*]: Do not switch – please, my brother – big brother – do not switch . . .

ALAN: What's the matter with you?

TERRY: Big brother – watch – over me. 'Let your light – so shine . . .'

ALAN: Are you drunk?

TERRY: Hey! You're clever. Definitely. You [*she reaches forward and digs a finger hard into* ALAN'*s chest*] have got clever. Leave you alone for a couple of years and what happens? You get clever.

ALAN: You are drunk.

TERRY [*obediently*]: I am drunk.

ALAN: Come into the sitting room.

TERRY: Should be dead.

ALAN [*abruptly*]: What?

TERRY: Yes. No – maybe – you know? Just a bit – round the edges?

ALAN: What're you talking about?

TERRY: Drunk?

ALAN: Come on! [ALAN *reaches down and takes hold of* TERRY'*s arm.*]

TERRY [*childish*]: Don't want to.

ALAN: Oh, for goodness' sake!

TERRY: Why can't I sit here?

ALAN: 'Cause you'll wake Ellen – and the kids – talking out here. Shouting your head off!

TERRY: Is Ellen – who's shouting?

ALAN: You are shouting.

TERRY: I am not! Believe me – if I was shouting! Ha! She . . . [TERRY *lifts her head and looks up the stairs. The light from the landing shines brightly into her face.*] Ellen – lovely Ellen – wouldn't sleep . . .

ALAN: You've been crying.

TERRY: Oh, yes. [TERRY *looks down quickly and her face hides in the shadows again.*] Sleeping the sleep of the satisfied? She doesn't go begging. Eh?

ALAN: Why?

TERRY [*chanting*]: Mary Ellen's just been laid, flat – on top

35

of a dustbin ... [TERRY *tilts her head to one side and giggles.*] ... laid? [TERRY *grimaces and hides her face in her hands.*] If you can't do better than that! Yes, I know. Sorry.

ALAN: Trouble?

TERRY: Alan.

  [*Silence.*]

ALAN: What?

TERRY: Nothing. Just – Alan – 'stead of Tom, Dick and Fred – Pete, Martin, Billy and Jim – John – David – darling, sweetie – lover – hey, you! Alan. Nice name – means you – means – us.

ALAN: What do you want?

TERRY: 'Into your hands, I commend ...' [TERRY *laughs.*] The things I say!

ALAN: What d'you mean?

TERRY: When I get drunk.

ALAN: What are you ...

TERRY: In vino – what?

ALAN: Veritas. Terry ...

TERRY: Only I haven't been drinking vino – nothing but 'the hard stuff' tonight.

ALAN: What are you trying to say, Terry?

  [TERRY *stands up on the middle of the three steps, face to face with* ALAN.]

TERRY: 'Father, I have sinned against heaven, and before thee ...'

  [ALAN *reaches out and slaps* TERRY's *face, not hard, not viciously, but effectively.*]

Hey!

ALAN: Now! Make a bit of sense.

TERRY: Will you put me to bed? Tuck me up warm and tell me a story?

ALAN: For goodness' sake!

TERRY: Stay with me – hold my hand – till I go safe to sleep?

ALAN: No, I won't.

TERRY: That's what I want.

ALAN: Pity.

> [*Silence.*
>
>> TERRY *steps forward down the last stairs into the hall.*]

TERRY: 'Scuse me.

ALAN: Where do you think you're going?

TERRY: No point staying here.

ALAN: You're in no state . . .

TERRY [*harshly*]: Does that worry you?

ALAN: You're not going out again. Not tonight.

TERRY: You're so masterful.

ALAN: You can stay here.

TERRY: Make a wonderful father.

ALAN: You can sleep on the sofa.

TERRY: I don't want to sleep on your sofa.

ALAN: That's all there is.

TERRY: I'll find a bed somewhere.

ALAN: At this time of night.

TERRY: Specially – this time of night. People glad to see me – plenty of them.

ALAN: I'll get the car out – look – I'll take you home.

TERRY: Ah! That's a good – that . . . [TERRY *stares at him silently for a moment.*] Hmm. Home. Take me home. Well, now, big brother – that raises a problem. Bit of a tiny problem. Where is my home?

ALAN [*coldly*]: I've got the address written down somewhere.

TERRY: Funny. Very – oh, yes.

> [*Silence.*]

ALAN: Lenny thrown you out?

TERRY: Leonard!

ALAN: Can't say I blame him.

TERRY: I left him –

ALAN: I didn't know.

TERRY: I didn't tell you.

> [*Silence.*]

ALAN: You're better off.

TERRY: Thanks.

ALAN: I always said he was no good for you. It couldn't work.

TERRY: Yes. Yes, I know. You always said ... [TERRY *steps in close to* ALAN *and speaks up into his face.*] What right – I mean, as far as I'm concerned, Ellen is no good for you. That doesn't give me the right – I don't tell you ... [TERRY *breaks off abruptly, in mid-sentence.*] Ah!

ALAN: I know what you think about Ellen.

TERRY: I don't think about Ellen. I think about you.

ALAN: Some day, I'll tell you what Ellen thinks about you.

TERRY: Ellen? Thinks!

ALAN: Might come as a surprise.

TERRY: I can – oh, boy – can I! Guess. Yes, I can. Hear – what she says about me.

ALAN: You've always known what other people thought about you.

TERRY: The worst!

ALAN: If you're looking for help – looking to me to help ...

TERRY: I am looking – brother of mine – for a place to sleep. On my own, preferably – 'cause I am sick to death ...

ALAN: I'll get some blankets.

TERRY: Make a cup of tea as well.

ALAN: Oh, yes?

TERRY: What else? The bodily comforts, sweetie. That's us, isn't it? The great providers – in time of trouble. A roof, a fire – one hot drink, one soft bed – the knife is six inches deep in his soul – and we feed him. Meat and two veg. We help him – 'the way to dusty death' – hmmmm? We make it easy for him – I mean, that's it – the whole bit – easy – and no fuss. Specially – no fuss!

ALAN: You are speaking English?

TERRY: Screwed up, Alan – like a nut with three bolts. Safety, I need – protection ...

ALAN: 'Cause I don't understand ...

TERRY: Warm – I'll sweat. Food – I'll throw up. Hands holding – comfort – close – and peace ...

ALAN: Wake the kids and you won't get much peace.
    [*Silence.*]

TERRY: I won't stay. Thanks all the same.

ALAN: What?

TERRY: It's too much trouble.

ALAN: It's no trouble at all. Ellen knows . . .

TERRY [*harshly*]: What – does Ellen know . . . ? I'm potty – sort of demented child – liable to turn up in the middle of the night – any night – and ask – what? – for sanctuary?

ALAN: No.

TERRY: I'd rather go – oh, you know – somewhere I have to pay. Somewhere I have – rights.

ALAN: For goodness' sake, Terry – the nearest hotel . . .

TERRY: People you pay don't – say no.

ALAN: Look – you're not in the centre of London, you know.

TERRY: I'll catch a bus.

ALAN: You'll stay here.

TERRY: I'll ring a doorbell. Pay up – look – happy – and go to sleep.

JESS'S VOICE [*startled*]: Terry, love – what's the matter?

CUT TO *the bathroom of the basement flat.*

[TERRY *is standing in front of the bathroom mirror, staring at her reflection.*]

JESS'S VOICE: Are you all right?

TERRY [*hesitantly*]: Words. A loss for words – Teresa Ann Stephens! No – the weight – dragging weight. I can't – move the words – times I can't – into my mouth – out of my mouth. They . . . [TERRY *rubs her throat with her hands.*] . . . strangle – here – in my throat – constrict.

JESS'S VOICE: I'll phone them, shall I? Tell them you can't come?

TERRY: What?

JESS: Your mother and father. I'll tell them . . .

TERRY: They don't know. I haven't told them. They don't – good grief! They don't expect me.

JESS: I thought – you know – you said . . .

TERRY: No! If I told them – I mean, the performance! [TERRY *shakes her head and then half laughs.*] If they knew I was coming!

39

JESS: Doesn't matter then, does it?

TERRY: Anyway, I might change my mind. What?

JESS: You don't have to go.

TERRY: Oh, yes.

JESS: Honey, I don't think you should.

TERRY: Come with me.

JESS: Oh, now – look!

TERRY [abruptly]: Sorry. No!

JESS: I will. Of course, I will.

TERRY: I don't know why I said that.

JESS: Just – I thought . . .

TERRY [laughing]: Of course, you don't want to come with me.

JESS: If it's been such a long time.

TERRY: Nobody could.

JESS: Your parents don't know me.

TERRY: Silly.

JESS: They'll want to talk . . .

TERRY [abruptly]: I don't want you to come with me.
　　　[Silence.]
　　Really – I can't think what made me – say . . . [TERRY turns away from the mirror and looks jerkily round the bathroom.] Where's my handbag got to now?

JESS: The bedroom.

TERRY: Oh, yes. [TERRY walks towards the door.]

JESS: I made some coffee.

TERRY: Oh. Yes – thanks. I'm not sure [she looks at her watch] if I've got time . . .

JESS [quietly]: Not to worry. I was making a cup for myself . . .

TERRY: Good. [TERRY steps out into the hall and walks uncertainly towards the bedroom.]

JESS'S VOICE: What will you do about eating?

TERRY: Oh. Well, if I don't have something with them, I'll probably . . . [TERRY clasps her hands together, laughing.] I can't think about that.
　　　[JESS watches TERRY from the bathroom doorway.]

JESS: There's nothing here. That's all.

TERRY: No. Right. [TERRY *walks forward into the bedroom and picks up her handbag from the bed.*]

JESS: I thought – if you're coming back . . .

TERRY: I won't. No. I'll – er – well, I might go to the club.

JESS: Oh. But, I thought – er – that is . . .

TERRY: What?

JESS: You don't go to the club any more.

TERRY: I haven't – no – for a while.

JESS: I thought you decided . . .

TERRY: No one I like – no one I want to see – goes there. Simple as that.

JESS: Well . . .

TERRY: Weekends – there's hardly anyone – none of the people . . . [TERRY *holds her handbag hard against her chest.*] Home for the weekend.

JESS: I can easily get some food.

TERRY: No, no – don't bother. They always put on some sort of meal Sundays.

[*Silence.*]

JESS: 'Kay.

TERRY: See you when I get back.

JESS: Have a good day.

CUT TO FILM: *Looking through the wire mesh fence, which encircles a children's playground. The playground is crowded to capacity, with children up to and including ten-year-olds, all playing wildly.*

Terry walks round the playground, looking through the fence. The camera moves with her as far as the corner of the fence and then she walks away towards the road at the far side of the playground. She reaches the road and stops for a moment at the curb, looking across at the houses facing her.

CUT: *Close shot of Terry as she walks forward across the road to the pavement on the far side. She walks across the pavement and opens the front gate of one of the houses. Watch her, as she walks into the front garden and along the path to the front door. She rings the doorbell.*

The house is a semi-detached, stucco-faced house, which was

41

*built in the early nineteen-thirties, in one of the outer London
suburbs.*

CUT TO *the hall of the Stephens' house.*

    [FATHER *is looking out of the house at* TERRY, *who is
standing on the doorstep.*]

FATHER'S VOICE: Hello, stranger.

TERRY: Hello, Dad.

    [*Pull back to include* FATHER, *as* TERRY *walks forward
into the house.* FATHER *holds the door wide open for her
to walk past.*]

FATHER: This is a surprise. I didn't know you were coming
today. Your mother didn't tell me.

TERRY: She didn't know.

FATHER: This is a surprise. [FATHER *shuts the front door and
then pushes it to make sure it has shut securely.*]

TERRY: Where is she?

FATHER: In the kitchen. [FATHER *turns to face* TERRY.]
I'm glad you've come. Now, I can get out of the drying-
up.

TERRY: You won't get away with that.

FATHER: It's always worth a try. Did you say your mother
doesn't know you're coming?

TERRY: No, she doesn't.

FATHER: We'll give her a surprise.

    [FATHER *turns and walks away, along the hall, towards
the kitchen.*

       FATHER *is seventy years old, just above average height,
but slightly stooped, with thinning, greying hair and the
fragments of a bright laughing personality.*]

TERRY: Not much for surprises, is she?

FATHER [*calling*]: Mother. Got a surprise for you out here.

MOTHER'S VOICE: What d'you say?

FATHER: Look who's here. [FATHER *opens the kitchen door.*]

MOTHER'S VOICE: I can't hear a word . . .

FATHER: Look who it is.

    [TERRY *follows her* FATHER *along the hall to the kitchen
door.*]

MOTHER'S VOICE: What are you talking about?
[TERRY *walks into the kitchen.*]

TERRY: Hello.

MOTHER: Oh.

FATHER: I knew you'd be surprised.

MOTHER: Hello, stranger.

TERRY: How are you?

MOTHER: Well as can be expected, I suppose. [MOTHER *is standing at the sink, surrounded by dirty plates and dishes.*]

FATHER: Didn't know Terry was coming by today, did you?

MOTHER: Are you going to start drying-up, or aren't you?

FATHER: Well, now – I thought, Terry – as she's here – and she's doing nothing.

MOTHER: Oh, did you?

TERRY: I don't mind.

MOTHER: Your father's only joking. He always does the drying-up – Sundays.

TERRY: Perhaps he deserves a holiday?

MOTHER: Is that what it is? Public holiday. Because our only daughter is gracious enough to pay us a visit . . .

FATHER: I was only joking.

TERRY [*firmly*]: No. I'd like to help with the washing-up. You go and sit down.

FATHER [*laughing*]: No, no. [FATHER *picks up the tea towel.*]

MOTHER: It'll take twice as long if you do. Much better let your father get on with it.

TERRY: All right. It'll take twice as long! We've got all afternoon.

MOTHER: You may have all afternoon. I've got plenty of things to keep me busy.

TERRY: Go on, Dad.
[FATHER *picks up a plate and starts to dry it.*]

FATHER: Would you like a cup of tea?

TERRY: Have a bit of a rest?

MOTHER: He's only just now got up.

FATHER: Pity you couldn't get here in time for dinner.

TERRY: No, thanks. Er – I mean – I don't want a cup of tea.

MOTHER: Coffee?

TERRY: Have you got any coffee?

MOTHER: Instant.

TERRY: Drink nothing else myself.

[FATHER *puts the plate down on the kitchen table.*]

FATHER: I'll put the kettle on.

MOTHER: Have you had anything to eat?

TERRY: Thanks. Yes, I have.

MOTHER: Have you?

TERRY: I had a sandwich – you know?

FATHER: That's not enough.

MOTHER: 'Bout all you ever eat.

TERRY: I usually manage a couple of meals a day.

MOTHER: You're looking tired.

TERRY: Thanks.

FATHER: Haven't you been well? [FATHER *fills the kettle at the cold tap.*]

TERRY: I'm in excellent health.

MOTHER: Doesn't look like it. [MOTHER *turns back to the sink and gets on with the washing-up.*]

TERRY: Doesn't feel like it now. Funny, when I came in, I felt splendid. Now – I need a six weeks' holiday.

MOTHER: Yes.

TERRY: Fat chance. [TERRY *picks up the tea towel.*]

FATHER: You'll get a holiday this year, will you?

TERRY: Shouldn't think so. Holidays come that bit expensive. [TERRY *picks up a plate and starts to dry it.*]

MOTHER: You can come with us.

TERRY [*carefully*]: Thanks.

MOTHER: Dull for you, I suppose.

[FATHER *puts the kettle on the gas stove and lights the gas.*]

FATHER: If you'd like to come with us . . .

TERRY: When are you going?

FATHER: Usual time. End of August. Thereabouts.

MOTHER: Thought we might go a little later this year, as a matter of fact.

TERRY: Break out? [TERRY *puts the plate down on the table.*]

MOTHER: The weather's often nice at the end of September.

TERRY: Depends where you are.

MOTHER: With your father being retired, we can go more or less any time.

TERRY: You're lucky. I've got a couple of weeks in June. If I'm still at the same place. If not, it's catch as catch can.

FATHER: It would be something to look forward to, wouldn't it, mother?

MOTHER: Are you?

TERRY: What?

MOTHER: Still working at the same place?

[TERRY *picks up a serving dish and starts to dry it.*]

TERRY: I don't know. Where was I?

MOTHER: Something to do with gramophone records?

TERRY: Oh, yes. No. I left.

FATHER: What are you doing now?

TERRY: Same thing. Different office.

FATHER: Nice people?

TERRY: Not particularly.

MOTHER: How many jobs have you had?

TERRY: Since when?

MOTHER: Since the – er – gramophone records.

TERRY: Can't remember. Two – maybe three.

MOTHER: Your father was with the same . . .

TERRY: Yes, I know. Still, makes a change – and I don't have the responsibility, do I? [TERRY *outlines a square on her chest with her finger.*] Ex-serviceman – wife and fifteen kids . . .

MOTHER: Your father was very proud of his job.

TERRY: How long were you there, Dad? [TERRY *puts the serving dish down.*]

FATHER: Goodness knows.

MOTHER: Thirty years.

TERRY: There's a coincidence. Just exactly as long as I've been alive. Thirty last month. Did you know that?

MOTHER: Yes, of course.

TERRY: I thought – since I didn't get a birthday card.

MOTHER: We didn't know where to send it, did we?

FATHER: Here. Let me do it. [FATHER *takes the tea towel from* TERRY.]

MOTHER: Your present's here – waiting for you.

TERRY: Oh, that's nice. What is it?

FATHER: Wait and see.

MOTHER: Where are you living now?

TERRY: Ah!

FATHER: It's well hidden.

TERRY: Rather proud of that. Sorry, Dad – what did you say?

FATHER: There's no point pulling the house to pieces, because you won't find it.

TERRY: Oh, no? I'll bet it's hidden in the same place it's always hidden.

MOTHER: It isn't hidden. Don't be ridiculous! It's in the back room. The kettle's boiling.

FATHER: Oh, yes. [FATHER *puts the tea towel down and walks across to the gas stove.*]

MOTHER: Proud of what?

TERRY: My new home.

MOTHER: Where is it?

TERRY: Oh well, I don't suppose you'd know the area. It's in . . .

MOTHER: I don't suppose we would.

TERRY: Sort of in Chelsea – between Earls Court and Chelsea.

FATHER: How do you make – er . . .

TERRY: I'll do it.

FATHER: Probably better if you do.

TERRY: Forsyth Street.

FATHER: Is it nice?

TERRY: Super.

MOTHER: Living on your own?

TERRY: Yes. Well, no – not exactly. Not at the moment.

MOTHER: I see.

TERRY: The rent's a bit more than I can afford, really. I'm sharing – with a girl friend.

FATHER: That's nice.

TERRY: It's not permanent.

MOTHER: No.

FATHER: I don't like to think of you living on your own.

    [TERRY *turns her head quickly to look at her* FATHER, *too quickly and the room swims.*]

TERRY: I'd like you to see it. It's a real home. My first – real home. Sitting room – really quite large – gets a lot of sun – and there are two bedrooms. I've got the bigger one.

FATHER: Sounds a lot better than – where was it? That room?

TERRY: Baron's Court.

FATHER: When I came to fetch you.

TERRY: That was guggy. Very guggy! [TERRY *shudders.*] Try not to think about that.

FATHER: Have you got a garden?

TERRY: No, I haven't.

FATHER: Pity. Nothing like a garden.

TERRY: I look out on a garden. [TERRY *puts a teaspoonful of instant coffee into a cup.*]

FATHER: Ah.

TERRY: There's a tree I'm getting very fond of. Looks in at my window. First thing I see in the morning, when I wake up. [TERRY *pours boiling water into the cup.*] Very splendid it looks at the moment, too. Red with blossom.

MOTHER: Milk? Sugar?

TERRY: Yes. [TERRY *looks round for the sugar.*]

FATHER: I'll get them.

TERRY: Must be above five hundred years old, I think. Tall! I can't see the top.

FATHER: Disappears in the clouds?

TERRY [*laughing*]: Well, no – not exactly. My bedroom's in the basement and the window cuts it off.

    [FATHER *puts the sugar bowl down beside* TERRY'S *cup.*]

FATHER [*firmly*]: Disappears in the clouds. You climb up it . . .

MOTHER: What's the matter, Terry?

TERRY: Nothing. Why? What d'you mean?

MOTHER: You're white as a sheet.

TERRY: Am I? [TERRY *puts her hands to her cheeks.*]

MOTHER: Ted – get the girl a chair.

FATHER: Here. [FATHER *pulls forward the chair, which stands back against the wall by the door.*] Come on, love.

> [MOTHER *takes the tea towel away from* FATHER *and dries her hands on it vigorously.*]

MOTHER: Well, that's done. You go and sit down, Ted.

FATHER: Have we finished?

MOTHER: I'll do the rest. Isn't there something you wanted to watch this afternoon?

FATHER: I thought Alan was coming to see us?

MOTHER: He said he might.

TERRY: That'll be jolly.

MOTHER: If he can get away.

FATHER: There's a film on this afternoon.

MOTHER: Certainly won't be here for a while yet. If he gets here at all.

TERRY: Ellen being difficult?

MOTHER: You might as well watch some of it – while you've got the chance.

> [FATHER *puts a hand on* TERRY's *shoulder.*]

FATHER: You're sure you're all right?

TERRY: Oh, yes. I felt – suddenly – felt it was hot in here – you know?

FATHER: Does get hot.

MOTHER: It looked like you were going to pass out.

FATHER: You don't get enough to eat.

TERRY: Oh, yes – I do! I'm a pig – an absolute pig. I never stop eating.

FATHER: This girl you're living with – is she a sensible girl? More sensible than you?

TERRY: Jess? Oh, yes. She's more sensible than God.

MOTHER: Jess? What sort of name is that?

> [FATHER *straightens up, turns and walks across to the refrigerator.*]

TERRY: Short for Jessica. Like Terry – short for Teresa?

MOTHER: Yes.

TERRY: I think we make a good pair.

MOTHER: How did we ever start calling you Terry?

TERRY: I wanted to be a boy.

MOTHER: It was Alan.

TERRY: I thought it was Dad.

FATHER: What? [FATHER *takes a bottle of milk out of the refrigerator.*]

TERRY: Called me Terry.

FATHER: Was it?

MOTHER: No. It was Alan.

TERRY: It wasn't.

FATHER: If your mother says it was Alan [*he shuts the door of the refrigerator*] it was Alan. She's never wrong about something like that.

MOTHER: Alan couldn't pronounce Teresa.

TERRY: He always was a backward child.

FATHER: There you are. [FATHER *puts the bottle of milk down on the table, next to* TERRY'S *cup of coffee.*]

MOTHER: Ted! Really! Put it in a jug.

FATHER: Terry doesn't mind.

MOTHER: I mind.

FATHER [*abruptly*]: All right. You put it in a jug.

   [*Silence.*]

   Sit there and have a rest. [FATHER *turns and walks out of the kitchen.*] I'll leave the door open, shall I?

TERRY: Thanks, Dad.

   [*Silence.*

      TERRY *watches her* FATHER *walk away along the hall, then turns and looks up at her* MOTHER.]

MOTHER: How d'you think he's looking?

TERRY: Much the same.

MOTHER: Do you? [MOTHER *shakes her head, picks up the bottle of milk and carries it back to the refrigerator.*] You never did look at other people.

TERRY: Older. He looks older.

MOTHER: He is older.

TERRY: Tired.

MOTHER: Doesn't know what to do with himself.

TERRY [*coldly*]: Gets under your feet?

> [MOTHER *shuts the door of the refrigerator and turns to look at* TERRY.]

MOTHER: Yes. Yes, he does.

TERRY: Perhaps you should put him in a home?

MOTHER: That's what I can expect, isn't it?

TERRY: Old people's home.

MOTHER: I know.

TERRY: You won't get old.

MOTHER: Soon as your father's gone.

TERRY: I'll be dead and buried, before you get old.

MOTHER: I can just see you. Alan – Ellen – and you. 'Well, then – now he's dead, what are we going to do with her? She can't stay here with us.'

TERRY: Ellen?

MOTHER: 'I've no room for her.'

TERRY: Me.

MOTHER: 'Much better put her away.'

TERRY [*laughing*]: Dear God!

MOTHER: 'Put her into a home.'

TERRY: Who'd have you? It's not easy – getting into one of those places. I've been trying for years. Seems like it might be the ideal place for me.

MOTHER: I'm serious.

TERRY: No, you're not. I hope you're not. It makes a pretty sick joke. If it's for real – eeech! I may just throw up. [TERRY *drinks some of her coffee.*]

MOTHER: Don't talk like that.

TERRY: Sorry, Mother. I'm so sorry. I may be – just a little bit sick.

MOTHER: I thought you were going to be.

TERRY: Sick?

> [*Silence.*]

So did I.

MOTHER: What's the matter with you?

TERRY: Nothing.

MOTHER: Don't be silly, child. Obviously . . .

TERRY [*abruptly*]: I'm perfectly all right.

MOTHER: . . . something's the matter. [MOTHER *walks across and shuts the kitchen door.*] Are you pregnant?

TERRY: No.

MOTHER: You've put on a lot of weight.

TERRY: Yes!

MOTHER: Have you seen a doctor?

TERRY: Not recently.

MOTHER: Have you got a doctor?

TERRY: No. Not at the moment. The last time I went out with him, he suggested a couple of things I didn't altogether fancy, so I haven't been out with him again.

MOTHER: Terry, why don't you stay the night? Go down and see Doctor Parker in the morning.

TERRY: If I want to see a doctor, I'll find one of my own. Thanks all the same.

MOTHER: Doctor Parker knows you better than anyone.

TERRY [*grinning*]: I wouldn't say that.

MOTHER: Go and see him.

TERRY: I don't want to see him.

MOTHER: Go and see – someone.

TERRY: I think I'll go and watch some telly. [TERRY *pushes her cup away and stands up.*]

MOTHER: If you haven't seen a doctor, how can you be certain . . .

TERRY [*harshly*]: 'Cause I know about things like that. I mean – yes, it may have come as a lovely surprise to you – Alan. 'Goodness, doctor, is that mine?' I know – 'cause I have to know. Not having the luxury of a husband, I might have to do something about it. Can we have the door open again?

[*Silence.*

MOTHER *turns away and opens the door.*]

Thank you.

MOTHER: Can you take a holiday?

TERRY: I have my living to earn.

MOTHER: We'll lend you – enough – for a holiday.

TERRY: I know how much that cost.

MOTHER: There's no need ...

TERRY [*interrupting*]: I'm all right! Really. Look ... [TERRY *spreads her arms wide and puts on a clown's expression of ecstasy.*] I'm all right. [TERRY *drops the pose abruptly.*] Let's talk ... [TERRY *gestures across the kitchen in the general direction of the house next door.*] Let's have a good old gossip – woman to woman! Tell me – How's Mrs Collins? And all the little Collinses – how are they? How's Mr Collins? Has he run off with Mrs Evans yet?

MOTHER: Go and watch television with your father.

TERRY: How's Timmy – what's his name? O'Brien! Has he got young Penelope in the family way? He's an ambitious lad. Somebody must be knocking on his door.

MOTHER: What's the good – even trying to have a serious conversation with you!

TERRY: It's all going on – out in the sinful suburbs. Oh, yes!

[*The front doorbell rings.*]

Shall I go?

MOTHER: If you don't mind. I just want to get the cake into the oven.

TERRY: Oh, no – come on! You're not going to bake a cake! Just because I've come to tea.

MOTHER: No. I'm making it for your father. I bake a cake for him every Sunday.

TERRY: Does he eat it?

[*The front doorbell rings again.*]

MOTHER: Hurry up with you, before it wakes your father.

TERRY: Yes, yes. On my way. [TERRY *walks out of the kitchen. She turns in the doorway and looks at her* MOTHER *for a moment.*]

MOTHER: Go along.

TERRY: That serious conversation – what would we talk about?

[TERRY *turns and walks away along the hall towards the front door. Halfway along the hall, suddenly, she splays her feet and waddles, Charlie Chaplin fashion, pretending to swing a cane in her right hand.*

The door of the front room opens and her FATHER *looks out.* TERRY *drops the performance just before he notices her.*]

FATHER: Is someone going to answer the door?

TERRY: Yes, Dad.

FATHER [*grumbling*]: Thought perhaps I was expected to do everything round here.

TERRY: Good film?

FATHER: Not bad. [FATHER *turns away and walks back into the front room.*] I've seen it before.

[TERRY *hurries on to the front door and opens it.*
ALAN *is standing on the doorstep.*]

TERRY: Well, hello.

[ALAN *walks into the hall.*]

ALAN: I didn't know you were going to be here.

TERRY: Funny – 'cause we were just now taking bets on whether you'd make it.

ALAN: I said I'd look in.

TERRY: Somehow Mother didn't altogether believe you would.

ALAN: Talking about Ellen again?

TERRY: Not a word!

MOTHER'S VOICE: Is that you, Alan?

ALAN: Yes, it is.

MOTHER'S VOICE: Just putting a cake in the oven.

ALAN: Oh, no! You – or me?

TERRY: Dad – she says.

ALAN: Every Sunday it's the same thing.

TERRY: You don't come round every Sunday. Do you?

ALAN: No. I mean, every Sunday I do come – oh, you know what I mean.

TERRY: You're putting on weight.

ALAN: You can talk.

TERRY: Thought I'd say it first.

[ALAN *walks round* TERRY *and carefully examines her general shape.*]

ALAN: I think it's a great improvement.

TERRY: You always did like your ladies fat.

ALAN: Ellen isn't fat.

TERRY: I wasn't talking about Ellen.

[*The door of the front room opens and* FATHER *looks out.*]

FATHER: Hello, Alan. How are you, old son?

ALAN: I'm all right, Dad. How are you?

FATHER: Not too bad, I suppose. Mustn't grumble.

TERRY: I'm splendid.

ALAN: If you weren't, you'd tell us, wouldn't you?

FATHER: Your mother said you were going to look in.

MOTHER'S VOICE: Alan.

ALAN: Ellen sends her love.

MOTHER'S VOICE: Come and talk to me.

FATHER: Pity she couldn't come with you.

ALAN: Watching a bit of telly?

FATHER: How're the kids?

ALAN [*calling*]: Just coming.

FATHER: Your mother's been looking forward to having a chat with you.

ALAN: They're fine.

FATHER: When are they coming to see us?

ALAN [*grinning*]: When are you coming to see them?

FATHER: Ask your mother about that.

ALAN: How's the garden?

FATHER: Thought I'd have a break from it, this week-end.

ALAN: Looks a bit sad, out in the front.

FATHER: You know what it is. Leave it for five minutes . . .

ALAN: Thought you'd be out there this afternoon. Missing all the sunshine.

FATHER: Feeling a bit . . . [*He shrugs.*] . . . you know.

ALAN: Thought I might come over next week. Give you a hand with the heavy work.

FATHER: I can manage it myself, perfectly well. I don't feel like it. Today. I want to see the film.

TERRY: You won't see much of it. Standing out here.

ALAN: I mean that, Dad. 'Bout coming to see us.

FATHER: Yes, of course. One of these fine days.

ALAN: You don't get out nearly enough.

TERRY: Leave him alone.

ALAN: I thought we might – all of us – you and mother – Ellen and the kids ...

TERRY: Olé!

ALAN: If it's nice, next weekend – all of us – get in the car and go out for a run. Might even have a picnic.

FATHER: We'll see.

ALAN: I talked to Ellen about it this morning.

FATHER: Depends on the weather.

TERRY: I'll pray for rain.

MOTHER'S VOICE: Are you coming to see me, Alan? Or aren't you!

FATHER: Go on.

ALAN: We'll talk about it later.

FATHER: That's right.

[ALAN *walks away along the hall, towards the kitchen.*]

TERRY: Wild horses wouldn't get me there.

FATHER: Come and watch the film.

TERRY: No.

FATHER: You'll enjoy it.

TERRY: You'll enjoy it more, on your own.

FATHER: Why don't you come and see us more often?
     [*Silence.*]

TERRY: Often enough, don't you think?

FATHER: I miss you.

     [TERRY *reaches out and rests a hand on his arm.*]
  Your mother hasn't been well. Just recently.

TERRY: Oh?

FATHER: She worries about you.

TERRY: Does she worry about you? [TERRY *draws her hand back and clasps her hands.*]

FATHER: Nothing to worry about.

TERRY: You look tired.

FATHER: I'm all right.

TERRY: Maybe you should get out more. Maybe Alan ...

FATHER: Your mother's always so busy.

     [*The kitchen door shuts.*

55

TERRY *and her* FATHER *both look along the hall at the kitchen door and then look at each other.*]

TERRY [*grinning*]: Secret session.

FATHER: Talking about Ellen.

TERRY: Talking about me.

FATHER: Come and see us, Terry. More often.

TERRY: You come and see my new home.

FATHER: I'd like to.

TERRY: But you won't.

FATHER: Yes. Yes, we will.

TERRY: It's nice. You'll like it.

FATHER: Talk to your mother.

TERRY: Go and watch your movie.

[FATHER *looks back into the room, round the door.*]

FATHER: I think there's going to be a fight. Come on.

TERRY: No, Dad. You go in. I'll just be a minute.

[FATHER *looks at* TERRY *and smiles.*]

FATHER: It's a long time since we had a chat.

[FATHER *nods turns away and walks back into the room. Silence.*

TERRY *closes her eyes and turns a slow complete circle on the spot. She rests both her hands against the banisters and then leans her head against her hands.*]

CUT TO FILM: *Terry's bedroom in her parents' house. Night.*

The room is at the front of the house, on the first floor. The curtains are pulled back and the room is in darkness, except for the light shining from the street outside.

Terry is lying in the bed, staring up at the ceiling. She has one of her arms up, under her head. The other rests at her side, on top of the bedclothes. She is younger than we've seen her so far.

TERRY'S VOICE: In glass enshrined, entombed – in glass, preserved, protected, 'prisoned flower, golden flower, safe

in glass, confined.

Delivered – yes – to any thousand eyes,

but held, withheld,

unheld.

56

No fist can shatter,
hand rape through
and sweat, salt sweat, the flower poison,
safe – in glass – secure.

The sun burns emptiness.
The flower blossoms cold.
The wind grasps hands and whispers leaves.
The flower stands in silence, motionless –
and safe.
The evening colours every living thing.
The flower shines transparent, safe – and dead.

The rain laughs hard against the glass,
the water sparkles,
splatters,
and the flower reaches
hands
towards the life,
the sound,
and finds the glass, cold glass,
press flat the fingers' flesh.

The flower weeps
and man cries 'Miracle.
'Inside and out,
'the water flickers down.
'The glass is no more barrier
'than thought.'
Now the fist can shatter,
now – the hand –
and now,
the flower darkens,
tears fall burning,
vanish
in the dust and blinding splinters
of the glass.
     [*Silence.*]

ALAN'S VOICE: Terry. Where are you? Terry?

CUT TO *Terry's bedroom in the Stephens' house. Day.*
[*Looking at the back of* TERRY'S *head, as she sits sideways on the bed, looking out of the window.*]

ALAN'S VOICE: Terry?
[TERRY *turns her head and looks at the door of the bedroom for a moment. Suddenly, she shudders and stands up.*]

TERRY: Here. I'm here.
[TERRY *walks round the bed and starts to dig among the scattered books on the shelves. The door opens and* ALAN *looks in.*]

ALAN: What're you doing?

TERRY: Nothing. There's a book I want. It's here – somewhere.

ALAN: I was looking for you.

TERRY: So – you found me.

ALAN: I want to talk to you.

TERRY: That's nice. [TERRY *continues to search through the books.*]

ALAN: Seriously. [ALAN *shuts the bedroom door.*]

TERRY [*grinning*]: Behind closed doors.

ALAN [*calmly*]: Mother thinks you're pregnant.

TERRY: Mother – thinks anyone above the age of consent, suffering from a sick headache and slightly overweight for an undersized rabbit, is very likely pregnant. It's all on account of her fertile imagination. [TERRY *throws her arms wide.*] Tara!

ALAN: Where have I heard that one before?

TERRY: She's made more girls pregnant than Don Juan. Where have you heard that one before?

ALAN: She's worried about you.

TERRY: I'm worried about Jim. Who's Jim? Jim is a man with three feet, four arms and two – heads. Everyone's worried . . .

ALAN: Why do you talk nonsense all the time?

TERRY: Anything else makes me so miserable. Once in a

while, I try – oh – asking for a packet of frozen peas. Even that has a sound – a melancholy . . .

ALAN: It's no wonder Lenny chucked you out.

TERRY: I – chucked Leonard out – if you want to put it that way. No, it's no wonder at all. We just weren't suited.

ALAN: Sorry.

TERRY: Please! Don't apologize. What else are families for? If not to be rude to each other.

ALAN: Are you?

TERRY: What?

ALAN: Oh, come on!

TERRY: Honestly, would I tell you, if I was?

ALAN: I hope so.

TERRY: You're potty.

ALAN: I might be able to help.

TERRY: That's the best offer I've had all week. People are pretty backward in coming forward.

ALAN: That's what families . . .

TERRY [interrupting]: No! Don't say it, love. Think it – all right. That's your business. Don't say it. 'Cause it's such a lie and I don't like to hear you lie.

ALAN: If you won't let us help you . . .

TERRY: Don't need help. Thanks very much. I needed help – a long time ago – and there was a great shortage of able-bodied people then, male and female. Now – I'll make it on my own. I have to – make it on my own. Here endeth the lesson. [TERRY raises her hand and starts to make the sign of the cross.] The Lord bless you . . . [TERRY stops abruptly and clasps her hands together.] D'you think there's any truth in the rumours coming out of Jerusalem . . . [TERRY points violently at ALAN.] You – wanted to talk to me.

[ALAN shakes his head, pityingly].
What did you want to talk about?

ALAN: You.

TERRY: My favourite subject! How did you guess? Cheeky monkey. [TERRY clambers on to the bed.] Would you like to hear my life story? No – of course, you wouldn't. I mean, everyone's got a perfectly good life story of their own. I had such a happy childhood. Happy, happy, happy! My mother – they should write a song about her. My father – the sort of man who went out into the world and lost the British Empire. My brother – well, it's early days yet, but you can be sure he'll follow in his father's golden footsteps – a useless life, a miserable marriage and a happy old age – contemplating the wonder of youth. Are you looking forward to being old? I am. I intend to be old as soon as possible. Stop work, stop play, stop life – go directly to jail, do not pass go, do not collect ... [TERRY *bounces down on to her knees.*] That's the story of my life! Do not collect two hundred pounds. Always happens when you most need it. Just when you're going to clinch Park Lane and Mayfair – pow! Go directly to jail! [TERRY *wraps her arms round her knees and sits back on the bed.*] I needed a hundred and fifty pounds, once. I really needed it. 'Course there was no one I could ask. The father – he didn't have one hundred and fifty half-pennies – and I wouldn't have asked him, anyway ... [TERRY *looks up at* ALAN *and laughs.*]

[*Singing*] La, la, la, – la-la, la, la! [TERRY *throws herself forward on her hands and knees.*] I left my violin at home, 'cause you might not ask and I'm too shy. [*She swings her legs round and off the bed, sitting back.*] Count down! Ten, nine, eight – whereupon – he leapt at his horse, 'cause women had gone out of style. [TERRY *lunges forward and flings her arms round* ALAN'S *neck.*] I love you too!

[ALAN *pulls her arms away from his neck firmly and holds her wrists, steadying her.*]

ALAN: If you stopped talking for a minute ...

TERRY: If I stopped talking, there'd be an ugly, black silence – deep as the world – and I might fall into it.

ALAN: Instead of which?

TERRY: I make a bridge of noise and run like the very devil – 'cause on the other side ...

ALAN: What?

TERRY: Something – better than this.

    [ALAN *laughs*.]

ALAN: I miss you.

TERRY: What've I said? Something funny?

ALAN: Not particularly.

TERRY: That's when you laugh. Of course! That is the sort of twisted idiot you are.

ALAN: I do – really – I miss you.

TERRY: Why is it so lonely?

ALAN: What?

TERRY: Everything. Everywhere! Lonely.

ALAN [*grinning*]: Poor old thing.

TERRY: Seriously.

ALAN: Seriously – if you must live on your own.

TERRY: Must! You're joking. I hope you're joking. On my own? What d'you think? I want to live on my own? I want to live in a crowd of ten thousand – and never let one of them go home. I want them round me, all round me – day and night – loving me. Terry, what do you think? Terry, what are you going to do? Terry! You think anyone wants to live – you must be potty! – on their own? What are they going to do at the weekend? What do I do at the weekend?

ALAN: Come home.

TERRY: Not home – this – isn't my home. If I've got a home – and I'm not sure about that – 'cause I don't know what the word means. If I've got a home . . .

ALAN: Fixed residence – I think. Dwelling house.

TERRY: It isn't here.

ALAN: Household.

TERRY: It's way off – in my mind – and till I find it . . .

ALAN: Got it! Fixed residence of family.

TERRY: This is a family?

ALAN: Isn't it?

TERRY: The outward and visible – maybe – if you don't look too closely.

FATHER'S VOICE: Tea's made.

ALAN: It's the only one you've got.

TERRY: Doesn't that make you sick? I mean, when you look round . . .

ALAN: Make the most of it.

TERRY: Other people's families . . .

ALAN: I want to talk to you.

FATHER'S VOICE: Come on, you two.

TERRY: There's never time, is there? If it isn't one thing, it's another. As the actress said – turning over.

ALAN: I want to know what's going on.

TERRY: Sweetie, your best friends won't tell you that.

[ALAN *catches hold of* TERRY'S *arms.*]

ALAN: Listen to me.

TERRY [*acting*]: Get off!

ALAN: Something – I don't know . . .

TERRY [*acting*]: I'll smash your face in!

FATHER'S VOICE: Your mother's poured out.

ALAN: Tell me about it.

TERRY [*acting*]: I've heard about people like you.

[*Silence.*]

FATHER'S VOICE: Don't let it get cold.

[ALAN *lets go of* TERRY *and she rubs her arms.*]

TERRY: If I liked anyone . . .

FATHER'S VOICE: Alan. Terry. D'you hear?

TERRY: I am pregnant.

CUT TO *the front room of the Stephens' house.*

[*Close shot of a circle of tea cups, as* MOTHER *pours tea into them.*]

MOTHER'S VOICE: Put your own sugar.

[*Pull back to include the table laid for tea and the four people sitting round it.*

FATHER *sits at the head of the table, with his back to the window.* ALAN *sits on the right side.* TERRY *sits on the left.* MOTHER *sits behind an array of cups, teapot, milk jug and sugar bowl, pouring tea.*]

MOTHER: Terry.

[TERRY *reaches forward and picks up one of the cups. She passes it to her* FATHER.]

FATHER: It's a long time since we've sat down, all of us together – and had tea.

ALAN: Yes, it is.

TERRY: Thought at least, we'd have the fatted calf.

MOTHER: We didn't know you were coming, did we?

[TERRY *picks up another cup and passes it to* ALAN.]

ALAN: Thanks.

FATHER: Feels like old times.

TERRY: Honestly, did we sit down to tea – like this? All of us? When we lived at home?

MOTHER: Yes, of course we did. Help yourself to bread and butter, Alan.

TERRY: Funny – I sort of think of it – in and out – grabbing a sticky bun – you know? Time out from playing in the garden.

MOTHER: Sunday tea, we always sat up.

ALAN: Specially when there were visitors.

TERRY: Oh, yes. But that was different.

FATHER: Any bread and butter for me?

ALAN: Sorry, Dad.

MOTHER: Not too much, Ted.

TERRY: I thought it all happened – sitting up for tea – after we left. When we came back.

MOTHER: If we only had tea, when you condescended to visit us . . .

TERRY: You'd starve to death! Yes.

FATHER: Pity the children aren't here, Alan. They'd make short work of this little lot.

ALAN: Most of it on the floor.

MOTHER: It's weeks now and I haven't seen hide nor hair of the children, Alan. Do you know that? Positively weeks.

ALAN [*laughing*]: It's ten days, at the very outside.

MOTHER: Sunday – three weeks. You brought them over in the car – and you didn't stay to tea.

TERRY: Poor starving little brats!

ALAN: Wednesday – week before last. Ellen brought them over herself.

MOTHER: She may have said she brought them.

ALAN: The children told me.

TERRY: Pass the jam.

    [ALAN *passes the jam dish to* TERRY.]

MOTHER: Does Ellen think I'm a bad influence on the children?

FATHER: What were you two talking about just now? Had to call you a dozen times.

TERRY: The state of the war.

FATHER: What war?

TERRY [*grinning*]: No war. Talking. Just – well, nothing in particular.

MOTHER: There's no need to make fun of your father.

TERRY: I'm sorry. What do you mean?

MOTHER: You know what I mean.

TERRY: No, I don't. If I did . . .

ALAN: I was telling Terry about this new job I've just been offered.

TERRY [*persistently*]: If I knew, I wouldn't . . .

FATHER: New job, Alan? What new job?

ALAN: It's by way of being promotion as a matter of fact.

FATHER: Promotion! That's good.

MOTHER: It's about time.

FATHER: They must be pleased with you.

ALAN: Yes, I think they are.

FATHER: That's good. Isn't it, Mother? That's very good!

MOTHER: Will it be more money?

ALAN: It would be. Really quite a lot more money.

TERRY: But you're not going to take it.

ALAN: Let's have the jam back. If you've finished with it?

    [TERRY *picks up the jam dish and holds it in her hand.*]

TERRY [*carefully*]: You're not going to take the job?

ALAN: I'm thinking about it. Jam?

    [TERRY *passes the jam dish to* ALAN.]

    [*Politely*] Thanks.

FATHER: You're not going to take it?

ALAN: I don't know.

FATHER: They'll expect you to take it, won't they? If it's a promotion?

ALAN: What they expect and what they get – those are two very different things. Dad.

TERRY: Tara!

MOTHER: Be quiet, Terry!

FATHER: I don't understand, Alan. If it's a promotion and if it's more money, why aren't you going to take it?

TERRY: In a nutshell, Dad. That puts it in a sweet, crunchy nutshell. I can't wait to hear the answer.

MOTHER: You listen to me, young lady. You're not too old . . .

TERRY [*laughing*]: To go across your knee? Oh, come on! Not too old – maybe – twice again too large.

MOTHER: You can still be sent out of the room.

TERRY [*harshly*]: You send me out of the room, sweetie, you send me out of the house.

FATHER: Don't speak to your mother like that.

TERRY: Goodness, is this my mother? I quite forgot. I thought it was my older sister. Lawks!

MOTHER: You think you're very clever, don't you?

TERRY: Sometimes – yes. I think I get by.

ALAN [*laughing*]: In a fairly large crowd.

FATHER [*persistently*]: Why aren't you going to take the job?

ALAN: Dad, look – I haven't decided what to do. Not yet.

TERRY: It means moving away from London?
    [*Silence.*]

ALAN: Yes, it does.

TERRY: Lock, stock and barrel! If I can refer to darling Ellen . . .

MOTHER: Is that what it means?

ALAN: Yes. That's what I'm thinking about. I don't know if it's a good thing . . .

TERRY: It's a good job?

MOTHER: What do you know about it?

TERRY: Presumably – it's a good job. Or you wouldn't be thinking about it.

ALAN: Yes, it's a good job.

TERRY: You'd like to take it.

MOTHER: How far away?

ALAN: Oh, well – quite far away.

FATHER: From London? Away from London?

ALAN: I shan't take it. Let's forget about it. I'm sorry I mentioned it.

TERRY: I bet you are.

MOTHER [*harshly*]: You mind your own business!

ALAN: Too many problems. The kids – they've only just started school.

TERRY: There are schools? Where you're – er – where you're not going?

ALAN: Ellen – and her friends. I don't think it's fair . . .

TERRY: Oh, she's quite a friendly soul. I mean, she's not my type, but . . .

MOTHER: Alan, if it's a good job . . .

ALAN: It's not that good!

MOTHER: . . . and you want to take it.

FATHER: We won't see you?

MOTHER: Then, you must take it.

ALAN: Thanks. I'll make up my own mind.

TERRY: Ha!

ALAN [*viciously*]: Shut up!

[*Silence.*]

TERRY: Sorry.

ALAN: Sniping. Endless sniping. Don't you ever get bored?

TERRY [*quietly*]: If you want to take the job . . .

MOTHER: You mustn't think about us, Alan. Your father and I can manage quite well. We've got the house. We've got enough money. The only thing that matters – really – is your career. We've tried to give you every possible chance, if this is the right thing for you to do – well, then – you must do it. That's all there is to it. After all, we're getting on now . . .

TERRY: Mrs Stephens, wife and mother, I present you with the Jesus of Nazareth award for suffering humanity. May God bless you and all who sail . . .

[MOTHER *slaps* TERRY *hard across the face.*]

MOTHER: You have a filthy mouth.

66

TERRY [*gasping*]: I'd better go and wash it.

MOTHER: How dare you speak like that in this house!

[FATHER *pushes back his chair and stands up.*]

Oh, yes. That's right!

TERRY: What – pray tell me, mother dear – is so special about this house?

[FATHER *walks round the table, passing behind* ALAN, *who half rises to speak to him.*]

MOTHER: I might've known . . .

TERRY: You think he is here? You think he is going to be offended, because your daughter . . .

MOTHER [*to* FATHER]: Coward!

TERRY: Why doesn't he strike me dead?

MOTHER: I will not have you making your cheap jokes . . .

TERRY: If they're so shocking, why doesn't he reach down – pow! – and strike me dead?

[FATHER *opens the door of the room and walks out into the hall.*]

MOTHER: You think you're so important?

TERRY: I think anyone, who needs – something – I don't know – anything. God knows . . .

MOTHER: Your friends think that's very funny, I suppose?

TERRY: Once and for all, the friends I've got – I haven't got any – you could butter on that piece of bread, eat and you still wouldn't choke on them.

ALAN: Terry, be quiet.

TERRY: Sweetie, I've only just got started.

MOTHER: You don't make me laugh.

TERRY: Five elephants and a camel, stuck in a phone box, wouldn't make you laugh.

MOTHER: If you can't control your tongue . . .

TERRY: You wouldn't let him take that job . . .

MOTHER: . . . I think it's better, if you don't come and see us any more.

ALAN: Mother, no.

TERRY: If it was everything he wanted – if it was ten million pounds a week!

MOTHER: You've upset your father.

TERRY: And – free milk for the kids!

MOTHER: We can manage – quite well . . .

TERRY: You've got the house. You've got enough money. Yes!

MOTHER: It's the same – every time you come and see us.

TERRY: This time – no. It's different this time.

ALAN: It's got nothing – I mean – this whole thing . . .

TERRY: You must take that job.

ALAN: No bloody must about it.

> [*Silence.*]

Sorry. I'm sorry. All the shouting – and it is my choice.

TERRY: I won't come and see you again.

ALAN: Terry – come on. You don't mean that.

TERRY: It hurts too much. It isn't fair. Everyone gets their chance to hurt you – once. Twice, if you're stupid, or maybe – love them. Families – any time they like. I don't think . . .

> [*Silence.*]

The way things are, I don't think I want to get hurt, not any more.

MOTHER: You don't know the meaning of the word.

> [*The front doorbell rings.*]

TERRY: Enter the uninvited guest.

MOTHER: See who it is, Alan.

TERRY: With the answer to all our problems.

> [ALAN *stands at the table, looking across at* TERRY.]

We won't say a word, till you get back.

> [*The front doorbell rings again.*]

Promise!

ALAN: It's probably Gordon. Look . . .

MOTHER: Answer the door.

ALAN: Both of you . . .

TERRY: Truce.

> [ALAN *turns and walks across to the door. He goes out.*]

MOTHER: Don't come and see us again.

TERRY: I won't.

> [*Silence.*
>
> MOTHER *begins to clear the table. Automatically,* TERRY *helps her.*]

MOTHER: I can manage.

[TERRY *puts the plate down and turns away from the table.*]

TERRY: I'll give you the address. In case you need – er – in case anything happens and you want to get in touch.

MOTHER: Thank you.

TERRY: I'm on the phone.

MOTHER: You might as well leave the number.

TERRY: I thought I would.

MOTHER: When is it due?

TERRY: Four – five months.

MOTHER: You ought to have a doctor look at you.

TERRY: I go to the hospital.

MOTHER: Hmm.

TERRY: They're very good. I'm going to have it in hospital.

MOTHER: They'll make you. If it's the first. [MOTHER *looks round at* TERRY.] It is the first?

TERRY: First I've had. Yes.

MOTHER: If you're anything like me, you'll have a rough time.

TERRY: That – seems to be the general opinion.

[*Silence.*]

MOTHER: You want to have it?

TERRY: Yes.

MOTHER: I didn't really – mean ... [*She shrugs.*] If you want to come and see us ...

TERRY: You meant it. Anyway, I don't want to. I've only got five months – at the most – five. I have to learn a great many things. Looking after myself – living on my own ...

MOTHER: I thought you said – er – Jessica. Isn't that her name? Isn't she living with you?

TERRY: For the moment. Yes. Just – for the moment.

MOTHER: Till – the baby?

TERRY: No.

[*Silence.*]

MOTHER: Do you want me to tell your father?

TERRY: You do what you want to do.

MOTHER: No. It's up to you.

TERRY: I'd rather – rather you didn't – if that's possible?
[MOTHER *nods her head.*]

MOTHER: You'll drop us a line.

TERRY: Not – not for a while.

MOTHER: When . . .

TERRY: Yes. Oh, yes. D'you have anything without tips?
[TERRY *holds up a packet of tipped cigarettes.*]

MOTHER: I don't think so.

TERRY: Smoked my last – on the train.
[*The chime of an ice-cream van tinkles outside in the street.*]

MOTHER: Oh, I must get . . . [MOTHER *stops and shrugs.*]
No need. No, I don't have to get any ice cream.
[TERRY *breaks the tip off one of the cigarettes and drops the tip into the grate.*]
Have you thought about – all the things? You'll need a
great many . . .

TERRY: I've thought. I've read. I've asked.

MOTHER: You've – told a lot of people?

TERRY: No one. It isn't something . . . [TERRY *shrugs and puts the cigarette into her mouth.*] Anyway, I have to go on
working. No – a few theoretical . . .

MOTHER: I always thought . . .

TERRY: Have you got a match?
[*Silence.*
MOTHER *walks across to the fireplace and picks up a box of matches which is lying on the mantelpiece.*]

MOTHER: If it had teeth, it would've bitten you.

TERRY: I'm really very frightened.

MOTHER: There's no need.
[MOTHER *strikes a match and lights* TERRY'S *cigarette, as* ALAN *walks back into the room.*]

ALAN: Gordon.

TERRY: I'll go and say good-bye to Dad.

ALAN: I've just palmed Gordon off on to him.

TERRY: He'll have to get out then, won't he?

ALAN: Put it a bit more graciously.

TERRY: What is he? Some sort of tender plant?

ALAN: Aren't we all?

TERRY: I'll tell him – 'daughter-talk'.

ALAN: That'll put the fear of God . . .

TERRY: What would we do without you?

ALAN: What?

TERRY: 'A very present help in time of trouble.' [TERRY *pats* ALAN'*s face gently.*]

ALAN: I suppose you know what you're talking about.

TERRY: What makes you think that? [TERRY *walks out of the room and along the hall towards the back room. With her hand on the door handle, she hesitates for a moment and then she opens the door and walks in.*]

[*Briskly*] Dad.

[TERRY *stops abruptly, seeing* GORDON LESTER, *who is sitting opposite her* FATHER, *talking to him, smoking a cigarette.*]

Sorry. I'm sorry. I didn't know . . .

GORDON: That's all right. Quite all right. [*He stands up and turns to face* TERRY.]

FATHER [*irritably*]: What is it, Terry?

TERRY: I want to say good-bye.

FATHER: Are you going?

TERRY: 'Fraid so.

GORDON: I'll leave you alone.

[GORDON LESTER *is the same age as* ALAN, *dressed in casual shirt and trousers.*]

FATHER: No. Don't go away.

TERRY: If you don't mind.

GORDON: Of course not.

FATHER: I was enjoying our chat.

GORDON: I'll wait – er – outside.

TERRY: Thanks.

FATHER: Don't go away.

TERRY: Mr – er . . .

GORDON: Lester. Gordon Lester.

TERRY: Mr Lester came to see Alan, Dad.

FATHER: He was at school with Alan. We were talking about it, talking about the old days.

TERRY: Yes, I know.

GORDON: When you've spoken to your daughter ...

FATHER: I was enjoying it.

TERRY: I want to say good-bye.

FATHER: They used to play football together.

TERRY: It won't take long.

FATHER: We were talking about it.

[GORDON *pulls the door open.*]

GORDON: Where is Alan?

TERRY: He's in the front room. He's talking to my mother. Don't disturb them.

GORDON: Oh.

TERRY: Is that – er – d'you have a cigarette without a tip?

GORDON: What? Oh, yes.

TERRY: Let me have one.

GORDON: Certainly. [GORDON *takes out a packet of cigarettes and offers it to* TERRY.]

TERRY: Thanks.

FATHER: I used to watch them play. I don't suppose you remember, Terry?

TERRY: I remember.

[GORDON *lights* TERRY'S *cigarette for her.*]

GORDON: You don't remember me.

TERRY: Should I?

GORDON: We used to know each other. We went to a couple of dances.

TERRY: I'm sorry.

GORDON: It's a long time ago.

FATHER: What d'you want to say, Terry?

TERRY: 'Scuse me.

GORDON: Yes, of course. [GORDON *walks out of the room and shuts the door.*]

TERRY: I want to say good-bye.

FATHER: Aren't you staying to supper?

TERRY: No, I can't. Sorry.

FATHER: Your mother'll be disappointed.

TERRY: Bit busy tonight.

FATHER: You're happy, are you?

TERRY: Yes. Why?

FATHER: You should be happy.

TERRY: Thanks. [TERRY *walks across to the fireplace and stubs out her first cigarette.*]

FATHER: When are we going to see you again?

TERRY: I don't know. Some time.

FATHER: Soon. Your mother misses you.

TERRY: Don't do too much. Don't let Alan break your back.

FATHER: I won't.

TERRY: He's on some sort of health kick.

FATHER: What?

TERRY: He's decided you need a lot of fresh air and exercise.

FATHER: D'you remember that picnic?

TERRY: Picnic? What picnic, Dad?

FATHER: On a hill. The side of a hill – and you went running. You fell over!

TERRY: Did that happen?

FATHER: I thought you were going to roll – clear down the hill.

TERRY: I thought I made it up.

FATHER: It was such a hot day. Your mother had the devil of a job, making you keep your clothes on.

TERRY: Funny.

FATHER: D'you remember climbing? There was just the one path – and that wasn't much of a path.

TERRY: I remember.

FATHER: I had to carry you. Alan went on, up the path and stood ...

> [*Silence.*]

He stood at the very top of the hill – and shouted down at us.

TERRY: Yes.

FATHER: 'Come on,' he shouted. 'Buck up.'

TERRY: 'Slow-coaches.'

FATHER: Your poor mother. She only just made it.

TERRY: It was a good thing she did. She was carrying the food.

FATHER: That was a day.

TERRY: I thought I made it up.

FATHER: That was a good day. Aren't you going to stay for supper?

TERRY: No.

FATHER: When are we going to see you again?

TERRY: Oh – you know. Soon.

FATHER: Yes. Make it soon. You were laughing and crying. Dirt all over your face – your clothes. You cut your knee. [FATHER shakes his head.]

TERRY: It was a good day.

FATHER: Yes. You've told your mother?

TERRY: Er – what?

FATHER: You're not staying to supper.

TERRY: Oh, yes.

FATHER: You know what she is. We've got your address, have we?

TERRY: I'll give it to Mother.

FATHER: Make sure you do.

[Silence.]

TERRY: 'Bye. [TERRY leans over and kisses her FATHER on the cheek.]

FATHER: Take care of yourself.

TERRY: I will. [TERRY straightens up and turns away.]

FATHER: Terry! What about your present? You can't go without your present.

TERRY: Oh. No – I suppose . . .

FATHER: 'Course you can't! [FATHER stands up and walks across to the sideboard.] I don't know what your mother would say, if you went without your present. [FATHER opens the sideboard and takes out a package wrapped in decorated paper.]

[Triumphantly] Now! [FATHER walks across to the door, carrying the package.]

[Calling] Mother!

TERRY: Dad! Oh, no. Look . . .

FATHER [*calling*]: Alan.

> [FATHER *opens the door and comes out into the hall.*
> TERRY *follows.*
>
> > GORDON LESTER *is sitting on the stairs.*
> >
> > FATHER *walks to the front room and opens the door.*]

FATHER: Can't let Terry go, without giving her present to her. [FATHER *walks into the front room.*]

TERRY: I'm sorry. You know what parents . . .

GORDON: It's all right. Don't worry, please.

TERRY [*mumbling*]: I don't want the . . .

> [TERRY *walks into the front room.*
>
> > FATHER *has put the package down among the debris of the tea, which has not been cleared away yet.*]

You don't have to . . .

FATHER: Go on, Terry. Open it.

> [MOTHER *is standing by the fireplace staring at* TERRY, *who shrugs and walks across to the table.*]

Can you guess what it is?

TERRY: No, no, I've no idea.

CUT TO FILM: *A monstrous selection of presents for very young children, laid out on the chairs, the sofa and on the floor, wrapped in the most garish paper, with bits and pieces of the presents breaking through the paper.*

CUT BACK TO *the Stephens' front room.*

> [*Close shot of* TERRY'S *hands as she undoes the ribbon tied round the package and struggles with the paper.*]

MOTHER'S VOICE: I don't know what all the fuss is about. It's only . . .

FATHER'S VOICE: Oh, now – don't tell her. Let her guess. Can you guess?

TERRY: Haven't the faintest idea.

CUT TO FILM: *A smaller selection of presents, with two central, large presents; a small bicycle for Alan and a large dolls' house for Terry.*

CUT BACK TO *the Stephens' front room.*

> [*Close shot of* TERRY'S *hands as they struggle with string tied round the box.* FATHER'S *hand reaches in with a penknife.*]

FATHER'S VOICE: Here you are. This'll help.

MOTHER'S VOICE: I don't know why you wrapped it up like – like – I don't know what!

> [TERRY'S *hands take the penknife.*]

FATHER'S VOICE: That's the fun, isn't it?

CUT TO FILM: *Looking along the length of a table laid for a twenty-first birthday party.*

VOICES [*discordant*]: 'Happy birthday to you. Happy birthday to you. Happy birthday, dear Terry . . .'

CUT BACK TO *the Stephens' front room.*

> [*Close shot of* TERRY'S *hand as she pulls a silk nightdress out of the box. Pull back to include* FATHER, MOTHER *and* ALAN, *who are standing round watching.*]

FATHER: Your mother chose it.

TERRY: Yes.

FATHER: You like it, don't you?

TERRY: Oh, yes. Thank you. [TERRY *kisses her* FATHER.]

FATHER: Couldn't think what else . . .

TERRY: It's super. Really. [TERRY *turns her face to her* MOTHER.] Thank you.

FATHER: Happy birthday.

> [TERRY *kisses her mother.*]

ALAN: I've got nothing for you.

TERRY: I'll leave an address. You can send it on to me.

FATHER: Just like a brother.

> [TERRY *puts the nightdress back into the box and shuts it.*]

MOTHER: If you don't like it, you can always go and change it. I asked them.

FATHER: Of course, she likes it.

TERRY: Yes. I like it.

> [*Silence.*]

Well, then.

MOTHER: You're welcome to stay for supper.

TERRY: No, thanks. Oh, I'll – er – have you got something I can write with?

ALAN: A pen, maybe?

TERRY: I'll let you have my address.

[ALAN *gives* TERRY *a pen and she tears a piece off the wrapping paper.*]

MOTHER: No, don't do that. I might find a use for it.

[MOTHER *picks up the wrapping paper and begins to fold it.*]

TERRY: You'd better see how your friend's getting on. He was looking distinctly sorry for himself a couple of minutes ago.

ALAN: Oh, for goodness' sake! [ALAN *goes out of the room, as* TERRY *finishes writing.*]

TERRY: There you are. Put it somewhere safe, so you can be sure and lose it.

[FATHER *takes the piece of paper and reads the address.*]

FATHER: 130A, Forsyth Street. [*He passes the piece of paper across to* MOTHER.]

CUT TO *the dining room of the Bricstone Club. Later that evening.*

TERRY: I was only three when my parents died.

LAWRENCE: How terrible!

TERRY [*thoughtfully*]: Yes.

[TERRY *and* GEOFFREY LAWRENCE *are sitting at a table laid for four people, but the club dining room is almost empty and there is no one else sitting at the table with them, or any of the nearby tables.*]

I suppose it was.

LAWRENCE: Both of them?

[LAWRENCE *is twenty-five years old, good-looking, sensitive, leaning forward to listen to* TERRY, *who is sitting facing him across the table.*]

TERRY: In a car crash. They were driving back from France together. It was just before the War.

[*The room is in shadowy darkness, except for the area round their table.*]

77

I didn't understand at the time. They told me, of course . . .

LAWRENCE: If you were only three . . .

TERRY: Just – Mummy and Daddy aren't . . . [TERRY *stops speaking for a moment and puts a hand up to her mouth.*] . . . aren't coming home.

LAWRENCE: Don't talk about it.

TERRY: Life went on.

LAWRENCE: Children accept things.

TERRY: I was living with my aunt and uncle. Staying with them – while my parents were away – and then . . . [TERRY *turns her cup in its saucer.*] I lived with them.

LAWRENCE: Nice house?

TERRY: Enormous. I think it was enormous. I . . . [TERRY *smiles briefly at him.*] Everything seems enormous – when you're a child.

LAWRENCE: Where was it?

TERRY: In the country. I had a beautiful pony. I rode him – nearly every day. Hardly ever went to school.

LAWRENCE: Obviously, you were very spoilt.

TERRY: I don't think so.

LAWRENCE: I was joking.

TERRY: They were so sweet. They never tried – oh, you know? They never pretended they – were my parents. They let me keep . . .

[*Silence.*]

LAWRENCE: They sound nice.

TERRY: They were super! Of course, they wanted me to stay there – with them. But, I thought – London! The big city. [TERRY *laughs and gestures.*]

LAWRENCE: You live here?

TERRY: Live here. Die here. I wouldn't want to live anywhere else now. I went back to see . . . [TERRY *breaks off, suddenly.*] I'm sorry. I must be boring you.

LAWRENCE: No. No, of course not. Would you like some more coffee?

TERRY: Yes, I would, as a matter of fact.

[LAWRENCE *turns in his chair and looks for* THE WAITER.]

Funny – I can talk to you.

LAWRENCE [*casually*]: I feel I've known you all my life. [LAWRENCE *catches* THE WAITER'S *eye and gestures at the two empty coffee cups*.]

TERRY: It's like that, isn't it? With some people you meet. [LAWRENCE *turns to face* TERRY.]

LAWRENCE: If you're lucky. Very lucky. I haven't enjoyed myself this much in ages.

TERRY: That's nice.

LAWRENCE: You're entirely to blame.

TERRY [*laughing*]: Blame!

LAWRENCE: I rather enjoy being miserable. It's so romantic. Pale and interesting! Hasn't anyone ever said that to you?

[TERRY *shakes her head and her hair flashes across her face. She pushes at it, a moment after it has fallen back into place*.]

No. The way you sparkle. They wouldn't, would they? [LAWRENCE *reaches out and takes hold of* TERRY'S *hand*.] Marianne – I thought ... [LAWRENCE *stops abruptly, grins and lets go of* TERRY'S *hand*.] Nothing – I thought. As usual.

TERRY [*gently*]: What did you think? [LAWRENCE *pulls a packet of cigarettes out of his pocket*.]

LAWRENCE: You went back to see – what? You were saying – just now.

TERRY: I went back to see my parents' house. Where we used to live.

LAWRENCE: Oh.

TERRY [*brightly*]: I could've saved myself the trouble. Redevelopment area. They've pulled it down. Pulled the whole street down.

LAWRENCE: No!

TERRY: Not a trace. Can I have a cigarette?

LAWRENCE: Sorry. Yes, of course. [LAWRENCE *opens the packet of cigarettes*.] Got them out for you.

TERRY: Might never have existed. So much ...

[THE WAITER *pours coffee into their two empty cups.*]

[*Laughing*] So much for sentimental journeys! [TERRY *takes a cigarette.*]

LAWRENCE: You are a fantastic creature.

TERRY: From outer space. Beware! I came in on the last Gemini capsule.

[LAWRENCE *lights her cigarette.*]

LAWRENCE: Pulled it down?

TERRY: Oh, yes. Putting up a block of flats. Hidjus!

LAWRENCE: I can imagine.

TERRY: I've got nothing against – [*laughing*] – as a matter of fact, yes – I have. I've got everything against building vast, ugly, squared-off blocks of flats. I hate them.

LAWRENCE: So do I.

TERRY: It's very reactionary of us. All the best people ...

LAWRENCE: We are the best people I know. [LAWRENCE *lights his cigarette.*] What do you do?

TERRY [*grinning*]: Well, now – that depends, doesn't it?

LAWRENCE [*grinning*]: How d'you mean?

TERRY [*elegantly*]: To what do you refer?

LAWRENCE: What do you do for a living!

TERRY: I'm sort of a 'Man Friday'.

LAWRENCE [*laughing*]: You could have fooled me.

TERRY: Sort of a white – female – 'Man Friday'.

LAWRENCE: Leaving no footprints in the sand.

TERRY: Not if I can help it. We're going to Germany to-morrow.

LAWRENCE [*casually*]: We?

TERRY: My boss. He's setting up a film. Sort of a co-production.

LAWRENCE: Sounds exciting.

TERRY: We went to America – when was that? Oh – couple of weeks back.

LAWRENCE: You certainly get around.

TERRY: Aeroplanes. Hotel rooms. Cases. You know? Packing and unpacking.

LAWRENCE: You like it?

TERRY: Oh, yes. I wouldn't do it, if I didn't like it.

LAWRENCE: That – doesn't necessarily follow.

TERRY: With some people – maybe. Not me.

LAWRENCE: For instance, I really loathe the job I have to do.

TERRY: You don't have to do it.

LAWRENCE: Hmm.

TERRY: Do you?

LAWRENCE: Don't tempt me. [LAWRENCE *knocks the ash off his cigarette into the saucer*.] Don't you want to go back to the country? The peace – all that space – and – nothing?

TERRY: When I'm old. Very, very old. Maybe – then. Yes. I had a very happy childhood. Does that sound strange?

LAWRENCE: No.

TERRY: They took such trouble. People should – take trouble – with children.

LAWRENCE: Sometimes, if there's a reason . . .

TERRY: It's easier? Yes. If they'd been my own parents, perhaps . . . [TERRY *stops, shrugs and grins*.] What shall we do now?

LAWRENCE: I don't know. What would you like to do?

TERRY: It's Sunday, isn't it. Oh!

LAWRENCE: Even the 'big city' gets pretty provincial on a Sunday night.

TERRY: At this time. Yes.

LAWRENCE: I've got a lot of super records. At my place. I don't know if you like . . .

TERRY: Music? Potty about it!

LAWRENCE [*diffidently*]: We could go back there. Play a few records.

TERRY: I think I'd like that.

LAWRENCE: All right. [LAWRENCE *looks round and beckons to* THE WAITER.]

LEONARD'S VOICE: Terry baby. Hey, hey, hey! [LEONARD NGANA *walks across the dining room, heading towards* TERRY *and* LAWRENCE.] Long time – long, long, long time – no see.

[*Light spreads across the room and gradually the special area round* TERRY'S *table fades into the general illumination.*]

TERRY: I knew I shouldn't have come here.

LEONARD: I thought maybe you didn't. Any more.

TERRY: I've been trying to kick the habit.

LEONARD: Great, you look, baby. Just great.

[LEONARD NGANA *is a Negro. He is thirty-three years old, tall and slim. He looks at* LAWRENCE *amiably.*]

TERRY: Geoffrey Lawrence.

LEONARD: Leonard Ngana. Hi.

[LEONARD *puts his hand out and* LAWRENCE *shakes it.*]

TERRY: His friends call him Lenny. I call him Leonard.

LEONARD: How you been?

TERRY: Fine.

LEONARD: I look to see you, every time I come in.

TERRY: Sorry you've been disappointed.

LEONARD: I thought maybe you'd found some place else.

TERRY: Where else is there you can make instant friends? Just – add a little gin.

LEONARD: You look – you know? A million dollars, baby.

TERRY: We're just going.

LEONARD: Hey – no! Have a drink with me.

TERRY: Another time.

LEONARD: Is there going to be another time?

TERRY: I shouldn't think so.

[LEONARD *laughs.*]

LEONARD: Now's as good a time . . .

TERRY [*harshly*]: Now – is a terrible time.

LAWRENCE: Terry?

LEONARD: How long you know Terry baby?

LAWRENCE: I met her tonight. [LAWRENCE *looks at* TERRY.] Terry?

TERRY: Do you want to stay here? Have a drink.

LAWRENCE: No.

[TERRY *stands up.*]

LEONARD: For old times' sake, baby.

TERRY: For old times' sake, I just might break this chair over your stupid, fat head.

[LEONARD *laughs, pulls back a chair and sits on it, opposite* TERRY.]

LEONARD: You look great!

TERRY: Don't be deceived by those laughing eyes and all the smiling teeth – all eighty-nine of them. Back there is a snake – a real, live, jungle snake.

LEONARD: I miss you, baby.

TERRY: I miss you, too. Like bad breath.

LEONARD: Take no notice, Geoff, baby. She's just an old-fashioned girl. Always calls a spade a nigger.

TERRY: Go away.

[LEONARD *stretches his arms wide.*]

LEONARD: I just now got here, ma'am.

TERRY: It'll come as a surprise to you, baby, but you 'just now got here' too late.

LEONARD: All booked-up for tonight?

TERRY: Five years too late.

LEONARD: You don't mean that.

[TERRY *leans across the table down towards* LEONARD.]

TERRY: I mean it.

LAWRENCE: I don't understand.

[TERRY *straightens up.*]

TERRY: Have you paid the bill?

LEONARD: 'Cause you are going to.

LAWRENCE: No, I haven't.

LEONARD: I hope you enjoyed your meal.

TERRY: I'd like to go.

LEONARD: I hope you're satisfied.

LAWRENCE: Yes, of course.

LEONARD: There's that story – 'bout the woman always pays? [*Laughing*] They just never heard 'bout little old Terry, when they said that.

LAWRENCE: Why does he call you Terry?

LEONARD: 'Cause that's her name.

TERRY: That's my name.

LAWRENCE: Terry?

TERRY: Teresa.

LEONARD: Which they all shorten to Terry . . .

LAWRENCE: But you said . . .

LEONARD: . . . 'cause, she makes out to be a woman, baby . . .

TERRY: Like you – 'make out' to be a man?

LEONARD: Hey, hey, hey!

LAWRENCE: Marianne.

TERRY: Sometimes, I like to think – sometimes . . . [TERRY *bends down and scoops up her handbag.*] I shouldn't have come here.

LEONARD: You been telling stories again, baby? You shouldn't do that. You know the Good God liable to find out.

TERRY: If God is good – I doubt it – I doubt he's there at all. But – if he is and he's good – then, what in hell are you doing here? Sitting here. What in hell . . .

[THE WAITER *hands the bill to* LAWRENCE.]

Did it hurt you?

LAWRENCE: What?

TERRY: Marianne. Did she hurt you?

LAWRENCE: No.

TERRY: Did she hurt anyone?

LEONARD: You going to cry. That's always the best bit. I like to see you cry.

LAWRENCE: When you're ready.

[TERRY *looks thoughtfully at* LAWRENCE, *who is waiting at the end of the table.*]

TERRY: I'm sorry.

LAWRENCE: No. It's all right. I don't begin to understand . . .

LEONARD: There ain't a man living . . .

TERRY [*viciously*]: Shut up!

[LEONARD *holds up his hands and laughs, happily.*]

LAWRENCE: Really. It's all right.

[TERRY *shakes her head wearily.*]

I haven't enjoyed myself . . .

TERRY: It was a super meal . . .

[*Silence.*]

LEONARD: I guess I'm going to cry now.

[TERRY *holds out her hand and* LAWRENCE *reaches to take it.*]

TERRY: Thanks.

LAWRENCE: I expect we'll – er . . .

TERRY: Yes, of course.

LAWRENCE: Good-bye.

TERRY: 'Bye, now.

[LAWRENCE *glances down at* LEONARD.]

LAWRENCE: Good-bye.

LEONARD: So long, baby.

[LAWRENCE *walks away, across the dining room.* TERRY *sits down, facing* LEONARD.]

What you and me going to do, baby?

CUT TO *Terry's bedroom in the basement flat. Night.*

[*Looking across* TERRY'S *bed, past her hands, as she rips first the top sheet and then the bottom sheet off the bed. Pull back as* TERRY *reaches down and picks up the top sheet, bundling the two sheets together in her arms and pushing them into a polythene bag. The other bedclothes are already scattered about the floor of the bedroom.* TERRY *walks towards the bedroom door.*

The telephone is ringing.]

JESS'S VOICE: Terry?

[*Sound of the front door shutting, as* TERRY *twists the polythene bag shut and stands up. She carries the bag with her, as she walks out of the bedroom.*]

Are you there?

[TERRY *walks into the hall and drops the polythene bag on the floor.*]

TERRY: Yes. [*She turns and walks back into her bedroom and picks up her coat from the chair in the corner.*]

LEONARD'S VOICE: Hello, little friend. Who are you?

[TERRY *grimaces, when she hears* JESS'S *sharp intake of breath at seeing* LEONARD *in the flat.*]

TERRY [*calling*]: It's all right Jess. He's harmless. [TERRY *pulls on her coat, as she walks back across the bedroom.*] All appearances to the contrary.

JESS'S VOICE: Terry.

[TERRY *walks out of the bedroom still struggling with her coat.*

    LEONARD *is standing in the kitchen doorway, drinking a glass of milk. He is wearing trousers and an open-necked shirt.* JESS *is standing back from him, in the doorway of the sitting room.*]

LEONARD: You frightened of me, little friend? I won't eat you.

TERRY: I wouldn't be too sure of that. [TERRY *reaches down and picks up the polythene bag. She walks along the hall, carrying it.*]

LEONARD: You didn't tell me you had a little friend living with you, baby.

TERRY: You didn't ask.

JESS: What's going on? Who . . .

TERRY: Jessica Adams – Leonard Ngana.

LEONARD: Hi, little friend.

TERRY: He's my husband. Was – my husband.

LEONARD: Still am, Terry, baby. Far as I hear it.

TERRY: Going to have to do something about that. Can't have the baby born with a name – Ngana.

LEONARD: You think you going to have a baby? [LEONARD *laughs.*] You really optimistic.

TERRY: I'm going to have a baby. Four – maybe five months from now.

LEONARD: My baby?

TERRY: How did we achieve that? Remote control? Be your ever-loving age, sweetie! No. Not your baby.

LEONARD: You my wife. You going to have my baby.

TERRY: Pink, with blonde hair, and blue eyes. I hope – one head, two arms and two legs. I'm going to the launderette, Jess. You come with me?

JESS: At this time of night?

TERRY: The sheets are dirty. I hate sleeping in dirty sheets.

LEONARD: You bitch.

TERRY: Nobody said you had to come home with me, sweetie. It was your idea.

LEONARD: What are you doing? Having a baby?

TERRY: It happens. Regularly. I haven't got the statistics to hand . . .

LEONARD: You said you didn't want a baby.

[*The telephone rings.*]

TERRY: I said – I didn't want your baby.

LEONARD: You wanted me.

TERRY: I got over that.

LEONARD: Bitch!

TERRY: Something you weren't ever going to believe.

JESS: Terry.

TERRY: Yes. Answer it. Go on. I thought, if I showed you . . .

[JESS *turns and walks into the sitting room.*]

I can take it – or leave it alone.

LEONARD: You didn't want a baby.

TERRY: Now – leave me alone. Leave me in peace.

LEONARD: You wouldn't have a baby.

TERRY: You think you'd make a good father?

LEONARD: What father you got for him? That man – what's his name? Lawrence? You going to make him the father?

TERRY: I can't make anyone the father. Elementary biology. It's already decided.

LEONARD: Who?

TERRY: I don't know.

[JESS *walks into the doorway of the sitting room.*]

JESS: Terry.

TERRY: I don't want to know.

JESS: It's your brother, Terry. He wants to speak to you.

TERRY: No.

JESS: It's important, he says. Urgent.

TERRY: Tell him I'm dead. Tell him I died of exposure. You – get yourself dressed and out of here.

JESS: Terry.

TERRY [*violently*]: Tell him – no!

LEONARD: You sick, baby. You know that?

TERRY: Everybody's sick, sweetie. Some of us walking – some of us – flat on our back. Go away.

> [LEONARD *pushes himself away from the doorpost and walks along the hall towards the bedroom.*]

JESS: I don't know what he wants to say ...

TERRY: I won't speak to him.

JESS: I think you should.

> [TERRY *launches herself through the doorway, into the sitting room.* JESS *follows her.* TERRY *walks towards the telephone, picks up the receiver and puts it down on the rest.*]

CUT TO *interior of a launderette. Night.*

> [*Close shot of the spy-hole of a Bendix washing machine in action. The water and the clothes swirl round in a chaos of motion.*]

TERRY'S VOICE: One of us – Alan – me – you know? Should have been a cripple – born – a cripple.

> [*Pull back to include* TERRY, *who is slumped in a chair, watching the clothes swirl in the machine.*]

That ...

> [TERRY *lifts her arm and points a finger at* JESS, *who is standing beside the machine.*]

... would have been perfect. Hmm? A lifetime's devotion. Fetching and carrying – oh, yes! – that is the answer. Feeding, washing, cleaning up after me – lifting me into bed.

> [*Silence.*]

Being brave.

> [*The all-night launderette is almost deserted. At the far end, a* YOUNG MAN *watches his washing, hopelessly, and behind the counter, an older* MAN *reads a magazine.*]

The mute gratitude shining in my face – her only reward – and it's enough! I can see her – refusing to die. Arguing with God. 'What will Terry do?' Calling God by his first name. She never calls anyone by their first name. 'She's helpless. I can't leave her. You must take Terry first.' God – I can see the tears in his tired, old eyes, running down – into his tired, old beard. A mother's breaking heart. [TERRY *opens her handbag and searches for a cigarette.*] I am a great disappointment to my mother. Oh, for goodness' sake!

> [TERRY *looks up at* JESS, *who is holding out a packet of cigarettes.* TERRY *takes one.*]

Healthy – like I am. Strong and standing – more or less, standing – on my own two feet. I just don't understand what's expected of a child. God, I promise . . . [TERRY *pushes the cigarette into her mouth and clenches her lips round it.*] Light?

> [JESS *pulls a box of matches out of her coat pocket.*]

A function in his life – that's all. Food and warmth, as long as he wants it – needs it. When he wants to go – goodbye. I promise.

> [JESS *lights* TERRY'S *cigarette.*]

'Cause, I'm going to see, believe me – he has none of the advantages I had.

JESS: You told her?

TERRY: I didn't have to tell her, sweetie. My mother can see a baby – clear ten months away.

JESS: What did she say?

TERRY: Write us a letter. Tell us what it is. Boy, girl – or monster. [TERRY *presses a hand against her stomach.*] No.

JESS: What did you say? [JESS *sits down beside* TERRY.]

TERRY: When I get home, I'm going to have a bath.

JESS: How – did you tell her?

TERRY: Didn't – tell . . .

> [*Silence.*]

JESS: Did you give her a chance? Did you let her . . .

TERRY [*fiercely*]: What?

JESS: I don't know. Act – like a mother. The way you talk about her . . .

TERRY: Can't be true? No. She's a – what is that expression – human being? Yes, she is. No, I didn't give her a chance. She had her chance. She didn't take it. Nobody gets two chances. I don't – nobody else . . .

[TERRY *stops speaking abruptly and, in the silence,* JESS *puts an arm round her shoulders.*]

Lonely. All lonely. But – yes – I am alone. I will be alone. Some time – so why not all the time?

JESS: You don't have to be.

TERRY: You – don't have to be. You – are you. [TERRY *sits forward and folds her arms against her stomach.*] I am a morass – good word – of self-pity. Yes, I am. That's how I am. How I live – from one day to the next. You live – and I'll live – and you be – whatever you are – and I'll be – 'cause that's the only . . . [TERRY *brings her hands up to her face and presses them against her cheeks.*] You think I want to be – I mean, every day I wake up and I think – no – not today. Today, I'm going to be happy – all day. Today, I'm going to sparkle. Today! By ten o'clock, it's gone. I'm dull. I'm dead. I'm me. I can't be different. Oh, I can be what you want, when I'm with you. I can be what he wants, when I'm with him – but I'm not with him – I'm not with you – all the time. I'm with me and I know and that's it. I mean, that [*she stands up*] is it.

CUT TO FILM: *Terry's bedroom in her parents' house. Night.*
The younger Terry is lying in the bed, staring up at the ceiling. She has one of her arms up, under her head. The other rests at her side on top of the bedclothes.

VOICE: The Lord bless you and keep you. The Lord let the light of his countenance shine over you. The Lord grant you his peace, now and for evermore.

CUT TO *Terry's bedroom in the basement flat. Night.*
[*Looking down over* JESS'S *shoulder at* TERRY, *who is lying in bed, with the bedclothes pulled up to her chin.* TERRY *is staring up at the ceiling, her eyes wide.*]

TERRY: I didn't say any of the things I wanted to say – the things to make it – oh – easy for her. The things would have made her – hate me. No. Things to disgust – sicken her – things – sicken me. Things I've done. Little men –

scurrying – lies I've told – love – I've made cheap. This baby. I don't know who – Jess – honestly, it could be one of five, six – it isn't important, but it would have helped her. I think it would have helped.

[*Silence.*]

I didn't say any of those things.

JESS: Better not.

TERRY: Still – I still – really – want her to love me. All my life, you know ... [TERRY *turns her head and looks up at* JESS.]

I can't remember once, when she said – really – not once, when she said 'I love you.' [TERRY *laughs.*] Oh boy! Here we go! Doesn't that make you feel sick? Even you?

[JESS *shakes her head.*]

I love you. The people who have said that – and got – what they asked for. Terry, I love you. Take your clothes off. Terry, I love you. Lie down on the bed. Terry, I love you! [TERRY *laughs.*] These things – you know? – I think them. I've never said – poor old Jess. Never once – put her arms round me – tight round me and said 'I love you.' Those bloody words. [TERRY *sits up and reaches for the small bottle of pills on her bedside table.*] Get me a glass of water, will you?

[JESS *hesitates and* TERRY *looks at her, angrily.*]

Something to empty my mind, sweetie. Not even to make me sleep. Look, I'm going to have this baby. I'm taking no chances on that. So – get me a glass of water.

[JESS *stands up and walks away across the bedroom.* TERRY *opens the bottle and pours two pills into the palm of her hand.*

The telephone starts to ring.]

[*Calling*] Don't answer it.

[TERRY *puts the top back on the bottle of pills and puts the bottle back on the bedside table.*

The telephone stops ringing.

TERRY *slumps back against the pillows and stretches her neck, rolling her head on her shoulders.*]

JESS'S VOICE: It's your brother again. [JESS *is standing in the bedroom doorway.*]

TERRY: I won't talk to him.

JESS: I told him you would.

TERRY: Now – go back and tell him I won't.

> [*Silence.*
>
> JESS *turns and walks out of the bedroom doorway.*
>
> TERRY *turns her head and looks thoughtfully at the telephone on her bedside table. She leans over, reaches down and pulls the extension lead out of its socket. She drops it on to the floor and lifts herself up to sit back against the pillows.*
>
> JESS *walks back into the bedroom, carrying a glass of water. She hands it to* TERRY.]

Thanks.

JESS: He seemed awfully upset.

TERRY: He can write. [TERRY *takes one of the pills, with a swallow of water.*] How long before you find your own flat, Jess? [TERRY *takes the other pill, with another swallow of water.*]

JESS: Oh. Well, I don't know – I mean . . .

TERRY: You can't stay here. Not forever. Did you think you could?

JESS: I thought you – wanted . . .

TERRY: I want somewhere I can be on my own, sweetie. That's the point.

JESS: Oh.

TERRY: Long as you had no place to go – well, of course – you're welcome. I've been in that state myself. Wouldn't wish it on my worst enemy.

JESS: I haven't really been looking.

TERRY: I think you should start – looking.

JESS [*hesitantly*]: But, you'll need . . .

TERRY: I've got everything I need.

> [*Silence.*]

JESS: Well.

TERRY: I should put an advertisement in the paper – one of the evening papers. It comes a bit expensive, but it saves traipsing round all those agents.

JESS: Yes, I will.

TERRY: Tomorrow. [TERRY *puts the glass down on the bedside table.*] I think I'll try and go to sleep.

JESS: I'd like to stay. Help you. I could – well, I could look after you.

TERRY: No, you couldn't.

JESS: You'll find this flat's a bit much . . .

TERRY: I thought about all that, when I took it on. I can cope.

JESS [*abruptly*]: Let me stay.

[TERRY *shakes her head. She turns on her side and settles down in the bed, pulling up the bedclothes.*]

TERRY: 'Night.

[*Silence.*]

JESS: Sleep well.

TERRY: Hmm.

[JESS *stands up.*]

JESS: Shall I put the light out?

TERRY [*murmuring*]: Thanks, love.

[JESS *looks down at* TERRY, *lying deep in the bedclothes with her eyes closed tight.*

JESS *reaches across and switches out the light.*]

JESS: See you in the morning.

[JESS *turns and walks away, across the bedroom, silhouetted against the light in the hall.*

Cut to a close-up of TERRY, *as her eyes flick open and she stares at the wall beside the bed.*

The sound of children laughing.]

CUT TO FILM: *Looking down the side slopes of Whipsnade Zoo, out across the countryside below.*

VOICES [*singing*]: 'All things bright and beautiful . . .'

[*The sound of the telephone ringing.*]

A child runs past the camera and away, down the slope. She is about three years old.

VOICE: The Lord curse you.

VOICES [*singing*]: 'All creatures great and small . . .'

[*The sound of children laughing.*]

The child falls over and rolls several times, before she scrambles back on to her feet, laughing.

VOICE: The Lord make his darkness cover you.

      [*The telephone goes on ringing.*]

VOICES [*singing*]: 'All things wise and wonderful . . .'

The child stands, waving to people, watching her, away up the hill.

VOICE: The Lord torment you . . .

VOICES [*singing*]: 'The Lord God made them all.'

CUT TO *Terry's bedroom.*

      [*Close-up of* TERRY.]

VOICE: . . . now – and for evermore.

      [*The sound of children laughing.*]

FADE OUT

PART TWO

NO SKILL OR SPECIAL KNOWLEDGE
IS REQUIRED

First transmitted by Theatre 625 on B.B.C.-2 on
9 October 1966 with the following cast:

FATHER	Maurice Denham
TERRY	Judi Dench
ALAN	Michael Bryant
MOTHER	Margery Mason
FATHER AS A YOUNG MAN	Frederick Pyne
FATHER'S FRIEND	Barry Stanton
TERRY AS A CHILD	Gaynor Jones
GORDON LESTER	Emrys James
MOTHER AS A YOUNG WOMAN	Ann Mitchell
LEONARD	Calvin Lockhart
ALAN AS A CHILD	Keith Kent
GERMAN SOLDIER	Leslie Southwick
FOUR ENGLISH SOLDIERS	Pat Gorman
	Christopher Denham
	John Scott Martin
	Stuart Baron
VICAR'S AND PHOTO- GRAPHER'S VOICES	Graham Leaman
Story Editor	James Brabazon
Designer	Richard Wilmot
Produced by	Michael Bakewell
Directed by	Christopher Morahan

FADE IN *the front room of the Stephens' house.*

> [*The family is at tea.* FATHER *is sitting at the head of the table, with his back to the window.* ALAN *sits on the right side.* TERRY *sits on the left.* MOTHER *sits at the end of the table, behind an array of teapot, milk jug and sugar bowl.*]

TERRY: May God bless you and all who sail . . .

> [MOTHER *slaps* TERRY *hard across the face.*]

MOTHER: You have a filthy mouth.

TERRY [*gasping*]: I'd better go and wash it.

MOTHER: How dare you speak like that in this house!

> [FATHER *pushes back his chair and stands up.*]

[*Bitterly*] Oh, yes. That's right.

TERRY: What – pray tell me, mother dear – is so special about this house?

> [*Swing with* FATHER, *as he walks round the table, passing behind* ALAN, *who half-rises to speak to him.*]

MOTHER: I might've known.

TERRY: You think he is here? You think he is going to be offended, because your daughter . . .

MOTHER [*to* FATHER]: Coward!

> [*Cut to close-up of* FATHER, *as he stands at the door.*]

TERRY'S VOICE: Why doesn't he strike me dead?

MOTHER'S VOICE: I will not have you making your cheap jokes . . .

TERRY'S VOICE: If they're so shocking . . .

> [FATHER *opens the door.*]

. . . why doesn't he reach down – pow! – and strike me dead?

> [FATHER *walks out of the room, into the hall. He hesitates momentarily, in the hall, outside the door of the front room.*]

MOTHER'S VOICE: You think you're so important?

TERRY'S VOICE: I think anyone, who needs . . .

MOTHER'S VOICE: You are not going out – understand me, Terry.

TERRY'S VOICE: ... something – I don't know – anything. God knows!

TERRY'S VOICE: Who's going to stop me?

MOTHER'S VOICE: Your friends think that's very funny.
I suppose?

TERRY'S VOICE: Once and for all ...

MOTHER'S VOICE: I'm going to stop you.

TERRY'S VOICE: The friends I've got – I haven't got any
– you could butter on that piece of bread ...

    [FATHER *walks away from the door of the front room,
    towards the back room. He shambles, head down.*]

MOTHER'S VOICE: You use this house like a hotel.

TERRY'S VOICE: ... eat – and you still wouldn't choke on
them.

MOTHER'S VOICE: When I was your age ...

ALAN'S VOICE: Terry, be quiet.

MOTHER'S VOICE: I had to be in the house
promptly ...

TERRY'S VOICE: Sweetie, I've only just got started.

MOTHER'S VOICE: ... at ten o'clock.

CUT TO *the back room.*

    [FATHER *walks in.*]

TERRY'S VOICE: When you were my age they didn't live
in houses.

MOTHER'S VOICE: If your father won't tell you!

TERRY'S VOICE: They still lived in caves.

MOTHER'S VOICE: How dare you speak to me like that!

    [*The sound of* TERRY *laughing.*]

  Wait till I tell your father.

TERRY'S VOICE: What d'you think he'll do?

MOTHER'S VOICE: He's altogether too soft with you,
young lady.

    [*The sound of* TERRY *laughing.*]

  If you had more control over the girl ...

TERRY'S VOICE: Daddy, it isn't fair.

MOTHER'S VOICE: If you showed a bit more gumption.

TERRY'S VOICE: Daddy, she won't let me wear this dress.

MOTHER'S VOICE: D'you think she respects you?

TERRY'S VOICE: It's my special dress. I bought it for Elizabeth's party.

MOTHER'S VOICE: You think she loves you more, because you're soft with her?

> [FATHER *shuts the door behind him and leans back against it.*
> *Silence.*]

SUPERIMPOSE TITLE: *No skill or special knowledge is required*

FADE TITLE.

VOICES [*singing*]: 'Keep the home fires burning, while your hearts are yearning . . .'

> [FATHER *moves away from the door, towards his chair by the fire.*]

MIX TO FILM: *A narrow, dark street in France, during the Great War. The street is shattered by shell fire and lit now only occasionally by the flash of shells, exploding some distance away.*

A group of men, six or seven of them, soldiers, are stumbling along the street, their arms round each other, staggering from side to side of the street and singing, not very loudly.

VOICES [*singing*]: 'Though your lads are far away, they dream of home . . .'

Four of the soldiers, still with their arms linked round each other's shoulders, still singing quietly, occasionally laughing, stagger along the street together.

VOICES [*singing*]: 'There's a silver lining through the dark clouds shining . . .'

Two of the soldiers are standing in a shop doorway. The shop is in ruins. They are struggling to light a cigarette, without showing a light. The match strikes and they grin drunkenly at each other in the light of the flame.

VOICES [*singing*]: 'Turn the dark cloud inside out, till the boys come home.'

One soldier reaches out and pats the other's face, gently. Then the match burns out and they laugh.

CUT TO *the back room.*

> [*Close shot of* FATHER'S *hand, as he switches on the electric fire.*]

MOTHER'S VOICE: If you spoke to her – like a father should – told her . . .

> [*Pull back as* FATHER *straightens up and rubs the palms of his hands briskly together.*]

Well then! I shouldn't have to – all the time – try and knock some sense into her head.

FATHER'S VOICE: There's not a lot wrong with the girl. Far as I can see. [FATHER *walks across to the french windows and looks out over the overrun garden.*]

MOTHER'S VOICE: How far can you see?

FATHER'S VOICE: If you didn't go on at her, the whole time.

MOTHER'S VOICE: If I didn't who would?

FATHER'S VOICE: She'll learn. Give her a bit of time. [FATHER *turns away from the french windows, shrugs his shoulders and rubs his hands together again.*]

MOTHER'S VOICE: Do nothing?

FATHER'S VOICE: That isn't what I meant.

MOTHER'S VOICE: Take the easy way?

FATHER'S VOICE: She has to make her own mistakes.

MOTHER'S VOICE: Fat lot of help she'll get from you, when she does.

CUT TO *Terry's bedroom in the Stephens' house. Night.*

> [*Looking across the room from the doorway. The room is dark and the only light, from the landing, throws* FATHER'S *shadow forward, across the bed.*]

FATHER'S VOICE [*quietly*]: Terry. Are you awake, Terry?

> [*Push forward across the room, to the bed.*]

Terry?

> [*The shape under the bedclothes rolls over suddenly and sits up.*]

TERRY: Dad. Oh, Dad!

> [*Looking across the bed, past* TERRY *sitting up in bed, at the silhouette of* FATHER, *against the light from the landing.*]

FATHER: Lovey, what is it? [FATHER *sits on the edge of the bed.*] What's the matter?

> [TERRY *reaches out her arms and puts them round her* FATHER'S *neck. She is sixteen years old.*]

There, now. There. I thought I heard you – crying – I thought – something's wrong. What is it?

> [TERRY *does not answer. She goes on sobbing.*]

You can tell me.

TERRY [*mumbling*]: Frightened, Dad. I'm so – frightened.

FATHER: What d'you say? Frightened, lovey? Frightened of what?

TERRY: What'll happen? Oh, Dad!

FATHER: Here, now. Look! I can't help, if I don't know what's bothering you. [FATHER *strokes her back gently.*]

TERRY: Did Mum send you?

FATHER: Your mother's sound asleep.

TERRY: I thought, maybe . . .

FATHER: D'you want to talk to her? Shall I fetch her?

TERRY: Oh no. Oh, no!

FATHER: What is it, lovey? Best tell me. Can't be that bad. Surely?

TERRY [*mumbling*]: Want to – tell – I want . . .

FATHER: Come on, then. Take a deep breath . . .

TERRY: When he said – I mean, I knew he'd want – well, it isn't so terrible, is it?

> [FATHER *stops stroking* TERRY'S *back for a moment.*]

FATHER: What?

TERRY [*quickly*]: Letting someone kiss you? That isn't so terrible?

FATHER: No, it isn't. [FATHER *starts stroking* TERRY'S *back again.*] Of course, it isn't. My goodness, is that what all this fuss is about?

TERRY: No! Christ, I wouldn't be crying! No, I mean . . .

> [FATHER *takes hold of* TERRY'S *shoulders and holds her a little away from him, looking at her.*]

FATHER: What has happened, Terry?

TERRY: I didn't know, Dad. He said – just . . .

CHILD'S VOICE: Why did Toby die?

    [TERRY *starts to cry again.*]

TERRY: I didn't know.

CUT TO *the back room.*

    [FATHER *is sitting in his chair, by the fire. He opens his cigarette case and carefully selects a cigarette from it.*]

CHILD'S VOICE: I didn't want him to die.

    [*The sound of a small child crying.*]

FATHER'S VOICE: Everyone has to die sometime, poppet. Even little dogs. Dear little dogs, like Toby.

CHILD'S VOICE [*startled*]: Everyone?

FATHER'S VOICE: And go to heaven.

CHILD'S VOICE: Will Alan die?

FATHER'S VOICE: And live with God.

CHILD'S VOICE: Will Mummy die?

FATHER'S VOICE: Er – happily ever after.

    [FATHER *puts the cigarette into his mouth and takes out his lighter.*]

CHILD'S VOICE: Will you die?

FATHER'S VOICE: Not for a long time yet, poppet.

CHILD'S VOICE: Will you die?

FATHER'S VOICE: That's enough talk about – er – people – and dying – let's talk . . .

CHILD'S VOICE: Will you?

FATHER'S VOICE: When I'm very old. Very, very old.

CHILD'S VOICE: Toby wasn't old.

    [FATHER *lights his cigarette.*]

TERRY'S VOICE [*harshly*]: He didn't tell me what would happen. He didn't tell me . . .

CUT TO *Terry's bedroom. Night.*

TERRY: . . . anything.

MOTHER: You stupid fool!

TERRY: He caught hold of me.

MOTHER: Who was it?

[*Looking across the bed, past* TERRY, *who is sitting back against the headboard, at* MOTHER, *who is standing in silhouette in the centre of the room, and at* FATHER, *who is standing in the doorway. The room is still in darkness.*]

TERRY: What difference does that make?

MOTHER: What difference! It makes a great deal of difference.

TERRY: He's all right.

MOTHER: Who was it?

TERRY: You don't have to worry about him.

MOTHER: Terry, I want to know who it was – and you are going to tell me. [MOTHER *advances on* TERRY.]

TERRY: Mum – he hurt me.

MOTHER: Timmy Evans. Was it that young . . .

TERRY: No.

MOTHER: Peter, was it? Peter Craske?

TERRY: Listen to me!

MOTHER: Tell me who it was.

TERRY: I won't.

FATHER: Mother – the girl's in no state . . .

MOTHER: All right, then! [MOTHER *turns her back on* TERRY *and faces* FATHER.] Suppose she's pregnant?

FATHER: She isn't. She can't be. No, of course not. Don't be ridiculous – it was only – I . . .

[MOTHER *lets him flounder, until he mumbles into silence.*]

MOTHER [*quietly*]: We'll have to know then.

TERRY: He hurt me.

MOTHER: Tell me who it was.

[TERRY *starts to cry again.*]

CHILD'S VOICE: Why does it rain?

CUT TO *the back room.*

[*Close shot of* FATHER'S *hand, as he drops the lighter back into his pocket.*]

FATHER'S VOICE: The flowers get thirsty and then it rains – and they drink the rain.

[FATHER *settles down into his comfortable chair.*]

CHILD'S VOICE: A flower hasn't got a mouth. How can a flower drink, it hasn't got a mouth?

FATHER: It doesn't need a mouth. The rain falls on the ground . . .

CHILD'S VOICE [*quietly*]: Hasn't got a mouth.

FATHER'S VOICE: Soaks into the ground . . .

CHILD'S VOICE: Why does it snow?

FATHER'S VOICE: In the winter, when the flowers go to sleep, the snow keeps them warm.

TERRY'S VOICE [*harshly*]: I didn't want to tell you.

CHILD'S VOICE: Snow's cold. How can it keep the flowers warm if it's cold?

FATHER'S VOICE: Ah! Snow feels cold. Yes. But, underneath . . .

TERRY'S VOICE: Dad made me tell you.

MOTHER'S VOICE [*scornfully*]: A secret?

CUT TO *Terry's bedroom. Night.*
[*Looking past* TERRY, *at* MOTHER, *as she moves close to* TERRY.]

MOTHER: Did you think – honestly – you could keep it a secret? You – and your father!

TERRY: I didn't want to tell you.

MOTHER: Six of one, love – and half a dozen! He would have told me anyway.

ALAN'S VOICE: Dad.

MOTHER: Your father tells me everything.

ALAN'S VOICE: Do you remember Gordon Lester?

CUT TO *the back room.*
[*Close shot of* FATHER, *as he sits back in his chair, staring blankly at the single glowing bar of the electric fire.*]

ALAN'S VOICE: Dad?
[*Pull back between* ALAN *and* GORDON LESTER, *as* FATHER *lifts his head and turns to look at* ALAN.]

FATHER: Sorry, Alan. What did you say?
[ALAN *glances briefly sideways at* GORDON *apologetically.*]
[*Abruptly*] Yes, of course. Gordon, of course. I remember Gordon. Used to go to school with Alan. Isn't that right?

GORDON: Yes, Mr Stephens. That's right.

[FATHER *pushes himself forward in his chair.*]

FATHER: It's nice to see you again. [FATHER *stands up and turns to face* ALAN *and* GORDON.]

GORDON: You're looking very well.

FATHER: Can't complain. Time hangs a bit heavy, of course. Retired now.

GORDON: Ah.

[FATHER *holds out his hand and* GORDON *shakes it.*]

ALAN: I was wondering . . .

FATHER [*irritably*]: What is it, Alan?

ALAN: I'm helping Mum with the table.

FATHER: What?

ALAN: I thought you might like to talk to Gordon.

FATHER: Of course I would. What d'you mean?

ALAN: While I help Mum . . .

FATHER: I don't know what you're talking about.

ALAN: I'll leave Gordon with you.

FATHER: Yes.

[*Silence.*]

ALAN: Yes.

FATHER: Will you have a cigarette?

GORDON: Oh, no. Have one of mine.

FATHER: Nonsense. [*Laboriously,* FATHER *takes out his cigarette case and opens it.*]

ALAN: See you.

[ALAN *and* GORDON *look at each other and grin.*]

FATHER: Here. [FATHER *offers his cigarette case.*]

GORDON: Thanks.

[ALAN *walks to the door.*]

ALAN: Won't be long.

GORDON: I'll be all right.

FATHER: Here, I've got a light.

GORDON: Oh, thanks.

[FATHER *puts his cigarette case away carefully and then he searches for his lighter.*]

Don't worry, Mr Stephens. I've got a match.

FATHER: No, no. It's here. Somewhere. I know I've got it.

[FATHER *finds his lighter and pulls it out of his pocket.*] Ah!
[FATHER *snaps the lighter alight and holds it out to*
GORDON, *who bends to it and lights his cigarette. He
glances up at* FATHER, *through the flame, and grins.*]

GORDON: Thanks.

[FATHER *lets the lighter snap shut.*]

He's very popular, Alan.

FATHER: Is he. Yes – well he's a good boy.

GORDON: I don't know what we'd do without him. Life
and soul of the Old Boys.

FATHER: Yes, I believe. [FATHER *gestures at the chairs on
either side of the fire.*] Sit down, Gordon. Make yourself
comfortable.

GORDON: Thanks.

FATHER: What is it you're up to, then. You two boys.

[FATHER *settles into his chair.* GORDON *watches him
waiting for him to make his selection.*]

GORDON: Final arrangement for the dinner.

FATHER: Oh, yes?

GORDON: Annual Old Boys' dinner. [GORDON *settles into
the chair on the opposite side of the fire.*]

FATHER: It's not too hot for you.

GORDON: What, no. Oh, no. Not at all.

FATHER: We can switch the fire off. [FATHER *sits forward
in his chair.*]

GORDON: No. It's fine. Really.

FATHER: I find it rather cold these days.

GORDON: It's been a terrible winter.

FATHER: Not so young now and if I go to sleep ...
[FATHER *settles back in his chair again.*]
[*Smiling*] I do go to sleep in the afternoons. Need a rest.

GORDON: Oh. [GORDON *shifts forward in his chair, and starts
to get up.*] Perhaps I should wait for Alan ...

FATHER: Nonsense.

GORDON: If I'm disturbing you?

FATHER: It makes a nice change, having someone to talk
to.

GORDON: If you're quite sure.

FATHER: The Old Boys' dinner?

GORDON: You'd never believe how much organization it takes.

FATHER: Does it? Yes.

GORDON: If it wasn't for Alan . . .

FATHER: He's always been popular.
　　[*Silence.*]
　　You used to have one of these bicycles – wasn't it you? With the drop handlebars.

GORDON: Did I? Oh, yes. That's right. For – pity's sake!

FATHER: It was blue and silver. It had – didn't it have some special sort of dynamo?

GORDON: Yes, it did.

FATHER: I remember.

GORDON: What a fantastic . . . [GORDON *looks round for an ashtray.*]

FATHER [*quickly*]: It's just beside you. On the table.

GORDON: Oh, yes.

FATHER: Alan was always after me to buy him one like it.
　　[GORDON *finds the ashtray and puts it on the arm of his chair.*]

GORDON: I must've sold that bike – when was it? Fifteen years ago, at least. At the very least!

FATHER: 'Gordon's got one . . .' [FATHER *knocks the ash off the end of his cigarette into an ashtray.*] I can remember Alan saying that. As if it was yesterday.

GORDON: I remember it now. Alan was always after me – would I let him ride it? [GORDON *laughs.*]

FATHER: 'Why can't I have one?'

GORDON: I never would.

FATHER: 'You get through your exams, Alan – and then we'll see.'

GORDON: My father used to say that.

FATHER: I would've let him have one. Didn't seem like much to ask. Only, his mother . . .

GORDON: You're a terrible lot. Parents.

FATHER: She was always more careful . . . [FATHER *stops abruptly.*] What d'you say?

GORDON [*smiling*]: Do this and then, you can have that. Maybe!

FATHER: Oh.

GORDON: Blackmail. That's what it is. Nothing more – nothing less.

FATHER: You wait till you've got some children of your own. See what you say then.

GORDON: Well, now – there you've got me.

FATHER: How d'you mean?

GORDON: I have to confess – two children.

FATHER: Oh. That's nice. What are they?

GORDON: Boy and a girl. The boy's older.

FATHER: Pigeon pair. Make a lot of trouble for you, I shouldn't wonder?

GORDON: I've got some photographs on me. I don't know . . .

FATHER: I'd love to see them.

[GORDON *reaches into his jacket for his wallet.*]

GORDON: No sooner said . . .

FATHER: Our front room's a picture gallery.

GORDON: I'm supposed to have taken them out this afternoon. We were going to have a picnic.

FATHER: Here you are, talking to an old man.

[GORDON *pulls out his wallet.*]

GORDON: I'm having a great time.

FATHER [*quietly*]: Are you?

[GORDON *takes several photographs out of his wallet and then looks up at* FATHER.]

GORDON: You're quite sure you want to see them?

FATHER: Hand them over.

GORDON [*grinning*]: On your own head! [GORDON *leans forward and holds out the photographs.*] They aren't very good. Er – the photos.

[FATHER *takes the photographs. He puts them down on the arm of his chair and reaches into the top pocket of his jacket. He takes out his glasses case.*]

Well, neither are the children, if it comes to that.

[FATHER *opens his glasses case and takes out his glasses.*]

FATHER: Have you seen the photographs Alan takes?
[FATHER *puts his glasses on.*]

GORDON: Alan! I make Alan look like Leonardo da Vinci.
[FATHER *picks up the photographs and looks at them.*]

FATHER: She's very pretty.

GORDON: Yes. Matter of fact – that's not at all bad.
[FATHER *puts the photograph to the bottom of the pack and looks at the next one.*]

CUT TO FILM: *Looking down the side slopes of Whipsnade Zoo, out across the countryside below, showing through the heat haze.*

FATHER'S VOICE: He's a sturdy lad.

GORDON'S VOICE: I suppose you could call him that.

A child runs away down the slope. She is about three years old.

FATHER'S VOICE: Takes after you.

GORDON'S VOICE [*laughing*]: God forbid! Oh, no – that's terrible.

FATHER'S VOICE: Nonsense.

The child falls over and rolls several times, before she scrambles back on to her feet, laughing.

FATHER'S VOICE [*calling*]: Careful, Terry. Be careful now.

The child stands waving to people watching her, away up the hill.

GORDON'S VOICE: It makes the poor child look like an idiot! I couldn't get the camera to work. She must've been sitting like that – oh, I don't know! Hours!

Looking up the hill, from the child's point of view, at a man and woman, sitting round a tablecloth spread on the ground and covered with the debris of a picnic.

FATHER'S VOICE [*calling*]: Don't go too far, Terry.

Looking down the hill at the child, as she turns away and lurches on slowly, down the hill.

FATHER'S VOICE: Is that your wife?

GORDON'S VOICE [*laughing*]: She wouldn't thank me for showing you that!

FATHER'S VOICE [*calling*]: Terry, darling. Stay where Daddy can see you.

The child disappears over a ridge of ground. The sound of children laughing.

GORDON'S VOICE: That's all. Now you can relax.

FATHER'S VOICE: You've got a lovely family.

FATHER'S VOICE [*calling*]: Terry!

GORDON'S VOICE: One day, I'll get hold of a cine camera . . .

CUT TO *the back room.*

[GORDON *sits back in his chair and puts the wallet away.*]

GORDON: . . . take a moving picture of them – 'cause they move. Like perpetual motion they move!

FATHER: I've got a photograph of you, somewhere.

GORDON: Me? Photograph . . .

FATHER: Yes. Didn't know that, did you? [FATHER *pushes his glasses case away in the top pocket of his coat.*]

GORDON: I don't think you have, Mr Stephens. I mean, I don't want . . .

FATHER: Getting so old, I don't know what I'm saying?

GORDON [*laughing*]: I hope I've got your memory, when I get to be – when . . .

FATHER: I can't think where it is just now, but I'll find it and when I do [*he points at* GORDON, *smiling*] I'll show it you and you'll have to apologize.

GORDON: With pleasure.

FATHER: You used to play football with Alan.

GORDON: You used to come and watch.

FATHER: D'you remember?

GORDON: Certainly, I remember. Every Saturday.

FATHER: I enjoyed watching those matches.

GORDON: Best supporter we ever had. Every match you didn't watch, we lost.

FATHER: I don't think you did.

GORDON: Certainly!

FATHER: The last year – weren't you captain?

GORDON: That's right.

FATHER: I've got the photograph. The team – you and Alan – all the boys.

GORDON: Oh, I see.

FATHER: Can't think where it is just now.

GORDON: I apologize.

FATHER: That was a very good team.

GORDON: Best team the school ever had.

FATHER: I went on, you know . . .

[*The door opens and* TERRY *walks briskly into the room.*]

TERRY: Dad. [*She stops abruptly, seeing the two men deep in conversation.*] Sorry. I'm sorry. I didn't know . . .

GORDON: That's all right. Quite all right. [GORDON *stands up and turns to face* TERRY.]

FATHER [*irritably*]: What is it, Terry?

TERRY: I want to say good-bye.

FATHER: Are you going?

TERRY: 'Fraid so.

CUT TO *the hall.*

[*Close shot of* FATHER.]

FATHER: Your mother doesn't mean half she says. You know that.

[*Swing to include* TERRY, *who is standing at the bottom of the stairs holding a small suitcase. She is in her teens.*]

TERRY: If she doesn't mean it, why does she say it?

FATHER: She gets excited. She doesn't think.

TERRY: She should think. Talking to me – why shouldn't she?

FATHER: She's upset.

TERRY: I should think she would be.

FATHER: If she thought – if she had any idea . . .

TERRY: You heard her. 'No better than a tart!' That's what she said.

FATHER: No, it isn't.

TERRY: It's what she meant.

FATHER: No.

TERRY: Bloody yes!

FATHER: Terry! Don't talk like that.

TERRY [*sincerely*]: I'm sorry.

FATHER: I want you to come back with me – now – into the front room and talk to your mother. Sensibly.

TERRY: No.

FATHER: I'm asking you.

TERRY: Why can't she come out here? Talk to me out here!
FATHER: For my sake?
TERRY: No, Dad. No. It isn't fair.
FATHER: I don't want you running off . . .
TERRY: Why is it always you?
FATHER: Living on your own.
TERRY: Why does she always make you . . .
FATHER: No more does your mother.
TERRY: If she didn't treat me . . .
FATHER: Come and talk to her?
TERRY: What does she think I am?
FATHER: She worries about you, Terry.
GORDON'S VOICE: I'll leave you alone.

CUT TO *the back room.*
FATHER: No. Don't go away.
TERRY: If you don't mind?
GORDON: Of course not.
FATHER: I was enjoying our chat.
GORDON: I'll wait – er – outside.
TERRY: Thanks.
FATHER: Don't go away.
TERRY: Mr – er . . .
GORDON: Lester. Gordon Lester.
TERRY: Mr Lester came to see Alan, Dad.
FATHER: He was at school with Alan. We were talking about it. Talking about the old days.
TERRY: Yes, I know.
GORDON: When you've spoken to your daughter . . .
TERRY: I want to say good-bye.
MOTHER'S VOICE [*harshly*]: All right. Good-bye!

CUT TO *the front room.*
FATHER: Mother!
MOTHER: Let her go. I won't stop her.
> [*Looking past* MOTHER, *at* FATHER, *who is standing in the centre of the room, and at* TERRY, *standing in the doorway.*]

See how she gets on without us.

TERRY: What's the use, Dad?

FATHER: Talk to the child.

MOTHER: No.

FATHER: Ask her to stay.

MOTHER: Never – in a million years.

FATHER: She's going away. She's going – to leave home.

TERRY: Yes, I am.

FATHER: She means it.

MOTHER: If you want her to stay, you talk to her.

TERRY: Alan can bring the rest of my stuff, when I've found a place to stay.

[FATHER *turns desperately to face* TERRY.]

FATHER: Yes, but Terry – tonight! Where are you going to stay tonight?

TERRY: I'll find somewhere.

MOTHER: No fear of that.

TERRY: What have I ever done to you!

MOTHER: What haven't you done!

TERRY: I don't know!

FATHER: If you'd stay tonight, Terry. If you'd just stay ...

TERRY: No.

MOTHER: Don't beg her to stay.

TERRY: I'll be all right. I've got some friends. They'll find me a corner – somewhere.

FATHER: Terry.

TERRY: I can't, Dad. I would. I'd stay for your sake ...

MOTHER: Oh, yes.

TERRY: I can't.

MOTHER: Your father!

CUT TO *the back room.*

FATHER: They used to play football together.

[*Pull back to include* TERRY *and* GORDON, *standing at the door.*]

TERRY: It won't take long.

FATHER: We were talking about it.

[GORDON *pulls the door open.*]

GORDON: Where is Alan?

TERRY: He's in the front room. He's talking to my mother. Don't disturb them.

GORDON: Oh.

TERRY: Is that – er – d'you have a cigarette without a tip?

GORDON: What? Oh, yes.

TERRY: Let me have one.

GORDON: Certainly. [GORDON *takes out a packet of cigarettes and offers it to* TERRY.]

TERRY: Thanks.

FATHER: I used to watch them play. I don't suppose you remember, Terry?

TERRY: I remember.

[GORDON *lights* TERRY'S *cigarette for her.*]

GORDON: You don't remember me.

TERRY: Should I?

GORDON: We used to know each other. We went to a couple of dances.

TERRY: I'm sorry.

GORDON: It's a long time ago.

FATHER: What d'you want to say, Terry?

TERRY: 'Scuse me.

GORDON: Yes, of course. [GORDON *walks out of the room and shuts the door.*]

TERRY: I want to say good-bye.

CUT TO *the hall.*

[TERRY *and her* FATHER *are standing at the front door.* TERRY *has just opened the door.*]

FATHER: I knew – I mean, some day – obviously, you'd leave home.

TERRY: With that tall, dark stranger Mum was always talking about.

FATHER: Some – nice boy. Yes.

TERRY: He didn't seem to come along, did he?

FATHER: I didn't think . . .

TERRY: I can't stay, Dad. Not any longer.

FATHER: I'll miss you.

TERRY [*laughing*]: Come with me.

FATHER'S VOICE: Aren't you staying to supper?

FATHER: You'll be all right? You can – I don't know – look after yourself?

TERRY: Nobody can hurt me, Dad.

TERRY'S VOICE: No, I can't. Sorry.

FATHER: When you find somewhere . . .

TERRY: I'll let you know.

> [*Suddenly* FATHER *catches hold of* TERRY *and hugs her tightly.*]

FATHER: It isn't happening. It can't be.

FATHER'S VOICE: Your mother'll be disappointed.

TERRY: I love you so much, Dad.

FATHER: I don't believe – I won't – believe . . .

TERRY: It is – Dad – it is happening!

TERRY'S VOICE: Bit busy tonight.

FATHER: What will it be like? Without you? What am I going to do?

CUT TO *the back room.*

FATHER: You're happy, are you?

TERRY: Yes. Why?

FATHER: You should be happy.

TERRY: Thanks. [TERRY *walks across to the fireplace and stubs out the cigarette she brought in with her.*]

FATHER: When are we going to see you again?

TERRY: I don't know. Some time.

FATHER: Soon. Your mother misses you.

TERRY: Don't do too much. Don't let Alan break your back.

FATHER: I won't.

TERRY: He's on some sort of health kick.

FATHER: What?

TERRY: He's decided you need a lot of fresh air and exercise.

FATHER: D'you remember that picnic?

TERRY: Picnic? What picnic, Dad?

FATHER: On a hill. The side of a hill – and you went running. You fell over!

TERRY: Did that happen?

FATHER: I thought you were going to roll – clear down the hill.

TERRY: I thought I made it up.

FATHER: It was such a hot day. Your mother had the devil of a job, making you keep your clothes on.

TERRY: Funny.

FATHER D'you remember climbing? There was just the one path – and that wasn't much of a path.

TERRY: I remember.

FATHER: I had to carry you. Alan went on, up the path and stood . . .

> [Silence.]

He stood at the very top of the hill – and shouted down at us.

TERRY: Yes.

FATHER: 'Come on,' he shouted. 'Buck up.'

TERRY: 'Slow-coaches.'

FATHER: Your poor mother. She only just made it.

TERRY. It was a good thing she did. She was carrying the food.

FATHER: That was a day.

TERRY: I thought I made it up.

FATHER: That was a good day. Aren't you going to stay for supper?

TERRY: No.

FATHER: When are we going to see you again?

TERRY: Oh – you know. Soon.

FATHER: Yes. Make it soon.

TERRY: I'll try to.

FATHER: You were laughing and crying.

> [The sound of a small child crying.]

Dirt all over your face – your clothes. You cut your knee.

CUT TO FILM: *Looking down over the Father's shoulder, into the face of the child he is carrying. The child's face is dirty and slightly scratched. She is crying.*

TERRY'S VOICE: It was a good day.

FATHER'S VOICE: Yes.

CHILD'S VOICE [*sobbing*]: I hurt myself.

Father scrambles up the slope, carefully.

FATHER'S VOICE: I told you, didn't I, poppet?

CHILD'S VOICE: I didn't want to hurt myself.

Long shot, looking down the slope, towards Father and the child in his arms.

FATHER'S VOICE: Scrambling about – and falling over. Running away! Didn't Daddy say? 'You'll hurt yourself.'

TERRY'S VOICE: I didn't know it would hurt.

CUT TO *Terry's bedroom.*

[*Looking across the bed past* TERRY, *at* FATHER'S *silhouette.*]

TERRY: He didn't tell me it would hurt. Nobody told me.

FATHER [*quietly*]: What happened?

TERRY: We went for a drive in his car.

FATHER: Yes?

TERRY: We went a long way – and it got late. I said, 'You must take me home' – and he laughed.

FATHER: Where did you go?

TERRY: I don't know. We went so fast. It – oh, it must've been a long way – and then, he stopped.

FATHER: Yes?

TERRY: He kissed me. He put his arms round me and held me – tight. He – then, he bit me – bit my ear and said things – whispered – things . . .

[*Silence.*]

I said – 'Take me home' – and he laughed again.

FATHER: What did he do?

TERRY: He – pulled at me – pulled – at my dress – and tore it. I tried to get away from him – and all the time – Daddy – he was laughing all the time.

FATHER [*harshly*]: What did he do?

TERRY [*childishly*]:Hurt me.

FATHER [*harshly*]: You – Terry – you let him . . .

TERRY [*fiercely*]: Let him! No. I couldn't stop him.

[*Silence.*]

FATHER: How far did he – how . . .

TERRY: He talked to me – gently – all the time – whispering in my ear – gently – as if he was – telling me a story. Like you, Dad.

FATHER: No.

TERRY: Some secret – story.

FATHER: Not – oh, no – not like . . . [FATHER *breaks away from* TERRY. *He pulls away from her, completely.*] No!

TERRY: I could feel his hands – on me – over me. All – over me.

FATHER: How could you let him – touch – Terry!

TERRY: It didn't seem – I don't know – listening to him – listening to what he was saying – soft things, tender things – love . . .

[TERRY *reaches out towards her* FATHER *and he jerks farther away from her, along the bed.*]

Daddy?

FATHER: You let him make – you – how could you . . .

TERRY: I didn't want him to stop. I didn't – oh, it was so – real – and everything else – nothing!

FATHER: I hate you.

TERRY: Floating – drifting – and his hands – all I could feel . . .

FATHER: Stop it.

TERRY: All – I could hear . . .

FATHER: Stop talking – stop . . .

TERRY: Then – and then – he hurt me. I cried out.

[*The sound of a woman's sudden cry of physical pain.*]

CUT TO *a hotel bedroom. Night.*

[*Looking across the large hotel room, towards the bed. The room is in darkness, except for the pattern of light striking across the floor, through the partially drawn curtains.*]

FATHER'S VOICE: Sorry. I'm sorry. I didn't know. Sarah.

[*Cut to a close-up of a* YOUNG WOMAN'S *face drenched in tears.*]

I didn't mean to hurt you. I wouldn't. Sarah, please – forgive me.

[*The* WOMAN *turns her face into the pillow, away from
the sound of the voice.*]

For all the world, I wouldn't hurt . . .

[*Cut to the long shot, looking across the room.*]

Sarah.

CUT TO *Terry's bedroom. Night.*

FATHER'S VOICE: Don't turn away.

TERRY: He thought – he told me – afterwards . . .

FATHER: I'll fetch your mother. [FATHER *stands up and
turns away from the bed and* TERRY.]

TERRY: No! Oh, no. Don't tell her.

FATHER: You must talk – er . . .

TERRY: It'll be all right. Look, he said . . . [TERRY
scrambles on to her knees in the bed.] Don't tell Mum.

FATHER [*mumbling*]: Must – tell her.

TERRY: I had to tell someone. I wanted to tell you.

FATHER: Your mother – don't be silly – must . . .

TERRY: I can't tell her.

[FATHER *walks quickly towards the bedroom door.*]

FATHER: Yes.

TERRY: I won't.

FATHER: We have to – tell your mother. She'll know –
what to do. [FATHER *stumbles out of the room and on to the
landing. He sways two or three steps and then lurches sideways
against the wall. He presses his face flat to the wall and brings his
hands up to his mouth. He retches and his body shudders. He
crouches slightly, against the wall.*]

FATHER'S VOICE: You've told your mother?

CUT TO *the back room.*

TERRY: Er – what?

FATHER: You're not staying to supper.

TERRY: Oh, yes.

FATHER: You know what she is. We've got your address,
have we?

TERRY: I'll give it to Mother.

FATHER: Make sure you do.

[*Silence.*]

TERRY: 'Bye. [TERRY *leans over and kisses her* FATHER *on the cheek.*]

FATHER: Take care of yourself.

TERRY: I will. [TERRY *straightens up and turns away.*]

FATHER: Terry! What about your present? You can't go without your present.

TERRY: Oh. No – I suppose . . .

FATHER: 'Course you can't! [FATHER *stands up and walks across to the sideboard.*] I don't know what your mother would say, if you went without your present. [*He opens the sideboard and takes out a package, wrapped in decorated paper.*]

[*Triumphantly*] Now! [*He walks across to the door, carrying the package.*]

[*Calling*] Mother!

TERRY: Dad! Oh, no. Look . . .

FATHER [*calling*]: Alan.

[*He opens the door and comes out into the hall.* TERRY *follows.*

GORDON LESTER *is sitting on the stairs.*

FATHER *walks to the front room and opens the door.*] Can't let Terry go, without giving her present to her.

[*He walks into the front room.*

MOTHER *and* ALAN *are facing one another.*]

MOTHER: Does she try to understand? Does anyone?

[FATHER *puts the package down on the table.*]

FATHER: Terry's present.

MOTHER: Oh, for – oh!

ALAN: Present? What present's that? [ALAN *walks across to the table.*]

FATHER: Terry's birthday present.

ALAN: Terry's birthday was – when was it?

MOTHER [*calmly*]: Last month.

FATHER: We've been keeping it for her.

TERRY: You don't have to . . . [TERRY *walks into the room.*]

FATHER: Go on, Terry. Open it.

[TERRY *looks at her* MOTHER, *who is standing by the fireplace, staring at her.*]

Can you guess what it is?

[TERRY *shrugs and walks across to the table.*]

TERRY: No. No, I've no idea. [TERRY *reaches for the ribbon and begins to untie it. She struggles with the paper.*]

MOTHER: I don't know what all the fuss is about. It's only . . .

FATHER: Oh, now – don't tell her. [FATHER *looks round angrily at* MOTHER.] Let her guess. Can you guess?

TERRY: Haven't the faintest idea.

[TERRY *struggles with the string round the box.* FATHER *turns back and steps towards the table, as he puts his hand into his pocket.*]

FATHER: Here you are. [FATHER *takes out a penknife and hands it to* TERRY.] This'll help.

MOTHER: I don't know why you wrapped it up like – like – I don't know what!

[TERRY *takes the penknife.*]

FATHER: That's the fun, isn't it?

[TERRY *cuts the string and takes the lid off the box. Wrapped in tissue paper is a silk nightdress.* TERRY *takes it out of the box.*]

Your mother chose it.

TERRY: Yes.

FATHER: You like it, don't you?

TERRY: Oh, yes. Thank you. [TERRY *kisses her* FATHER.]

FATHER: Couldn't think what else . . .

TERRY: It's super. Really. [TERRY *turns to face her* MOTHER.] Thank you.

FATHER: Happy birthday.

[TERRY *walks across and kisses her* MOTHER.]

ALAN: I've got nothing for you.

TERRY: I'll leave an address. You can send it on to me.

FATHER: Just like a brother.

[TERRY *puts the nightdress back into the box and shuts it.*]

MOTHER: If you don't like it, you can always go and change it. I asked them.

FATHER: Of course, she likes it.

TERRY: Yes. I like it.

[*Silence.*]

Well, then.

MOTHER: You're welcome to stay to supper.

TERRY: No, thanks. Oh, I'll – er – have you got something I can write with?

ALAN: A pen, maybe?

TERRY: I'll let you have my address.

[ALAN *gives* TERRY *a pencil and she tears a piece off the wrapping paper.*]

MOTHER: No, don't do that. I might find a use for it.

[MOTHER *picks up the wrapping paper and begins to fold it.*]

TERRY: You'd better see how your friend's getting on. He was looking distinctly sorry for himself a couple of minutes ago.

ALAN: Oh, for goodness' sake! [ALAN *goes out of the room, as* TERRY *finishes writing.*]

TERRY: There you are. Put it somewhere safe, so you can be sure and lose it.

[FATHER *takes the piece of paper and reads the address.*]

FATHER: 130A, Forsyth Street. [FATHER *lifts his head and looks at* TERRY.]

TERRY [*brightly*]: You'll never find it on your own. When you come and see me . . .

CUT TO FILM: *Close-up of a small piece of paper, with an address written on it.*

TERRY'S VOICE: . . . give me plenty of warning. I'll make signs in chalk all along the pavements. It's really quite – well, it was – quite a smart neighbourhood, just – difficult for the stranger to find his way. They sell survival kits at all the chemists.

FATHER'S VOICE: We'll find it.

High shot, looking down a twisting staircase, at Father, as he walks slowly upwards, with his hand on the banisters. He pauses on each landing and looks at the doors.

TERRY'S VOICE: Don't speak too soon. Better men than

you have perished! The white man's grave – or is it burden? Anyway, if you are white, you need a passport.

MOTHER'S VOICE: You should be happy enough there.

TERRY'S VOICE: Yes, I'm very happy. Thank you.

FATHER'S VOICE: We'll come and see you, Terry. Soon – very soon.

He reaches the top landing, looks at the left-hand door and then knocks on it.

TERRY'S VOICE: Yes, Dad. Please. It would be nice. I'd like to show it off to you.

He steps back from the door and waits. The door opens and Terry looks out.

TERRY'S VOICE: Dad. Oh, Dad. Thank you.

MOTHER'S VOICE: Have to be a weekend, I suppose?

Close-up of Father.

TERRY'S VOICE: Thank you for coming.

TERRY'S VOICE: Unless you like to make it an evening?

Terry steps out of the room and presses herself into her Father's arms. He holds her tightly. There are tears in his eyes.

FATHER'S VOICE: Sounded like you might need a bit of help.

FATHER'S VOICE: We don't get out much in the evening. Do we, Mother?

TERRY'S VOICE: Stuck watching telly, I suppose?

MOTHER'S VOICE: We watch television. Yes.

TERRY'S VOICE: I've got a set.

TERRY'S VOICE: Come in. Please.

CUT TO *Terry's bed-sitting room in Baron's Court.*

[*Looking across the tiny room at* TERRY *and her* FATHER *as they walk through the doorway.*]

TERRY: I won't be a minute. I'm all packed. [TERRY *pulls the door shut.*]

FATHER: It's not easy to find, is it?

TERRY: I'll get my suitcase.

FATHER: Like a rabbit warren.

[TERRY *pulls the cupboard door open and jerks out a small and battered suitcase.*]

TERRY: Yes.

FATHER: Baron's Court. Funny name for a place – well, something like this.

TERRY: I'll just put a brush through my hair. [TERRY *pulls back a plywood partition and looks at her face in a small mirror over a wash basin.*]

FATHER: Is this all you've got?

TERRY: Oh, God! I look awful! Sorry, Dad – what did you say?

FATHER: Is this all you've got? The two of you?

TERRY: Yes.

FATHER: It isn't much.

[TERRY *pulls at her hair with a brush.*]

TERRY: No. It isn't easy – finding somewhere . . .

FATHER: If you need a bit of money. We haven't got much.

TERRY: It isn't a question of money, Dad. Not really. [TERRY *turns to face her* FATHER.]

FATHER: Lovey! [FATHER *clasps his hands together.*]

TERRY: What? What is it?

FATHER: You look so – tired. I've never seen you – look . . .

TERRY [*briskly*]: I haven't been sleeping too well just lately. [TERRY'S *face is haggard, and her eyes are sunk deep in their sockets. Her hair hangs lank round her shoulders.*]

FATHER: It's more – lovey – more than [*he shrugs his shoulders*] not sleeping.

TERRY: Take me home, Dad. I'll be all right – there. Take me – anywhere. I don't care.

[FATHER *holds out his arms and* TERRY *almost runs towards him. She hides in his arms.*]

FATHER: We've got your old room waiting for you. Come on.

TERRY [*mumbling*]: It isn't him – Dad. I love him. It's this – all this – and living . . . [TERRY *pushes back and looks at her* FATHER.] You can't call it living. Scrambling – fighting every day – all day – and people looking at you. Dad, it shouldn't – I love him – just because I love – it shouldn't.

FATHER: You can tell us all about it, when I get you home.
[FATHER *slips an arm round her shoulders and pulls her close.*]

TERRY: You do understand? Dad – you do – it isn't
Leonard – I love . . .

FATHER: Yes, of course.

TERRY: I hate this place. I live here – and – oh, God! I
hate it. Hate it!

FATHER: Your room's just the same. Just like it always was.

TERRY: I love him.

FATHER: You'll be happy there.

TERRY: I can't live . . .

FATHER: Comfortable.

TERRY: . . . like a pig, Dad – here – in this filth!

FATHER: Come on, lovey.

TERRY: It's all we can get.

FATHER: Shh. [FATHER *strokes her back gently.*] Baby.

TERRY: And Mum . . .

FATHER: Your mother can't wait to see you.

TERRY [*mumbling*]: Hates me.

FATHER: Nonsense. What nonsense! She would have come
with me, but you know what she is. Wanted to have
everything nice for you – spick and span! You know your
mother.

TERRY: She said – didn't she say – 'Wait and see, my girl,'
– she said – 'You'll come home – begging us . . .'

FATHER: All forgotten, baby. All forgotten.

TERRY: She was right.
[FATHER *leads* TERRY *across to her case and picks
it up.*]

FATHER: The sooner we get home . . .
[*The door opens and* LEONARD NGANA *steps into the
doorway.*]

LEONARD: Well now, baby – what's all this here? What's
going on?

TERRY: I'm going home.

LEONARD: You going home? Who says you going home,
baby? [LEONARD *shuts the door behind him.*] I don't say
you going home.

TERRY: Please. Let me go.

LEONARD: This your Daddy?

FATHER: I'm Terry's father. Yes.

LEONARD: Hi, Daddy, baby! How come you fixing to steal my wife away from me?

FATHER: Terry wants to come home. I'm taking her home.

LEONARD: No.

TERRY: I can't stay here.

LEONARD: You [*he points at* TERRY] are my wife, baby. You just naturally got to stay here.

FATHER: I'm taking my daughter home, where she belongs.

LEONARD: Here, Daddy, baby – here – where she belongs. With her rightful husband. You wasn't there, but she married me. I got papers to show.

FATHER: I won't let her live in this – this – filth. Look at it!

LEONARD: You think I want to live in filth? You think, if I could get me a better place, if I could afford me a better place – you think I'd live here?

FATHER: All right. [FATHER *steps away from* TERRY, *to face* LEONARD.] Get yourself somewhere better. Don't make her – make my daughter . . .

LEONARD: My wife!

FATHER: If you love her . . .

LEONARD [*angrily*]: I love her! [LEONARD *walks round* FATHER, *towards* TERRY. *He tries to touch her, but she shrinks away from him.*]
[*Gently*] I love you.

FATHER: You love her – and you keep her – in a pig-sty like this!

LEONARD: You think I want her living – here – baby, how many times I got to say . . . [LEONARD *turns away angrily from* FATHER, *turning in a circle, and smashes his hand down flat on a battered, old chest of drawers.*] What you think I am? You think I'm an animal – I want to live in my own mess? [LEONARD *turns and faces* FATHER, *almost weeping.*] That what you think?

FATHER: If you love my daughter, I think you could do better . . .

LEONARD: Baby, try – you – try being black – like I'm black! 'Cause I'm black – look at me. [LEONARD *rips his shirt open.*] Clear down – I'm black. You be like that and then – you come and tell me – do better!

FATHER [*hesitantly*]: All this – talk – all the time – how badly people – I don't know – treat you! You make an excuse . . .

LEONARD: That what you think?

FATHER: What do you do?

LEONARD: I look for work, baby.

FATHER: If you want – really – want to get out of here . . .

LEONARD: I want to. You believe me. I throw up. Every morning I wake up – here – look at these walls – and Terry – in the bed, next to me – and all I can see – those filthy walls . . . [LEONARD *smashes his first against one of the walls.*] And this! [LEONARD *catches hold of the plyboard partition and nearly rips it off its hinges.*] What is this! The rats – you can hear the rats – you know that? And the – all . . . [LEONARD *throws his hands wide and almost touches the walls on either side of the room.*] The mess! Terry – living here. I love her – you know? I throw up!

[*Silence.*]

[*Calmer*] And this – believe me, Daddy, baby – this is the best I can do. [*Laughing*] 'Cause this land [*he points at* FATHER] is your land!

FATHER: I'm taking Terry home.

LEONARD [*coldly*]: You got a piece of paper says you can take my wife out of here?

FATHER: She 'phoned me – this morning . . .

LEONARD [*grinning*]: I knew there was something cooking, baby. I just naturally knew.

FATHER: She said – 'Come and take me home.'

LEONARD: That what you said?

TERRY: I love you.

LEONARD [*harshly*]: You say that – 'Come and take me home'?

TERRY: I can't live here.

LEONARD: This the only place we got.

TERRY: Living here, Leonard – it makes me – ill. It makes me . . .

LEONARD [*gently*]: I know, baby. Me too. But, we going to break out. I promise. We not staying here. Don't you know that?

TERRY: You say that.

LEONARD: I mean it. Baby, when we got started, I told you – 'It'll be rough.' I told you that.

TERRY: I know.

LEONARD: Too rough?

FATHER: You can't expect any – well, decent . . .

LEONARD: Daddy, baby, I can expect. Yeah, I get disappointed. But, I can expect.

FATHER: Any decent girl – here – well!

LEONARD: You want to go with him?

TERRY: I want him to take me.

LEONARD: I'll stop him. If I can, baby. I need you.

TERRY: Dad.

[*Silence.*

LEONARD *turns to face* FATHER.]

LEONARD: You hear what she says? You got to take her.

FATHER: She sent for me.

LEONARD: Yeah. Now – she won't walk out that door, without you carry her – and I'm flat down there – with the rats. Where I belong. Right?

FATHER: She wants to come home.

LEONARD: She wants a lot of things, Daddy, baby.

FATHER: She told me . . .

LEONARD: Now, she's telling you – take me!

FATHER: Terry.

LEONARD: That's the way it is.

FATHER: Come on, lovey.

LEONARD: No, baby – you don't dig. She wants you fighting for her. You have to – take her – out of all this filth – up high on that white horse all you fathers are supposed to have. Riding whip in one hand, golden reins in the other.

FATHER: Your mother's waiting for you.

LEONARD: You got to fight, Daddy – 'cause I'm fighting. I want this girl. I've got her and I'm going to keep her. It's a big man's going to take her away from me.

[*Silence.*]

You that big man?

FATHER: You sent for me.

LEONARD: Go 'way, Daddy, baby.

FATHER: You told me . . .

LEONARD: Go 'way!

[*Silence.*]

FATHER: When you're ready, Terry – when you want to come home – we'll be waiting for you.

LEONARD: She ain't coming home. She just now really left.

[*Silence.*

FATHER turns and walks to the door. He turns the handle and pulls the door open. He doesn't turn to look back, but he hesitates for a moment.

High shot, looking down at the landing, as he walks out of the room. He pulls the door shut, turns and walks away, down the stairs.]

CUT TO *the hall of the Stephens' house.*

[*Close-up of* FATHER, *as he walks out of the front room.*]

TERRY'S VOICE: 'Bye, now.

[*Pull back to include* TERRY, *as she walks with her* FATHER *to the front door.*]

FATHER: Keep in touch.

[TERRY *glances at* GORDON LESTER, *as they walk past him.*]

TERRY: Nice to see you again.

GORDON: And you. [GORDON LESTER *stands up and puts out a hand, hesitantly.*] Er – I hope it won't be – so long . . .

TERRY: I hope so, too. [TERRY *shakes hands with him.*]

FATHER [*irritably*]: D'you hear me, Terry?

TERRY: Yes, Dad. Yes, of course. Anyway . . . [TERRY *smiles briefly at* GORDON LESTER *and then turns back to her*

FATHER. *She slips an arm round his waist.*] . . . you – are coming to see my new flat.

FATHER: You write to us.

TERRY [*laughing*]: Oh, Dad. You know I can't write my own name – let alone . . .

ALAN'S VOICE: Terry.

> [TERRY *turns her head and looks back at* ALAN, *over her* FATHER'S *shoulder.*]

Look after yourself.

TERRY: Fireproof! You know me. I'm the one – pulled up the ladder.

> [ALAN *turns his head slightly and looks in to the front room. Silence.*]

[*Coldly*] Lots of things to do, sweetie. Sorry.

ALAN: The fate of nations?

TERRY: Something like that.

FATHER: Why can't you stay to supper?

TERRY: 'Cause there are people expecting me. [TERRY *turns back to her* FATHER, *grins and kisses him on the cheek.*] Your daughter is a very popular girl.

FATHER: You come all this way . . .

TERRY: Just 'cause I love you. [TERRY *opens the front door.*]

FATHER: I haven't had a chance to talk to you.

TERRY: All the more reason to come and see me – settled in my new home.

FATHER [*abruptly*]: Don't rush off.

TERRY: There's nothing I'd like better – Dad, you know that! A quiet evening with you . . . [TERRY *stands in the doorway.*] But – needs must . . . [TERRY *reaches out and touches her* FATHER, *gently, on the side of the face.*] 'Bye, now. [TERRY *turns away from the house.*]

CUT TO FILM: *Looking across the small square suburban front garden of the Stephens' house. Terry steps down on to the path and walks towards the front gate. She is wearing a light-coloured, belted mackintosh, and carrying a small suitcase.*

FATHER'S VOICE: I'll walk with you, Terry. As far as the bus.

She reaches the front gate and pulls it open. Father stands in the doorway, watching.

TERRY'S VOICE: No. Dad, Thanks all the same.

CUT. *Terry turns and looks back at the house. She is wearing a lightweight spring coat and she is not carrying the small suitcase.*

FATHER'S VOICE: It's no trouble. I can just do with the walk. Wait there. I'll change my shoes. Won't be a moment.

Father stands in the doorway.

TERRY'S VOICE: No, Dad. Don't bother.

CUT. *Looking along the path to the front gate. A young girl in school uniform is standing at the gate, with a satchel over her arm.*

CHILD'S VOICE: I'm late as it is.

She turns and runs across the road, away from the house.

CUT TO *the hall of the Stephens' house.*
[*Close-up of* FATHER.]

FATHER [*calling*]: Mind how you go.

MOTHER'S VOICE: She's old enough. She can look after herself.

FATHER: I don't know what gets into her. [FATHER *stands, staring out of the house at* TERRY, *as she walks away.*]

GORDON'S VOICE: She's changed, hasn't she? I hardly recognized her . . .

MOTHER'S VOICE: Oh, yes.

GORDON'S VOICE: . . . as the same girl.

MOTHER'S VOICE: Terry's changed.

FATHER: Six months. [FATHER *shuts the door and turns to face the group in the hall.*]

GORDON [*smiling*]: If I'd had any idea . . .

FATHER [*interrupting*]: Must be six months, since we last saw Terry.

MOTHER: More than that.

FATHER: Is it? Yes, I suppose it is.

ALAN: D'you mind waiting a bit longer?

GORDON: Well, as a matter of fact, old son . . .

FATHER: I think we ought to go and see that – what is it? – new flat she's living in.

MOTHER: If there's time.

FATHER: You've got the address?

ALAN: Just have a word . . .

GORDON: . . . wouldn't it be better . . .

FATHER [*fiercely*]: You have got the address?

MOTHER: Yes, I have.

FATHER: She seemed to want us to go.

MOTHER: Let me make you a cup of tea, Gordon?

GORDON: Oh, no. Really, Mrs Stephens.

MOTHER: I hate to think . . .

ALAN: I'll talk to Dad . . .

FATHER: I'd like to see where she's living.

ALAN: Five minutes.

MOTHER [*laughing*]: Not even a cup of tea!

FATHER: I want to go, anyway.

MOTHER [*abruptly*]: Yes, Ted.
    [*Silence.*]

FATHER: Don't you?

MOTHER: If there's time.

ALAN: Dad . . .

GORDON: I'll give you a call later.

ALAN: Can I talk to you, Dad?

FATHER: Who's the girl – what did Terry say . . .

MOTHER: Jessica.

GORDON: When you're at home.

FATHER: Do you know her?

MOTHER: No, I don't.

ALAN: Dad.

FATHER: Who is she? What sort of girl is she? What does she do?

MOTHER: How should I know?

FATHER: How did Terry meet her? How does Terry come to be sharing . . . [FATHER *breaks off abruptly and shakes his head.*]

ALAN: I'm sorry.

FATHER: We don't know any of her friends. [FATHER *walks through the group away, along the hall.*]

GORDON: Forget it.

[*Watch* FATHER, *as he walks towards the back room.*]

ALAN'S VOICE [*desperately*]: Mum!

MOTHER'S VOICE: I'll look after Gordon.

GORDON'S VOICE: There's no need.

ALAN'S VOICE: Dad.

[FATHER *walks into the back room, pushing the door wide open. He walks into the centre of the room and stops. He slaps his hands together.*]

FATHER: Treats this house like a hotel.

[ALAN *follows his* FATHER *into the room.*]

Coming and going – just as she pleases.

ALAN: Dad.

FATHER: Your mother's right. Absolutely – right!

ALAN: Can I talk to you, Dad?

FATHER: What's happened to her? [FATHER *takes his cigarette case out of his pocket and opens it.*] Always rushing off – where? Where does she go?

ALAN: Should I take the job, Dad?

[FATHER *selects a cigarette for himself, carefully*].

FATHER: She's not the same girl.

ALAN: It means I shall have to leave England.

FATHER: He's right. The boy's right. [FATHER *gestures with the cigarette in the general direction of the hall.*] What's-his-name?

ALAN: It means I'll have to go abroad.

FATHER: I can hardly recognize her.

ALAN: I shall have to live – abroad.

FATHER: I want to know!

ALAN: Dad! Listen to me. Will you listen to me?

[*Silence.*]

FATHER: What does your mother say? [FATHER *puts the cigarette into his mouth.*]

ALAN: You know what she says! 'Don't think about us, Alan. Take the job.'

[FATHER *turns away and puts the cigarette case away into his coat pocket.*]

'If you want to take it . . .'

[FATHER *takes out his cigarette lighter.*]

FATHER: Well, then – if that's what your mother says . . .

ALAN: What do you say? Dad! I'm asking you.

FATHER: I think she's right. If you want to take the job.

[FATHER *lights his cigarette.*]

ALAN [*angrily*]: Of course.

[ALAN *breaks off and controls himself.*
Silence.]

[*Calmer*] I want to take the job.

FATHER: That's all there is to it. [FATHER *drops his lighter back into his pocket and walks across to the windows.*]

ALAN: The thing is – I mean, if I take the job . . . [ALAN *walks across to the window and stands, sideways on to his* FATHER, *looking at him.*] It isn't just – you know – a few months . . .

FATHER: Why did she marry him?

[*Silence.*]

ALAN [*wearily*]: I don't know, Dad. She was in love with him, I suppose.

FATHER: How could she – what d'you mean – love him – love someone . . .

ALAN: If you talk to Terry . . .

FATHER: Anyway, what does it mean?

ALAN: . . . you might get an answer. Talk to me . . .

FATHER: Love! What does that mean? [FATHER *turns on his heels to face* ALAN.] Did you see him? I saw him.

ALAN: Yes, I did.

FATHER: Black as the ace of spades!

ALAN: I met him once. I liked him.

FATHER: You liked him?

ALAN: Yes. I liked him and Terry – loved him.

FATHER: That's all you've got to say, is it? Terry – loved him! That's supposed to explain – that . . . [FATHER *walks away from* ALAN.]

ALAN [*violently*]: Dad, will you listen to me? Will you stop – for a minute – just one minute – will you stop thinking about your precious daughter? Will you – and think about me?

134

[*Silence.*]

I have to tell him tomorrow.

FATHER: What? Tell him what? Tomorrow?

ALAN: He gave me the weekend to think about it.

[*Silence.*]

FATHER: What're you talking about?

ALAN: The job – whether I should take the job.

FATHER: Of course, you should take it. You'd be a fool not to. It's a good job. Isn't it a good job?

ALAN [*quietly*]: Yes, it is.

FATHER: He expects you to take it, doesn't he?

ALAN: Yes, he expects me to take it.

FATHER: It isn't everyone gets a chance . . .

[FATHER *trails into silence.*
Silence.]

You'll go away?

ALAN: Yes.

FATHER: How long – er – when will we see you?

ALAN: I don't know. He said something about home leave – every two years.

FATHER: You'll take Ellen – and the children?

ALAN: Yes, of course.

FATHER: Terry won't come home again.

ALAN: She'll come home.

FATHER: I don't think so. What does your mother say?

ALAN: As far as Terry's concerned . . .

FATHER: You. What does she say about you – and going . . . [FATHER *stubs out his cigarette.*] Where?

ALAN: Australia.

FATHER: What does she say?

ALAN: I should go.

[FATHER *looks up at* ALAN *and nods his head.*]

FATHER: She's right.

ALAN [*violently*]: She hasn't thought about it. You – haven't thought . . . [ALAN *clasps his hands together.*] I know – Terry – I mean, how much you care . . . [ALAN *gestures vaguely.*]

FATHER: Watching her – you know? Walking away – I thought . . . [FATHER *shakes his head slowly.*]

ALAN: Just – please – before I go home – think. Will you? If it's too much I don't have to take the job. It doesn't mean that much to me. All I want you to do . . .

FATHER: Ellen wants you to take it.

[*Silence.*]

ALAN: Yes.

FATHER: She's a sensible girl.

ALAN: She's got no family – no one she has to – leave . . .

FATHER: She's lucky.

ALAN: But she understands.

FATHER: I like Ellen.

ALAN: If I say – no. If I tell him . . .

FATHER: You can't say – no. [FATHER *puts a hand on* ALAN'S *shoulder.*]

ALAN: If you want me to. You and Mum . . .

FATHER: You can't throw away a chance like this.

ALAN: Dad – when I get on that boat – when . . . [ALAN *rubs his hand across his forehead.*] I mean – that's it.

FATHER: You'll go by boat, will you?

ALAN: Two years.

FATHER: Halfway round the world.

ALAN: Even then, I'm not sure.

FATHER: Do the kids know? They'll have the time of their young lives! Are they looking forward to it?

ALAN: I haven't told them. I haven't decided.

FATHER: What I wouldn't give . . . [*Smiling and nodding his head,* FATHER *takes out his cigarette case and opens it.*] I shouldn't really. I'm smoking too much. But I tell your mother – if I can't smoke too much, at my age! [FATHER *takes a cigarette and puts it into his mouth.*] What a wonderful opportunity.

ALAN: I might never . . .

[*Silence.*]

FATHER: Your mother's going to miss those kids of yours. What does she say about it? [FATHER *puts his cigarette case away carefully, as he takes out his lighter.*] She likes to have some kids about the house. It's the noise, I think. Makes all the difference to her. She's not the same woman.

[FATHER *lights his cigarette and stands at the window, looking out at the garden. He hums the tune of* 'Keep the Home Fires Burning' *quietly to himself.*] You're right about the garden. It is a mess. I don't know. I can't seem to get interested in it these days. [FATHER *drops his lighter back into his pocket.*] I used to look forward to Sunday. Hmm. D'you remember? I used to dig the garden – every Sunday – digging – planting – lifting the potatoes. There's always something to do in a garden. That's the beauty of it.

ALAN: Dad, I'm going away.

FATHER: It's best. Really. [FATHER *turns his head and looks at* ALAN.] We can't have you spoiling your chances. They only come once.

ALAN [*simply*]: If you want me to stay?

FATHER [*brightly*]: Of course, I don't know what the Old Boys will do without you. Gordon was telling me – 'Alan,' he said, 'life and soul of the Old Boys.'

ALAN: They'll manage.

FATHER: It's not so easy. Something like that – depends on one man, as often as not – depends on the enthusiasm of one man.

ALAN: They'll find someone else.

FATHER: A man – who cares.

ALAN: I won't be sorry . . .

[FATHER *pats* ALAN *on the shoulder as he turns and walks away from the window.*]

FATHER: You've given a lot of your time . . .

ALAN [*violently*]: Dad, I don't care . . . [ALAN *stops, clamps his mouth shut, and then suddenly relaxes.*] They'll find some other idiot ready to give up half his life – and all his friends . . .

FATHER: It's more than that.

ALAN: It isn't important.

FATHER: Don't make it seem ridiculous!

ALAN: I took it on . . .

FATHER: Just because – now . . .

ALAN: You know why I took it on?

FATHER: You were always popular.

ALAN: You – wanted me to.

FATHER [*abruptly*]: I – wanted you to.

ALAN: Yes.

FATHER: I didn't care. One way or the other.

ALAN: I asked you – 'Dad, should I . . .'

FATHER: Why do you always make me – try to make me – responsible.

ALAN: I told you – 'I can't spare the time. I've got enough to do . . .'

FATHER: I am not – responsible.

ALAN: 'Should I take it on?'

FATHER: You do things – the things you do . . .

ALAN: 'Yes' – you said. Yes!

FATHER: You make up your own mind.

ALAN: 'Keep in touch with your old friends!' Didn't you say that?

FATHER: Yes.

ALAN: 'You'll never regret . . .'

FATHER: Look at Terry!

ALAN: '. . . time spent, keeping . . .'

FATHER: Has she kept in touch – with her old friends?

ALAN [*shaking*]: I don't want to talk about Terry.

FATHER: Is she happy?

ALAN: Am I happy?

[*Silence.*]

How would you know.

FATHER: You've got everything.

ALAN: Oh, yes.

FATHER: More – ten thousand times . . .

ALAN: Than you ever had? Right. And you never stop telling me – you and Mother – both!

FATHER: You should be happy.

[ALAN *rubs his hand across his forehead.*]

ALAN [*quietly*]: Every time. I promise myself – every time . . . [ALAN *pulls his hand down to his mouth and presses it against his lips. He shakes his head.*]

[*Muffled*] Sorry, Dad. I'm sorry. [ALAN *turns and walks towards the door.*]

FATHER: Where are you going?

ALAN: Let's call it a day. Let's – you know?

FATHER [*violently*]: I'm talking to you!

[ALAN *stops walking and stands, quite still.*]

ALAN: Yes. I can hear you.

FATHER: Don't turn your back on me, when I'm talking to you.

[*Slowly,* ALAN *turns to face his* FATHER.]

At least, have the courtesy . . .

ALAN: What do you want to say to me?

FATHER [*coldly*]: Don't talk to me like that.

ALAN: Don't talk to me like a father.

FATHER: You mind what . . .

ALAN: You're too late – and I'm too old.

FATHER: Respect. We'll have a little – respect . . .

ALAN: Try and talk to me, as if I might – I mean, possibly – might have something to say . . . [ALAN *stops and takes in a deep, shuddering breath.*] I don't know why – any more – I don't . . .

FATHER: I don't know what you're talking about.

ALAN: Doesn't that remind you of Terry? Just a bit, Dad – remind you . . .

FATHER [*coldly*]: I got the impression you didn't want to talk about Terry.

[*Silence.*]

ALAN [*quietly*]: That's right.

FATHER: I've had to listen – I've lost count of the times . . .

ALAN: I don't think you've listened to me, since I was four – five years old – and talking – was door, table, sweetie – Dada.

FATHER: If there was a chance I might understand what you were saying, I'd be glad to listen.

ALAN: If there was a chance you might listen, I'd try to make you understand.

[*Silence.*]

What's the point, Dad?

FATHER [*simply*]: Why can't I talk to you?

ALAN: I've thought about that.

FATHER: I miss – most of all, I miss – d'you know? Talking to you – and Terry. I don't remember what we talked about. I don't suppose it was particularly important. [*Smiling*] I'm sure it wasn't – but – talking.

ALAN: We didn't talk.

FATHER [*urgently*]: Yes.

ALAN: I'll go and find Mum.

FATHER: We did – talk.

ALAN: I've got to go home. I can't stay to supper.

FATHER: I remember – evenings – we used to talk.

ALAN: I don't know what you remember. What you want to remember. Talking – no. Not you and me. Terry – maybe – once in a golden while – but not often. Not even with Terry. Next time you see her, ask her – 'cause she's in a mood to tell you.

FATHER: What is it you know about Terry?

ALAN: She won't come home – you're right. She won't come here again.

FATHER: I talked to her. We had a good talk.

ALAN: This time – this last time, she came . . .

FATHER: You don't like Terry.

ALAN: She's my sister.

FATHER: Why don't you like her?

ALAN: I like the people I have to like – the people I see – every day.

FATHER: You should – like . . .

ALAN: I should love her. She's family – isn't she? You should love family.

FATHER: You don't love her.

ALAN: No.

FATHER: She's not happy.

ALAN: She came to tell you that.

FATHER: If only – if she'd . . .

ALAN [*quietly*]: Kept in touch?

FATHER: If she was nearer – home. If she came to see us more often.

ALAN: You wouldn't wish that on her, would you? Honestly?

FATHER [*simply*]: I don't know what you mean.

ALAN: Poor old Terry.

FATHER: I would like to understand.

ALAN: About Terry?

FATHER: Yes.

ALAN: She needs to – oh, I don't know – grow up. She needs – she has to be on her own! [ALAN *shakes his head.*] No. She has to recognize – she is – I mean, now really is – on her own. Accept it – and then, get on with it.

FATHER: Get on with what?

ALAN: That isn't important.

FATHER: What's happening to her, Alan?

ALAN: She didn't know she was on her own. She thought – all these people round me, I'm not – you know – alone.

FATHER: She's not alone!

ALAN: She came to tell you, Dad. She knows.

FATHER: She's got us.

ALAN: Now, she can work from that – fact.

FATHER: She's always got her family.

ALAN: She doesn't have to waste any more time, running around – running away – hiding.

FATHER: Your mother.

ALAN: You taught her to hide.

FATHER: Me.

ALAN: She had to – unteach – herself.

FATHER: Some times, Alan – talking to you – I feel . . .

ALAN: She won't come back.

FATHER: . . . I'm talking to a stranger.

ALAN: I'll take the job. [ALAN *turns away and walks towards the door.*]

FATHER: It's a wonderful opportunity.

ALAN: Right. You're right.

FATHER: It isn't everyone . . .

[*The door opens and* MOTHER *looks into the room.*]

MOTHER: Alan, poor Gordon's still waiting . . . [MOTHER *stops abruptly, looks at* ALAN *and then looks past him at* FATHER.]

ALAN: Yes, I know. I'm just coming.

[MOTHER *steps into the doorway and stops* ALAN *getting out of the room.*]

MOTHER [*quietly*]: What've you been talking about?

ALAN: Hey, no! Look – I've kept Gordon . . .

MOTHER: What have you been saying to your father?

ALAN: Please! Mum.

MOTHER: Look at him.

[*Silence.*]

ALAN: I asked him, should I take the job?

FATHER: I think he should. Don't you, Mother?

MOTHER: I think he should make up his own mind.

ALAN: I have. I'm taking the job. 'Off to Tipperary in the morning . . .' [ALAN *reaches out to take hold of his* MOTHER'S *shoulder and move her out of the doorway.*] Now – if you'll just get out of the way!

MOTHER: I want to know what's been going on – between you and your father.

FATHER: Is Gordon still here, Mother? Did you say he was still here?

MOTHER: Yes, I did.

ALAN: We talked about Terry – just a bit about Terry. That's all.

[FATHER *walks towards the door.*]

FATHER: He must be wondering what's happening. Kept hanging about . . .

ALAN: He's got a family of his own.

MOTHER: What do you know about Terry?

FATHER: Something I want to show him.

ALAN: That's the great thing, isn't it?

FATHER: Out of the way, you two! Blocking the traffic!

ALAN: Everyone's got one. Everyone understands – about families.

FATHER [*calling*]: Gordon. [FATHER *walks briskly between* MOTHER *and* ALAN, *out into the hall.*] Something I want to show you. [GORDON *walks out of the front room.*]

GORDON: What's that, Mr Stephens? What d'you say?

FATHER: I was talking about a photograph. You remember?

142

GORDON: Oh. Yes. But, look . . . [GORDON *glances at his watch*.] . . . really, I don't think . . .

FATHER: I know where it is. I've just remembered. Talking to Alan . . . [FATHER *walks past* GORDON *and on into the front room. He goes to the sideboard.*] . . . I suddenly thought — I know where that photograph is. I saw it, just the other day.

[FATHER *kneels down in front of the sideboard and opens the double doors.*

GORDON *follows* FATHER *as far as the doorway and stands there.*]

GORDON: I'm terribly sorry, Mr Stephens . . .

FATHER: Just the other day. [FATHER *begins to sort through the assembled bits and pieces, pushed away into the sideboard.*] I don't know why I didn't think of it before. [FATHER *takes out an envelope of photographs, triumphantly.*] I'm sure it's here. I'm absolutely sure!

GORDON: My wife's expecting me back in time for tea and it's already . . . [GORDON *looks at his watch again.*] I'm hopelessly late, already.

FATHER: I won't be a moment, now, finding it.

GORDON: I thought Mrs Stephens was going to tell Alan.

[FATHER *drops the photographs and the envelope on to the floor.*]

FATHER: Damn!

GORDON: I just want to let him know . . .

FATHER: Fingers and thumbs. All . . . [FATHER *begins to sort through the photographs, on the floor.*] . . . fingers . . .

GORDON: Perhaps we'd better leave it for today, Mr Stephens? Some other time . . .

FATHER: More haste . . . [FATHER *mutters to himself, as he picks up one photograph after another, discarding them quickly, dropping them on to the floor.*]

ALAN'S VOICE: Gordon, old love! I'm sorry.

GORDON [*irritably*]: There you are. [GORDON *turns and walks out into the hall to speak to* ALAN.]

ALAN'S VOICE: Yes, I know. Look . . .

GORDON'S VOICE: I thought it was all arranged. I thought we were going to talk . . .

ALAN'S VOICE: I know!

[*Push in towards* FATHER, *searching through the photographs.*]

GORDON'S VOICE: It was your idea I should meet you here.

ALAN'S VOICE: What about tomorrow? Lunch? I can get away for an hour.

GORDON'S VOICE: Tomorrow's out of the question.

[FATHER *sits back on his heels, looking at a photograph.*]

ALAN'S VOICE: In the evening?

[*Cut to close-up of a faded, old-fashioned photograph of a small house in a country setting.*]

GORDON'S VOICE: I don't know.

FATHER'S VOICE: I've often thought of going back there.

ALAN'S VOICE: I could come round to your house?

MOTHER'S VOICE: What on earth for?

[*Cut to* FATHER, *sitting back and looking at the photograph.*]

MOTHER'S VOICE: If you'd like to talk in the back room, you won't be disturbed.

FATHER'S VOICE: I'd like to see the old place again.

GORDON'S VOICE: No, I'm sorry! I really can't wait any longer.

MOTHER'S VOICE: The people you used to know – well, they must be dead by now.

ALAN'S VOICE: Shall we say tomorrow evening?

[FATHER *drops the photograph on to the floor and picks up another.*]

MOTHER'S VOICE: I'm sorry, we've wasted so much of your time.

GORDON'S VOICE: No. Oh, no.

MOTHER'S VOICE: It isn't often we see Alan, these days.

GORDON'S VOICE: I didn't mean . . .

ALAN'S VOICE: About six?

[FATHER *picks up another photograph and smiles.*]

GORDON'S VOICE: Mrs Stephens, please . . .

MOTHER'S VOICE: It's perfectly all right, Gordon. I quite understand.

[*Cut to a faded, old-fashioned photograph of a group of people, posed artificially. A woman sitting and a man standing at her shoulder, with three children around them, varying in age from four to twelve.*]

VOICE: Smile, everybody. Smile, please.

GORDON'S VOICE: My wife is expecting me back for tea.

MOTHER'S VOICE: Ellen will be wondering where you've got to, Alan.

WOMAN'S VOICE: Teddy, smile.

[*Cut to* FATHER, *looking at the two photographs.*]

ALAN'S VOICE: Tomorrow evening, then?

CHILD'S VOICE [*grimly*]: I can't smile.

GORDON'S VOICE: Can you make it seven? Six is a bit early.

ALAN'S VOICE: Seven it is!

[FATHER *puts the two photographs down and sits back on his heels again, thoughtfully*].

FATHER: I was sure – absolutely sure.

[*The sound of the front door being opened.*]

MOTHER'S VOICE: What're you looking for?

[*Pull back to include* MOTHER, *as* FATHER *turns to look at her.*]

FATHER: There's a photograph I want to show Gordon.

MOTHER: He's gone.

FATHER: Has he? Oh, well.

MOTHER: His wife's expecting him home for tea.

FATHER: Oh, yes. He did say – something ... [FATHER *looks at the photographs on the floor in front of him.*]

MOTHER: What photograph is it?

FATHER: The school team. D'you remember? It was taken their last year. Gordon was captain and Alan was centre forward.

MOTHER: You won't find it there, will you?

FATHER: I thought I saw it.

MOTHER: Not with those photographs. They're all as old as the hills.

[FATHER *reaches down and rests his hand on the floor. He pushes on it and lifts himself up on to his feet again, slowly.*]

FATHER: Funny, because . . .
　　[FATHER *shakes his head.*
　　　Silence.]
　[*Suddenly*] He's gone?
MOTHER: He couldn't wait any longer.
FATHER: He's a nice boy, Gordon.
　　[*The sound of a car being started, outside the house.*]
I like him.
MOTHER: What were you and Alan talking about?
FATHER: Whether or not he should take this new job he's
been offered. [FATHER *walks across to the window and looks
at the road outside.*]
MOTHER: That's all?
FATHER: He wanted to ask me, should he take it?
MOTHER: You were talking a long time.
　　[FATHER *waves and nods, as the car drives away.*]
FATHER: I wish I could have found that photograph.
MOTHER: I thought you were a bit upset.
FATHER: Me? Upset? When?
MOTHER: When I walked in. I wondered what Alan could've
said – to upset you?
FATHER: I wasn't upset. [FATHER *turns and stands with his
back to the window.*]
MOTHER: I thought you looked upset.
　　[*The sound of the front door being shut.*]
FATHER [*calling*]: Alan?
ALAN'S VOICE: Just coming, Dad.
MOTHER: If he said something . . .
FATHER [*abruptly*]: He didn't.
　　[ALAN *walks into the room.*]
ALAN: Poor old Gordon.
FATHER: He had to get off, did he?
ALAN [*laughing*]: Just about half an hour late!
FATHER: I had a photograph I wanted to show him.
ALAN: Oh? Did you?
FATHER: Photograph of the school team.
ALAN: You haven't still got that!
FATHER: Yes, I have.

MOTHER: You know your father.

ALAN: Where is it?

MOTHER: He never throws anything away.

ALAN: But that photograph! It's ages old.

MOTHER: Look at these. [MOTHER *walks across to the side-board and bends down to pick up the scattered photographs.*] How long d'you think he's been keeping these?

FATHER: It's all right, Mother. I'll do that.

MOTHER: You sit down.

FATHER: I'll pick them up.

MOTHER: You're looking tired.

ALAN: Where is it, Dad?

FATHER: What's that?

ALAN: The photograph. I'd like to see it.

MOTHER: Alan – no!

FATHER: I can't remember.

MOTHER: Don't get him started.

ALAN: I thought you said . . .

FATHER: Isn't it silly?

MOTHER: You'll find it.

[FATHER *kneels down beside* MOTHER *and starts to help her pick up the photographs.*]

No – give them to me.

FATHER: I'll put them away.

[ALAN *reaches down between his* FATHER *and* MOTHER.]

ALAN: Now, now, children! Mustn't squabble. [ALAN *takes one of the photographs his* FATHER *is holding.*]

MOTHER: It wouldn't hurt you to get down and help, would it?

ALAN: I haven't seen this before, have I?

FATHER: Yes, you have.

ALAN: Don't think so. I don't remember . . .

FATHER: Let me have a look at it.

[FATHER *presses a hand down on the floor and starts to raise himself up on to his feet.* MOTHER *reaches out to help him.*]

Thanks. I can manage.

[MOTHER *watches* FATHER *struggle on to his feet.*]

Now, then. [FATHER *takes the photograph and looks at it.*] I used to live here. When I was a boy. I must have shown it to you.

MOTHER: Every other Sunday, for the last five years. [*Silence.*]

FATHER: I've often thought, I'd like to go back and see the old place.

ALAN: Really?

FATHER: Make a nice trip, wouldn't it?

ALAN: You could go this summer.

MOTHER: Don't put ideas into his head.

FATHER: As a matter of fact, only last summer [*he walks across to the window*] I was walking in the park – and the trees . . .

MOTHER: Leave him alone!

FATHER: The trees looked so beautiful.

ALAN: You could stay there, couldn't you? There must be a hotel – of sorts?

FATHER: I went for a walk . . .

ALAN: Come on! When was the last time you two had a proper holiday?

FATHER: I was on my own . . .

MOTHER: When you were children. [MOTHER *shuts the double doors of the sideboard.*]

FATHER: . . . walking on my own – and I thought . . . [FATHER *rests a hand on the window sill.*]

ALAN: It's good and time you had another.

FATHER: I thought then – it isn't a bit like it used to be – at home . . . [FATHER *shakes his head and smiles to himself.*]

ALAN: You know what I think?

FATHER: You could walk a mile and never meet another soul.

ALAN: You and Mum – get yourselves packed – and soon as the sun shines – off you go! That's what I think.

MOTHER: God knows there's little enough to keep us here.

FATHER: Something about the sun – in the trees – over head, it made me think – breaking and moving – smiling – like home, I thought. Why don't I go back and see the old place?

ALAN: People do. Lots of people.

MOTHER: When they get to your father's age?

ALAN: Yes. That's right.

MOTHER: It's very likely changed. It's a long time.

ALAN: Go and see.

MOTHER: Your father won't know anybody living there now.

ALAN: Does that matter?

MOTHER: And nobody – will know him. [MOTHER *takes the photograph away from* ALAN.]

FATHER: I certainly would like to see the old place. Once – before . . .

[MOTHER *looks angrily at* ALAN.]

MOTHER: Think! Why don't you think? [MOTHER *turns away and pulls one of the sideboard doors open.*]

FATHER: No. Don't put it away.

[MOTHER *straightens up and turns to face* FATHER, *as he walks across the room towards her.*]

I'd like to have another look at it.

MOTHER: You never stop looking at it.

[FATHER *takes the photograph.*]

FATHER: Staying to supper, Alan?

ALAN: No, Dad. No, I'm not. Some work to do, as a matter of fact. I brought it home with me – Friday. I haven't looked at it yet.

FATHER: You always did that. Left everything – till the very last minute. Didn't he, Mother?

ALAN: They gave us too much homework.

FATHER: Sunday evenings – head down – over some book or other.

MOTHER: You were always out playing football.

ALAN [*laughing*]: I don't think I was. I don't think I was all that keen.

FATHER: When was the last time I saw Gordon?

ALAN: He was at my wedding.

FATHER: Was that the last time?

ALAN: I don't know. Probably.

MOTHER: Ellen will be wondering what's happened to you.

149

ALAN: I doubt it. She knows where I am – and she's past thinking about accidents, by now. Knocked down and killed – leaving a wife . . .

MOTHER: Don't joke about things like that, Alan!

FATHER: Was he your best man?

ALAN: No, Dad.

MOTHER: Norman Driscoll.

FATHER: Yes, of course. That's right. How is Norman these days?

ALAN: I haven't seen him – oh – two years? Might be three. He moved to Southampton.

FATHER: Did he? Oh.

MOTHER: I hope Ellen will find time, before you all leave for Australia – to bring the children over to see us?

ALAN: I'm sure she will.

MOTHER: I would like to see my grandchildren once more, before . . .

ALAN: She would have come with me this afternoon, and brought the kids . . .

FATHER [*suddenly*]: I know where it is. Yes. [FATHER *edges between* ALAN *and* MOTHER.] Yes, of course!

ALAN: Look, Dad – don't run away.

FATHER: What an idiot I am!

ALAN: I'll have to go in a couple of minutes.

FATHER: I've thought now. I know.

> [FATHER *walks out into the hall.*
> *Looking across the hall, at the doorway of the front room, as* FATHER *walks out and crosses to the bottom of the stairs. He starts to climb the stairs.*]

ALAN'S VOICE: Dad.

> [FATHER *stops halfway up the stairs and turns his head, to look over the banisters.*
> *Cut to a close shot of* ALAN, *standing in the doorway.*]

ALAN [*grinning*]: Don't take all night.

> [*Cut to a high shot, looking down at* FATHER.]

FATHER: I know just where it is. I'd like you to see it.

ALAN'S VOICE: I'd like to see it.

> [FATHER *nods, turns and walks on, up the stairs.*]

MOTHER'S VOICE: Alan, come here. I want to talk to you.

ALAN'S VOICE: Now, look!

MOTHER'S VOICE: I will not have you . . .

ALAN'S VOICE: What did I say . . .

MOTHER'S VOICE: Shut the door.

> [*The door shuts, as* FATHER *reaches the corner of the stairs, turns and walks out of sight. He walks into the main bedroom, a depressing room with twin beds, set square. He shuts the door carefully behind him and then, for a moment, he stands quite still, just inside the room. He walks slowly towards a chair, in the corner of the room, and sits on it.*
>
> *The camera slowly pushes in towards him, as the voices begin.*]

FATHER'S VOICE [*laughing*]: I'll make the world stop. Yes, I will. I'll make it go backwards.

> [*The sound of a* YOUNG WOMAN *laughing.*]

There'll never be night. I . . .

CUT TO *a sitting room. Evening.*

FATHER'S VOICE: . . . will make day . . .

> [*Looking through a haze of light, across the room, at the figures of a* YOUNG MAN *and a* YOUNG WOMAN, *sitting close together on a sofa.*]

. . . eternal day – everlasting – and I'll love you . . .

> [*The sound of a* YOUNG WOMAN *crying.*]

CUT TO *the hotel bedroom. Night.*

FATHER'S VOICE . . . Sarah . . .

> [*Close-up of a* YOUNG WOMAN'S *face drenched in tears, pressed sideways against the pillows.*]

FATHER'S VOICE: . . . love you – all that everlasting day.

FATHER'S VOICE: Sarah, don't turn away.

FATHER'S VOICE: I'll make the sun shine in the middle of the night.

> [*The sound of a* YOUNG WOMAN *laughing.*]

FATHER'S VOICE: I didn't mean to hurt you. I wouldn't . . .

CUT TO FILM: *Looking up at a ceiling of leaves and the sun crackling through, moving slowly.*

FATHER'S VOICE: . . . hurt you.

FATHER'S VOICE: I'll make the stars fall in your lap. You want the stars? You can have them.

FATHER'S VOICE: Look at me, Sarah. Don't cry.

CUT: *Looking the length of an avenue of trees in a large formal garden, at the figures of a young man and woman, walking arm in arm.*

FATHER'S VOICE: We'll have children – hundreds – of children.

CUT TO *the sitting room. Evening.*

FATHER'S VOICE: We'll make them together, you and I, Sarah.

> [*Looking through a haze of light at the two figures.*]

We'll make them – with love – and then, we'll make them happy. We'll make them laugh . . .

CUT TO *the hotel bedroom.*

> [*Looking across the hotel room, towards the bed. The room is in darkness, except for the pattern of light striking across the floor.*]

FATHER'S VOICE: . . . like we laugh, Sarah.

> [*The sound of a woman's sudden cry of physical pain.*]

'Cause we can laugh.

CUT TO *the Stephens' bedroom.*

> [*Close-up of* FATHER, *sitting in the chair.*]

FATHER'S VOICE: That's what we'll give them.

CUT TO *Terry's bedroom.*

FATHER'S VOICE: Happiness and laughter.

> [*Looking past* FATHER, *who is standing in the doorway of the room, towards the bed, where* TERRY *is crouched, looking up at her* MOTHER, *who is standing over her.*]

I know that people – other people – say these things . . .

[MOTHER *slaps* TERRY *hard across the face and* FATHER *steps into the darkness of the room.*]
... these same things – but I mean them.
[MOTHER *turns furiously to face him.*]
Really, Sarah ...

CUT TO *the sitting room. Evening.*
FATHER'S VOICE: ... mean them. I've seen ...
[*Looking through a haze of light at the two figures.*]
... things – done things – in the war – and if I can't make sense – now ... if there isn't a reason – if you – aren't the reason ...

CUT TO FILM: *The two soldiers are sitting in the corner of the shop doorway, smoking the single cigarette between them. They have their arms round each other's shoulders and their heads together. One of them is speaking quietly into the other soldier's ear. A long way off, shells thud with a dull monotony.*
FATHER'S VOICE: If I get out of this – when! – I get out, I'll make sure – hear me? I'll make bloody sure, I see things better. A whole lot better.
FATHER'S VOICE: Sarah, I won the prize everyone else was fighting for.

CUT TO *the Stephens' bedroom.*
[*Close-up of* FATHER'S *face.*]
FATHER'S VOICE: I'm alive.
ALAN'S VOICE: Dad.
[*Pull back to include* ALAN, *who is standing in the bedroom doorway.*]
Hey!
[FATHER *turns his head and looks at* ALAN.]
What are you doing?
[FATHER *stares at* ALAN, *without answering, without seeming to hear the question.*]
Did you find it?
FATHER: What? Find what?

ALAN: The photograph. [ALAN *walks into the room.*] You said you knew where it was. Did you . . .

FATHER [*abruptly*]: No, I didn't. [FATHER *stands up and walks across the room, away from* ALAN, *towards the window.*]

ALAN: Are you all right?

FATHER: I'm fine. Yes. Why d'you ask?

ALAN: Just thought you looked – I don't know – a bit strange.

FATHER [*harshly*]: Why do you always quarrel with your mother?

ALAN [*grinning*]: I beg your pardon!

FATHER: You never see each other, without you're quarelling, these days.

ALAN: You're not serious?

FATHER: First, Terry.

ALAN: You know, I've had just about . . .

FATHER: Then – you.

ALAN: I've had more than enough!

    [FATHER *turns to face* ALAN, *across the twin beds.*]

FATHER: Don't you know how much it upsets her? Don't you have any idea . . .

ALAN: I'm going home, Dad. I just came to say good-bye.

FATHER: You children! You never think . . .

ALAN: Good-bye.

FATHER: Why can't you be – kind to her? Once in a while . . .

    [ALAN *turns away and walks back to the doorway.*]

    . . . try to understand.

ALAN [*coldly*]: I'll look in and see you during the week sometime. I can't say exactly when it's likely to be.

FATHER: If it isn't possible . . .

ALAN: Thursday, maybe – Friday.

FATHER: If you can't try . . .

ALAN: Don't say it, Dad.

    [*Silence.*]

  Don't send me away.

FATHER: Will you take the job?

ALAN: Yes, I think so. [ALAN *rests a hand against the edge of the door and shakes his head.*] Yes, I know. I'll tell him tomorrow.

FATHER: It's the sort of job ...

[*Silence.*]

Exciting. It sounds exciting. [FATHER *takes his cigarette case out of his pocket and opens it. He counts the number of cigarettes he has left in the case.*]

ALAN: The same job I'm doing now. A different office in a different country. The same job. Facts and figures. People and percentages.

FATHER: You always make things sound ... [FATHER *looks up at* ALAN *and slants his head slightly.*] I don't know – dull. More dull than they are. Than they have to be.

ALAN: It's the way they look – to me. The way they seem.

[FATHER *takes a cigarette out of his case and puts it into his mouth, carefully.*]

FATHER: It's going to be funny – you – halfway round the world.

ALAN: Will it make that much difference?

FATHER [*simply*]: I don't understand what you mean.

ALAN: Nothing. [ALAN *shakes his head.*] I don't know why I said it. [ALAN *takes his hand away from the door and straightens up. He looks at his* FATHER.] I don't have to take the job.

FATHER: Yes, you do. Of course, you do!

[*Silence.*]

ALAN: If you say so.

FATHER: I was thinking – d'you know something? I can't remember things we did together. When you were a boy. I try to – and I can't.

ALAN [*coldly*]: You used to come and watch me play football every Saturday afternoon.

FATHER: Yes, I did, didn't I? I know I did.

ALAN: Mum says, if you stay up here much longer, you'll miss some programme you want to see on the telly.

FATHER: I wish I could find that photograph.

ALAN: You'll find it.

FATHER: Oh, yes.

ALAN: You coming down?

[FATHER *shakes his head.*]

What shall I tell Mum?

FATHER [*quietly*]: Tell her, I'll come down, when I'm ready to come down.

ALAN: Right, then. That's what I'll tell her.

FATHER: Would you like – er ... [FATHER *holds out his open cigarette case towards* ALAN.] Cigarette?

ALAN: Thanks, Dad – no. I don't smoke.

FATHER: No, of course, you don't. It's Terry ...

ALAN: Yes.

FATHER: What is it, Alan? What's wrong?

[*Silence.*]

I try and talk to her. I try ... [FATHER *shuts his cigarette case and puts it away into his pocket.*] She just isn't my little girl any more, is she?

ALAN: No.

FATHER: See, there's something happening to her and I want to help – her – if I knew ...

ALAN: Ask Mum.

[ALAN *turns and walks out of the room.*

FATHER *takes his lighter out of his pocket and lights his cigarette.*]

CHILD'S VOICE: No, Daddy – please!

FATHER'S VOICE: It's all right, baby. Daddy won't hurt you.

CUT TO FILM: *Close shot of a small child's leg, centering on a graze across the knee and on Father's hands, dabbing at the graze gently, with a damp handkerchief.*

CHILD'S VOICE [*panic*]: Don't touch it!

FATHER'S VOICE: We must get it clean, baby. We can't have any nasty dirt ...

The leg strains away from the hands holding it.

CHILD'S VOICE: You're hurting. Hurting!

FATHER'S VOICE: I know, baby.

CUT TO *the Stephens' bedroom.*

[FATHER *is standing at the window, looking at the road outside.*]

FATHER'S VOICE: Not much longer.
> [*The sound of a car starting.*]

CHILD'S VOICE: No, please – Daddy!
> [FATHER *waves and nods his head.*]

FATHER'S VOICE: If we don't get it clean – well, it might never get better.

CUT TO FILM: *Looking down the side slopes of Whipsnade Zoo, out across the countryside below, showing through the heat haze.*

CHILD'S VOICE: Mummy. I want Mummy.

Sound of a small child crying bitterly.

CUT TO *the Stephens' bedroom.*
> [*Close shot of* FATHER, *as he turns his back to the window and his face into the shadow. The light in the sky outside the window is fading.*]

FATHER'S VOICE: Well, now – that's a bit silly, isn't it?

CHILD'S VOICE: You hurt me.

FATHER'S VOICE: Yes, but – look – it's all done now. Daddy's tied it up in a nice, clean bandage. That's rather good.
> [FATHER *draws on his cigarette.*]

CHILD'S VOICE: Still hurts.

FATHER'S VOICE: We could play hospitals. Would you like to play hospitals?

MOTHER'S VOICE [*calling*]: What are you doing up there?
> [*The sound of a jet, flying high over the house.*]

FATHER'S VOICE: You be the patient. I'll be the doctor?

CHILD'S VOICE: No.

FATHER'S VOICE: Oh, come on, baby. You're going to play with Daddy, aren't you? You're not going to make him cry?

CHILD'S VOICE: Tell me a story.

CUT TO *a small air raid shelter. Night.*

FATHER: Yes, all right.
> [*The sounds of the London blitz smash at the night sky outside the Anderson shelter. There are two camp beds in*

the shelter, one on each side of the doorway. MOTHER *is asleep, half-sitting, on the left of the doorway and* FATHER *is sitting on the right.* MOTHER *has a small* BOY *asleep across her lap and* FATHER *is nursing a little* GIRL.]

What story would you like?

CHILD: 'Bout the princess – and how she was taken away . . .

MOTHER'S VOICE [*calling*]: Ted!

[*A stick of small bombs falls in a line towards the shelter.*]

FATHER: Oh, yes.

CHILD: And – 'bout her Daddy finding her again.

FATHER: I remember.

CHILD: I like that story.

MOTHER'S VOICE [*calling*]: Ted – for goodness' sake!

FATHER: You make yourself comfortable and while I tell you the story, you go to sleep.

CHILD: If I go to sleep, I'll miss the end.

FATHER: I'll tell it to you again – tomorrow.

[*Local anti-aircraft guns start firing close to the shelter and, instinctively,* FATHER *holds the little* GIRL *closer.*]

FATHER'S VOICE: Once upon a time, there was a beautiful princess . . .

CUT TO FILM: *Looking down into a deep crater, gouged out of the battlefield mud, at two British soldiers, cowering in the bottom of the crater.*

FATHER'S VOICE: . . . a very beautiful princess – with golden hair and blue, blue eyes. She lived in a land where the sun shone all day and it was always summer.

[*The sound of aircraft, flying low overhead.*]

MOTHER'S VOICE [*calling*]: Are you going to stay up there for ever?

A German soldier stumbles over the top and falls down towards the two soldiers. He is carrying a rifle, with fixed bayonet.

FATHER'S VOICE: Her father was the king and he was very handsome.

CHILD'S VOICE [*murmuring*]: Hmm.

One of the British soldiers turns and tries to scramble up the far side of the crater.

FATHER'S VOICE: Her mother was the queen and she was so kind, everybody loved her.

CHILD'S VOICE: She used to give them presents – lots and lots of presents.

The other soldier, his feet sticking in the mud, catches at the boots of the climbing soldier and pulls him back towards him. They struggle over each other, trying to escape.

FATHER'S VOICE: That's right.

　　[*The anti-aircraft guns crash shells into the night sky.*]

CHILD'S VOICE: One day – go on, Daddy.

FATHER'S VOICE: One day, the king gave a great party for his daughter, the princess, and he invited everyone in the land specially to come and have a lovely time.

The German bayonet plunges forward. The lower soldier looks back over his shoulder, at the German soldier. His mouth is wide open, screaming in panic fear. He pulls hard at the other soldier's legs and tumbles him down on top of him.

CHILD'S VOICE: With cakes and things – and ice cream.

　　[*A bomb whines through the sky and explodes, no more than a hundred yards away from the shelter.*]

FATHER'S VOICE: More ice cream than you could eat in a month of Sundays.

The bayonet thrusts deep into the back of one soldier, shielding the other, who pulls a knife free from his belt.

FATHER'S VOICE: Now, there was a man at the party and he loved the princess very much indeed.

　　[*The sounds of people shouting and struggling, away in the distance, where the bomb landed.*]

CHILD'S VOICE: But he was sad, wasn't he?

He thrusts the knife up into the stomach of the German soldier.

FATHER'S VOICE: He was always trying to speak to the princess, when she was alone. But there were so many people with her, he never could. He used to watch her wherever she went . . .

A high shot, remote, looking down into the crater and the chaos of the three bodies, lying in the mud and water, at the bottom of the crater.

CHILD'S VOICE [*eagerly*]: His own daughter . . .

FATHER'S VOICE [*laughing*]: You know the story better than I do. You tell it.

CUT TO *the Stephens' bedroom.*

    [MOTHER *is standing in the doorway.*]

MOTHER: Still looking for that photograph?

CHILD'S VOICE: Oh, no – Daddy! No. You tell it.

FATHER: I can't think where it's got to.

MOTHER: Let's have a bit of light on the subject. It's got quite dark. [MOTHER *switches on the centre light.*]

FATHER: It doesn't matter now.

MOTHER: I'll help you look for it.

FATHER: I don't know where to start.

    [*Silence.*]

He doesn't look well, does he? Alan.

MOTHER: Well enough. Have you looked in these drawers?

FATHER: She leads him a bit of a dance, doesn't she?

MOTHER: She wants him to take that job.

FATHER: He's going to take it. He said so.

    [MOTHER *pulls one of the drawers open.*]

I've looked there. It isn't . . . [FATHER *shrugs and turns back to look out of the window again.*] I don't know where it is. Anyway, it doesn't matter now.

MOTHER: You wanted to look at it.

FATHER: I wanted to show it to Gordon.

    [*Silence.*]

If he does take the job – if he does – go to Australia – I shan't see him again.

MOTHER: Nonsense! You know, there's a case in the attic.

FATHER [*harshly*]: It doesn't matter!

    [*Silence.*]

MOTHER: He'll be back in two years. He said so.

FATHER: He said he wasn't certain.

    [MOTHER *shuts the drawer quietly.*]

MOTHER: Two years isn't very long.

FATHER: He kept saying – did I want him to take the job. He kept asking me.

MOTHER: Perhaps he isn't all that keen on taking it.

FATHER: Seems like a good job.

MOTHER: He's happy enough, where he is.

FATHER: She wants him to take it?

MOTHER: It's a promotion, isn't it?

FATHER: But, if he's happy enough . . .

MOTHER: She's ambitious for him.

FATHER [angrily]: If they want to go – if they've made up their minds – why . . . [FATHER takes his cigarette out of his mouth and looks for an ashtray.]

MOTHER: Here. Give it to me.

FATHER: There's never an ashtray!

　　　[MOTHER walks forward to take the cigarette from him, but FATHER turns away and opens the window.]

What does he want me to say? What does he expect . . . [FATHER drops the cigarette out of the window.]

MOTHER: Don't worry about it.

FATHER: If he goes, I shan't see him again. [FATHER shuts the window again.]

MOTHER: Of course, you will.

FATHER: I don't like to think of him – halfway round the other side of the world.

MOTHER: Will it really make that much difference?

FATHER [quickly]: He said that.

　　　[FATHER turns to face MOTHER, who is standing close behind him.]

Alan – said . . .

　　　[Silence.]

What did he mean?

MOTHER: If it was Terry . . .

FATHER: Why did she come and see us today?

MOTHER: She got up this morning and she thought to herself . . .

FATHER: What did she want?

MOTHER: She wanted to see you.

FATHER: I hardly spoke to the girl. I had to spend most of the afternoon talking to – Gordon.

MOTHER: I don't know why she came to see us. I don't know why Terry does anything. It's many, many years, since . . .

FATHER: Alan says – d'you know? He says, she won't come and see us again.

MOTHER: Alan says a lot of things.

FATHER: He said, there was a reason – he said – there was something Terry wanted to say.

MOTHER: She said nothing to me. Come on. Let's go downstairs.

FATHER: Why won't she come and see us again?

MOTHER: She will. Of course, she will.

FATHER: She isn't happy.

MOTHER: Terry!

FATHER: I didn't think she looked happy.

MOTHER: She's never happier, Terry – as long as there's a drama of some kind going on.

FATHER: What drama?

[MOTHER *turns away and walks back towards the door.*]

MOTHER: I'm going downstairs. You can stay up here, if you want to.

FATHER: Why do you fight with the girl?

MOTHER: You heard what she said to me.

FATHER: You never give her a chance.

MOTHER: You were sitting there.

FATHER: She's only a child.

MOTHER [*blandly*]: The day she treats me like a mother, I'll treat her like a daughter.

FATHER: When she said, 'Good-bye' – didn't you think – somehow, I thought . . .

MOTHER: It was six months – more – this time. She'll come and see you again.

FATHER: She should come and see me.

MOTHER: She will.

FATHER: I'm her father.

MOTHER: She always has come back and – she always will. In the meantime . . .

FATHER: Don't fight with her.

MOTHER: Come on. You've been up here most of the evening already. [MOTHER *puts an arm through his and holds on tight.*]

FATHER: I was looking for that photograph.

MOTHER: You can look tomorrow.

FATHER: I'd like to find it.

MOTHER: We'll both look – tomorrow.

FATHER: I can give it to Alan. He can show it to Gordon.

MOTHER: Yes.

FATHER: It was talking to Gordon, I remembered I still had it.

MOTHER: Did you have a nice talk with Gordon?

FATHER: Yes, I did. I like him. He's a nice boy.

MOTHER: You must've found a lot to talk about. He was in there with you . . .

FATHER: School, mostly – going to school with Alan. He said Alan was top boy at school.

MOTHER: So he was.

FATHER: They were all – jealous of him.

MOTHER: He did very well. He always did very well.

FATHER: Yes, he did.

MOTHER: His teachers always said . . .

FATHER: Oh – and he showed me some photos.

MOTHER: What photos?

FATHER: His children. He's got a fine-looking boy – and a girl.

MOTHER: I wish I'd seen them.

FATHER: The boy's about the age Alan – er – no . . .

MOTHER: Michael.

FATHER: The girl's younger.

MOTHER: A pigeon pair.

FATHER: Yes, that's what I said.

MOTHER: I thought they might stay to supper. Both of them – Alan and Gordon.

FATHER: He showed me a picture of his wife, too. She's very pretty.

MOTHER: Is she local?

FATHER: I didn't know her.

MOTHER: You could've shown him some pictures of Michael and little Sarah.

FATHER: Really, they don't like us at all, do they, Sarah?

MOTHER: Like us? Who?

FATHER: Terry. Alan. They come and see us – you're their mother and I'm – their father.

[MOTHER *rubs* FATHER'S *shoulder with her free hand.*]

MOTHER: They're very lucky.

FATHER: We live here. They come here.

MOTHER: Not very often, they don't.

FATHER: I suppose we should be thankful they come and see us at all.

MOTHER [*indignantly*]: No. No, I won't – be thankful!

FATHER: It's a duty, isn't it?

MOTHER: They like to see you.

FATHER: There's not a lot – I was thinking, this afternoon – there's no pleasure – for them.

MOTHER: Precious little for us! When they carry on the way they did today.

FATHER: I like to see them.

MOTHER: Yes.

FATHER: If there was – I mean, if I could – if it was possible to be – whatever Alan – whatever he wants me to be.

MOTHER: He loves you.

FATHER: He kept asking – 'Should I, Dad? Should I take the job?' I don't know! How can I know? I mean, most of his life – what do I know about that? What do I know about him – any more?

MOTHER: He shouldn't have asked you.

FATHER [*violently*]: I'm his father. Yes – if he wants – advice – is that what he wants?

MOTHER: He has to make up his own mind.

FATHER: If I don't know about the job – what sort of thing . . .

> [MOTHER *clasps her hands tightly round* FATHER'S *arms.*]

MOTHER: He can't come running to you.

FATHER: Half the time, when he's talking to me, I don't understand – I don't have the faintest idea . . .

MOTHER: He can't push the decision on to you.

FATHER: 'If you want me to stay . . .' [FATHER *pulls his arm away from* MOTHER'S *hands and turns back, to look out of the window again.*] 'If you ask me . . .'

MOTHER: It isn't fair.

FATHER: I don't know what he wants me to say.

MOTHER [*gently*]: He thinks you can tell him what to do. You're his father. He thinks you can tell him and, because you're his father – what you tell him, will be right?

FATHER: No. No, that isn't what he thinks.

MOTHER: Alan never has been able to make up his own mind. He's always had to ask someone.

FATHER: He knows I won't see him again, if he goes off to Australia. He knows I'll be . . . [FATHER *presses his palms down, against the window sill.*] He wants me to ask him to stay. He wants me – to beg him to stay.

MOTHER: Oh, no. [MOTHER *steps close behind him and puts her hands on his arms.*] He's asking for help.

FATHER: He thinks I need him. He thinks I'll – miss him so much . . . [FATHER *breaks off abruptly.*] I will. Yes.

MOTHER [*gently*]: He wants you to tell him what he should do.

FATHER: He said . . . [FATHER *breaks away from* MOTHER, *turning to face her.*] Do you know what he said? He said, we didn't talk together. When he was home, when he was a boy – he said . . . [FATHER *slants his head slightly, looking at* MOTHER.] We did, didn't we? We used to sit and talk. I remember. Alan – and me – by the hour. Talk about everything under the sun.

MOTHER: That's right.

FATHER: Why did he say it?

MOTHER: I don't know.

FATHER: Denying . . . [FATHER *leaves the single word hanging in the air.*]

MOTHER: I lit the fire in the front room. Why don't we go down and get a bit warm. It's cold. Don't you think it's cold in here?

FATHER: They had a good childhood.

MOTHER: It's still winter, really. You want it to be summer so much, you forget . . .

FATHER: Why does he have to pretend – now – as if . . . [FATHER *shakes his head.*]

MOTHER: They had a wonderful childhood.

FATHER: Yes.

MOTHER: If every child . . .

FATHER [*abruptly*]: I remember my father! [FATHER *takes his cigarette case out of his pocket.*]

MOTHER: Now, don't have another one. You're smoking too much. Wait till after supper.

FATHER: I remember . . . [FATHER *puts his cigarette case away again.*] They had a wonderful childhood.

MOTHER: Of course, they did.

FATHER: D'you remember that picnic? I was only thinking about it today.

MOTHER: What picnic?

FATHER: On the side of a hill, looking down – I can't remember where.

MOTHER: Oh, yes.

FATHER: I can see it so clearly. Terry ran away and fell over. She cut her knee. [FATHER *stops suddenly and looks at* MOTHER, *sharply.*] You do remember?

MOTHER: Certainly, I remember. There was a path. A very narrow path. Yes!

FATHER: That's right.

MOTHER: The three of you left me to carry the food. All by myself.

FATHER: Terry said – I was talking about it to her – asking – did she remember?

[*Silence.*]

She said – 'Did it happen?'

MOTHER: I can remember carrying the basket.

FATHER: She said – 'I thought I made it up.'

MOTHER: I thought I was going to have a heart attack.

FATHER: I thought I made it up.

MOTHER: Naturally, it began to rain. D'you remember that?

FATHER: After tea.

MOTHER: We just got to shelter.

FATHER: Running – across the grass – and Alan . . .

MOTHER: Shouting with excitement.

FATHER: I was carrying Terry.

MOTHER [*simultaneously*]: I was carrying Terry.

FATHER: She couldn't walk, she said.

MOTHER: As a matter of fact . . .

FATHER [*laughing*]: 'My knee hurts.'

MOTHER: I think it was you . . .

FATHER: Some funny sort of shelter.

MOTHER: . . . carrying Terry.

FATHER: It couldn't have been a bus shelter?

MOTHER [*laughing*]: We were a long way from buses!

FATHER: 'I'm too ill to walk,' she said. She had a scratch the size of my finger nail!

MOTHER [*laughing*]: Little madam!

FATHER: I don't even recognize her now.

MOTHER [*quietly*]: No.

FATHER: Perhaps we should go and see her?

MOTHER: If you want to.

FATHER: See this new place she's got?

MOTHER: Yes.

FATHER: I'd like to know where she's living. The sort of place it is.

MOTHER: We can talk about it later.

FATHER: You'll come with me?

MOTHER: If there's time.

FATHER: She wants us to go.

MOTHER: She wants you to go.

FATHER [*abruptly*]: I can't go on my own.

MOTHER: You can. Of course you can.

FATHER: I want to see her.

MOTHER: Yes, I know. Go – and see her.

FATHER: If you won't come with me, how can I go?

MOTHER: It won't – believe me! – it won't make a scrap of difference to Terry, whether I come with you or not.

FATHER: It makes a lot of difference to me.

    [*Silence.*]

MOTHER: Tell me when you're thinking of going, I'll see if I can manage . . .

FATHER: Sarah, the girl needs you!

MOTHER [*harshly*]: 'The girl' – told me today – precisely – what she needs – wants! – from me. She wants to be left alone. That . . . [MOTHER *stops abruptly and takes in a deep, shuddering breath.*]

    [*Quietly*] That is what she wants and I am only too happy to oblige her.

FATHER: Something's happening to Terry. I don't know what it is. She wouldn't tell me. She told Alan. Perhaps she told you.

MOTHER: She told me.

FATHER: Whatever it is . . .

MOTHER: She's pregnant. It's a fairly normal condition for a woman Terry's age. It's a pity she hasn't got a father for it, of course, but I don't suppose it matters to her, one way or the other.

    [*Silence.*]

    Yes.

FATHER: Terry.

TERRY'S VOICE: He kissed me.

MOTHER: She always told you the good things she did.

TERRY'S VOICE: He put his arms round me . . .

MOTHER: The things she wanted you to know about.

CUT TO *Terry's bedroom. Night.*

    [*Looking across the bed, past* TERRY, *at* FATHER'S *silhouette.*]

TERRY: ... and held me – tight. He – then, he bit me – bit my ear and said things – whispered – things ...
[*Silence.*]
I said – 'Take me home' – and he laughed again.

CUT TO *the hotel bedroom. Day.*
[*The curtains are drawn back and the room is lit with great clarity by the cold morning sunlight.*]
FATHER'S VOICE: What did he do?
[*A table is set at the end of the double bed. The* YOUNG MAN *and the* WOMAN *are eating breakfast, in complete silence.*]
TERRY'S VOICE: He – pulled at me – pulled – at my dress – and tore it.
[*The* YOUNG MAN *is wearing a dressing gown and the* YOUNG WOMAN *a brand new négligé. They do not look at each other across the table as they eat.*]
I tried to get away from him ...

CUT TO FILM: *The two soldiers are standing in the shop doorway. The match strikes and they grin drunkenly at each other in the light of the flame.*
TERRY'S VOICE: ... And all the time – Daddy – he was laughing all the time.
The sound of two men laughing, quietly, drunkenly.
FATHER'S VOICE [*harshly*]: What did he do?
One soldier reaches out and pats the other's face, gently. Then the match burns out and they laugh.
TERRY'S VOICE [*childishly*]: Hurt me.
MAN'S VOICE: Show them the big stick. Let them know who's master.
The two soldiers sink down in the doorway, pressed close to each other, still laughing.
FATHER'S VOICE [*harshly*]: You – Terry – you let him ...

CUT TO *the hotel bedroom. Night.*
[*Looking across the hotel room, towards the bed. The room*

is in darkness, except for the pattern of light striking across the floor.]

TERRY'S VOICE [*fiercely*]: Let him! No. I couldn't stop him.

CUT TO *the landing outside Terry's bedroom.*

[FATHER *sways two or three steps along the landing and then he lurches sideways against the wall.*]

TERRY'S VOICE: I could feel his hands – on me – over me.

[FATHER *presses his face flat to the wall and brings his hands up to his mouth.*]

I didn't want him to stop.

[FATHER *retches and his body shudders. He crouches slightly against the wall.*]

I love him.

CUT TO *the front room.*

[TERRY *is standing with her back to the fireplace, speaking to her* MOTHER *and* FATHER. *She is wearing a cotton summer frock, smart and neat and pretty.*]

TERRY: I'm going to marry Leonard.

[*Pull back between her* MOTHER *and* FATHER, *who are standing close together by the table.*]

I'm asking – 'cause you are my parents and I would – believe it or not – I would like you to be there – to see me – married.

MOTHER [*quietly*]: Your father can do as he pleases, of course.

TERRY: Will you come?

MOTHER: No, I won't.

TERRY: Dad?

FATHER: Give us a chance, Terry, love. You've sprung this whole thing . . .

TERRY: I'm asking you – both of you – will you come and see your daughter married?

MOTHER: What do you care?

TERRY: If you don't know . . .

MOTHER: Stand up on your own. You want to marry him . . .

TERRY: I love him.

MOTHER: Right, then. You don't need us there.

TERRY: Dad?

FATHER: I thought – I always thought, Terry, the day you got married . . .

TERRY: It won't be like that.

FATHER: The greatest day of my life – seeing you . . .

TERRY: Leonard – me – and if you won't come . . .

FATHER: We haven't even met him.

TERRY [harshly]: You won't meet him.

FATHER: That isn't true.

TERRY: Dad, I've asked you and asked you – and never once – never . . .

FATHER: You could've brought him here.

MOTHER: No.

TERRY [viciously]: You should listen – Dad – you should really listen to some of the stupid things you say.

FATHER: There's no need . . .

TERRY: I couldn't bring him here. She – wouldn't let him in the house.

MOTHER: No, I wouldn't.

TERRY: I wanted you to meet him. Dear God! He's the man I love.

MOTHER: Oh, yes!

TERRY: You should be happy.

MOTHER: Love!

TERRY: Someone – loves me – wants me . . .

MOTHER [harshly]: Yes!

TERRY: Wants to live with me.

FATHER: Plenty of young men . . .

TERRY: This – young man – the rest of his life – he wants to take care of me.

MOTHER: It won't work.

FATHER: It isn't so much we won't meet him. Your mother says . . .

TERRY: I know what she says. I know . . . [TERRY points at her MOTHER.] Look at her!

MOTHER: Some boy from round here . . .

TERRY: Some – white – boy.

MOTHER: ... wasn't good enough for you.

TERRY: White! Black! What difference does it make! For pity's sake!

MOTHER [*harshly*]: You'll find out.

TERRY: He loves me.

MOTHER: Wait. That's all I say. Wait!

TERRY: I love him. I want to be with him – live with him.

MOTHER: Yes.

TERRY: Can't you be happy?

MOTHER: You've found something you like and you're going to keep it, whatever happens to us, aren't you – whatever people think about us.

TERRY: What can people think – about you? What – in the name of sweet heaven ...

MOTHER: You [*she walks towards* TERRY] have found something – satisfies – you.

FATHER: Mother.

MOTHER: Really – satisfies ...

TERRY: You stupid – stupid!

FATHER: Terry, don't speak to your mother ...

TERRY: I haven't slept with Leonard.

FATHER: Terry, don't ...

TERRY [*violently*]: Shut up!
     [*Silence.*]

MOTHER: Now – yes – you see?

TERRY [*quietly*]: I haven't slept with him. I would, very likely, if he asked me to.

MOTHER: That is the sort of girl ...

TERRY: He loves me.

MOTHER: Our daughter!

TERRY: He wants to look after me.

MOTHER: One day – mark my words ...

TERRY [*screaming*]: He is not an animal.
     [*Silence.*]

MOTHER: You'll come back to us.

FATHER: Sarah, leave the girl alone.

MOTHER: ... You'll beg us ...

TERRY: No.

MOTHER: . . . on your knees, you'll beg us.

TERRY: Oh, no!

MOTHER: 'Forgive me!'

TERRY [*quietly*]: I'll never ask you for anything, ever again, the whole of my life.

MOTHER: One day . . .

FATHER: Can't we be reasonable? Can't we talk . . .

TERRY: I thought you'd come, Dad. I knew she wouldn't. She wouldn't cross the road and pick me up, if I was bleeding – dying – dead.

MOTHER: Marry this man, you might as well be dead.

TERRY: I thought you . . .

FATHER'S VOICE: I would've gone.

TERRY: . . . loved me.

CUT TO *the front room. The present.*

> [FATHER *is sitting at the table. There is one place laid and there is a plate of eggs and bacon in front of him.*]

FATHER: I wanted to go.

TERRY'S VOICE: I thought you'd want to see me married.

MOTHER: Eat it. Now I've cooked it for you, at least eat it, before it gets cold.

FATHER: I wanted to go. [FATHER *picks up the knife and fork.*]

MOTHER: What are you talking about? [MOTHER *walks round the table and sits on the chair facing* FATHER.]

FATHER: Terry's wedding. I would've gone.

> [*Silence.*]

MOTHER: I didn't stop you.

FATHER: You wouldn't come with me.

MOTHER: If you'd wanted to go you would've gone.

FATHER: That's easy to say.

MOTHER: That's true.

FATHER: I wanted to go. [FATHER *starts to eat his supper.*] For Terry – I wanted to do it for her.

MOTHER [*coldly*]: You'd do anything for Terry?

FATHER: Yes. Yes, I would.

MOTHER: Liar.

> [FATHER *lifts his head sharply and looks across the table at* MOTHER.]

You ruined that girl.

FATHER: Terry. Ruined – Terry?

MOTHER: Letting her think . . . [MOTHER *pulls her lower lip back between her teeth and stops.*]

FATHER: Go on. Say it. Say what you mean.

MOTHER: All her life, you let her think you could do anything. All she had to do was ask.

FATHER: Isn't that natural? Only natural?

MOTHER: If it's a lie?

FATHER: All right. I couldn't stop the sun in the sky.

MOTHER: You couldn't stop the girl at school, who used to bully her.

FATHER: At school? The girl . . .

MOTHER: You couldn't stop the man . . . [MOTHER *shakes her head.*] Ten thousand – little things. Things – that matter.

FATHER: Man? What man? What d'you mean?

MOTHER: A man stopped her. She was coming home from school. He . . . [MOTHER *gestures vaguely.*] . . . exposed . . .

FATHER: She didn't tell me about that.

MOTHER: It was ten years before she told me – and then [*she shrugs wearily*] she was angry – she used it – against me – attacking . . .

FATHER: Nobody can stop – I mean, accidents . . .

MOTHER [*vehemently*]: You – made her think you could. You told her . . .

FATHER: She was only a child.

MOTHER: 'Anything happens – anything you do' – I heard you!

FATHER: Is it wrong – is that what you're saying? Wrong to tell a child . . .

MOTHER: 'Come and talk to me, I'll understand. I'll help you.' How many times did she come to you?

FATHER: When she was a baby . . .

MOTHER: When she was a woman!

FATHER: She needed you!

MOTHER: You wouldn't let her – need – me. You made her think – every time – you ... [MOTHER *reaches her hands across the table, palms down against the surface of the wood*.] You didn't tell her about pain, you said – 'Don't worry, baby – Daddy'll take it away.' You didn't tell her about death – you said – 'No one dies.'

FATHER: What was I supposed to tell her?

MOTHER: 'They go to Heaven.'

FATHER: How could I know?

MOTHER: You didn't tell her about Heaven, you sent her to Sunday School. Let them ...

FATHER: I said what my father – said ...

MOTHER: You love her.

FATHER: Yes.

MOTHER: I know you love her.

FATHER: More than – more – I love her.

MOTHER: The things she does – you blame me. She hurts you – and you blame me.

FATHER: I made her.

MOTHER: It isn't my fault. When she hurts you, it isn't my fault.

FATHER [*harshly*]: It isn't mine.

MOTHER: No.

FATHER: Is that what you're saying?

MOTHER: No ... [MOTHER *slams her hands down on the surface of the table*.] ... I'm not – Ted – I sat there – half my life – and let her ...

FATHER: It isn't my fault.

MOTHER: Everything that happened ...

FATHER: You can't blame me.

MOTHER: If I'd talked to her – if I could have talked to her ...

[FATHER *pushes his plate away*.]

FATHER: What's the point! [FATHER *stands up*.] There's no point!

MOTHER: She won't come back.

175

FATHER: You want to blame me.

MOTHER: She's gone.

FATHER: I tried – and tried – with the girl.

MOTHER: You can't have her.

FATHER: I wanted to help her.

MOTHER: You can't – live – with her.

FATHER: I can't expect you to believe – to understand ...

MOTHER: Even in memories, you can't ... [MOTHER *pushes her chair back and stands up, facing* FATHER.] She isn't coming back.

    [*Silence.*]

FATHER [*quietly*]: She isn't coming back.

MOTHER [*simply*]: Me, Ted. You have to live with me.

FATHER: She told you.

MOTHER: All these years – pretending – now ...

FATHER [*simultaneously*]: And you – live with Alan? Is that the idea? You'd like that. He wouldn't ... [FATHER *stumbles over the words, chokes on them.*]

MOTHER: Alan's going away, too.

FATHER [*mumbling*]: ... hurt you.

MOTHER: We can't – either one of us ...

FATHER [*harshly*]: You can stop him!

MOTHER: I don't want to stop him.

FATHER: You stopped me. Every chance I ever got. 'You're happy enough where you are.'

MOTHER: I think it's right for Alan, taking this job.

FATHER: 'We've got enough money. We've got our home.'

MOTHER: It's a wonderful opportunity.

FATHER: 'Our children.'

MOTHER: He'll get on.

FATHER: You want him to get on.

MOTHER: He's bright. He should get on. He won't be happy, if he doesn't.

FATHER: Did you think – in that job – did you ever think – was I happy?

    [*Silence.*]

MOTHER: You stayed in that job, because you wanted to stay there. It suited you.

FATHER: It was nothing. Pieces of paper – and ticking them. Passing them to Mr Collingham. [*Violently*] Nothing!

MOTHER: You wanted to stay there.

FATHER: How do you know what I wanted?

MOTHER: I've lived with you – thirty-six years.

FATHER: You don't know what I want. You don't have the faintest idea.

MOTHER: The job suited you.

FATHER: It was nothing!

MOTHER: If you wanted to get on . . .

FATHER: Every chance I got.

MOTHER: If you'd come to me . . .

FATHER: Oh, yes!

MOTHER: Told me . . .

FATHER: What? What could I say? A house – two children – just barely making ends meet.

MOTHER: If you'd said – 'I want to chuck it, I want to start again. I want to go – oh, I don't know – anywhere!'

FATHER: Australia?

MOTHER: I would've packed up. I would've gone with you . . .

FATHER [*harshly*]: I know. Anywhere!

MOTHER [*simply*]: Yes.

FATHER: And now, it's too late.

　　[*Silence.*]

　　I remember my mother was frightened sick of my father. I remember . . .

MOTHER: Perhaps, one day . . .

FATHER: . . . I heard them talking.

MOTHER: . . . you'll know.

FATHER: I walked into the room and I saw my father hit – my mother – across the face. They were quarrelling. I don't know what it was all about. He hit her and she started to cry. I picked up a knife and pushed it into his stomach, deep into his stomach – low.

　　[*Silence.*]

　　No, I didn't. Of course, I didn't. Children don't murder

their parents. [FATHER *takes his cigarette case out of his pocket.*] You don't mind if I have a cigarette now, do you?

[MOTHER *shakes her head.*]

She was so frightened of him, she used to hide me away, when he was in the house. He never saw me, unless he sent for me, of course. Twice a year. Once – on my birthday. Once – at Christmas. [FATHER *selects a cigarette from his case, carefully.*]

[*Smiling*] It was a long time ago. Things have changed since then. Changed for the better. I used to see my children almost every day. We used to go – on picnics together. [FATHER *puts the cigarette into his mouth and turns it slightly, wetting it. He puts the case away, carefully.*]

MOTHER: You do blame me.

FATHER: One day, I was crying. It was nothing important. I think I must've cut myself – it was something quite trivial. But, I was crying. [FATHER *takes his cigarette lighter out of his pocket.*] My mother put her hand over my mouth, so he wouldn't hear me. So he wouldn't be angry. Children shouldn't cry – shouldn't be heard – crying. I almost suffocated. [FATHER *lights his cigarette.*] I loved my father.

MOTHER: You blame me for everything.

[FATHER *drops his lighter back into his pocket.*]

FATHER: I respected him. He was a man you could respect.

MOTHER: I'm sorry.

FATHER: You don't mind if Alan goes to Australia. Why should you? [*Suddenly,* FATHER *shrugs his shoulders, as if feeling cold.*] I think I'll go to bed. There's nothing I want to watch on telly tonight, is there?

[MOTHER *shakes her head.*]

Alan – Ellen – the children – let them go to Australia. Let them stay there – two years – three – five – ten! You're still young. You'll be here when they come back. You'll be alive. [FATHER *walks slowly across the room towards the door.*] I won't. I'll be dead. [*At the door,* FATHER *turns and looks at* MOTHER.] I hate you, d'you know that? Not for anything you've done – just – for being younger

– for having – more years to live. You will be alive, when I'm dead.

[*Silence.*]

I don't want to die. [FATHER *pulls the door open and turns to walk out into the hall.*]

MOTHER: Ted.

FATHER [*quietly*]: I don't go out any more. You don't know why. You think ... [FATHER *glances back at her.*] 'He's getting old, stupid. Can't take things in, any more.' I hate – everyone – yes – almost everyone I see, Sarah – I hate them. They'll be here. They'll be alive – and I'll be dead – in the earth – rotting.

[*Silence.*]

'Till death do us part.' I always thought – if I thought about it – [*violently*] and I thought about it! Everyone will die, before I die. I'll live for ever. I've got to. 'Cause I'm so – frightened – hmm? – of dying. Isn't that silly? An old man like me – why should I want to stay alive? What is there left? What can I do?

MOTHER: I didn't know.

FATHER: You didn't think. I've got nothing left, Sarah – just – living – and you'll still be living – when I'm dead. [FATHER *shrugs and turns away. He walks slowly into the hall.*] Don't stay down here all night. You've had a tiring day. [FATHER *walks slowly across the hall to the bottom of the stairs. He rests a hand on the banisters as he steps on to the bottom stair. He begins to walk, with some effort, up the stairs.*]

TERRY'S VOICE: You like it? You do like it?

FATHER'S VOICE: Yes, of course, I like it.

TERRY'S VOICE: Isn't it the most beautiful dress you've ever seen? Isn't it?

CUT TO *the front room.*

[*The room is prepared for a birthday party. It is decorated with paper streamers and balloons. A table is laid for a party tea.*

In front of the table, a CHILD *of six is swirling round and round, fluffing out her party dress, waist high.*]

TERRY'S VOICE: It's the most beautiful dress in the world. Nobody – [*shouting*] nobody ...

FATHER'S VOICE [*laughing*]: Terry! Not so loud.

TERRY'S VOICE: ... ever had a dress – so very – very – very ... [*The* CHILD *stops spinning and stands, legs slightly apart, breathless, and looking at the camera.*] ... beautiful!

FATHER'S VOICE: No, they didn't.

TERRY'S VOICE: Did they?

CUT TO *a bedroom. Day.*

> [*A* YOUNG WOMAN, *in a bridal dress, which is rather battered after the wedding ceremony, is standing at the end of a double bed, looking nervously at the camera.*]

FATHER'S VOICE: I never saw such a beautiful dress – such a beautiful girl – ever ...

> [*Hesitantly, the* YOUNG WOMAN *puts a hand to her forehead and brushes at her hair and bridal veil.*]

... in my whole life.

WOMAN'S VOICE: I'm so happy.

TERRY'S VOICE: Happy, happy, happy!

CUT TO *the front room.*

> [*The* CHILD *has her arms round her* FATHER'S *neck and her feet off the ground.*]

TERRY'S VOICE: I'm so happy.

> [*The two figures are whirling wildly, laughing.*]

WOMAN'S VOICE: I love you.

TERRY'S VOICE: Why can't it always be parties – and presents – and – fun!

CUT TO *the bedroom. Day.*

TERRY'S VOICE: Daddy – why?

> [*The* YOUNG MAN *is embracing the* YOUNG WOMAN *tightly. He is wearing a stiff, formal suit.*]

FATHER'S VOICE: I love you too.

WOMAN'S VOICE: We'll always be happy.

TERRY'S VOICE [*laughing*]: Happy, happy, happy!

WOMAN'S VOICE: Always and always.

FATHER'S VOICE: Always and always.

> [*The* YOUNG MAN *pulls back slightly from the* YOUNG WOMAN *and looks at her, down into her face.*]

World without end!

MAN'S VOICE: Show them the big stick!

CUT TO FILM: *The two soldiers are sitting in the corner of the shop doorway, smoking the single cigarette between them. They have their arms round each other's shoulders and their heads together. A long way off, shells thud with a dull monotony.*

MAN'S VOICE: Let them know who's master. That's what they understand. Tears afterwards – bound to be tears! Got to make you feel – you know? But that's what they want. That's what they respect. Show them the big stick.

CUT TO *the hotel bedroom. Night.*

> [*Looking across the width of the room, framing the* YOUNG MAN'S *silhouette on the left, to the door from the bathroom, which is open. The* YOUNG WOMAN *stands in the doorway wearing a brand new négligé, hesitant before walking into the room, towards the bed.*]

FATHER'S VOICE: Such a beautiful girl.

> [*The light shines through the négligé from the bathroom, slightly balanced by the light at the side of the bed.*]

WOMAN'S VOICE: Will you be – gentle – with me?

CUT TO FILM: *Looking down the side slopes of Whipsnade Zoo, out across the countryside below, showing through the heat haze.*

FATHER'S VOICE: One day, the princess – only she was the queen now, of course. She'd been the queen for many years.

CHILD'S VOICE [*murmuring*]: And beautiful.

Pan slowly up to the sky and hold on the white cloud formations drifting.

FATHER'S VOICE: Oh, yes. She was beautiful – still – very beautiful.

CUT TO *the air raid shelter. Night.*
> [*The sounds of the London blitz thunder outside the shelter and the oil lamp flickers.*]

FATHER: But she was old.
> [*The* CHILD *is cradled in his arms with her head against his chest.*]

And all her family, children – grandchildren – great-grand-children – came to see her. They stood round her bed and slowly, she opened her eyes to look at them . . .

MOTHER'S VOICE: She's asleep, Ted. No need to go on.
> [*Camera swings to* MOTHER, *who is sitting on the other side of the shelter.*]

FATHER'S VOICE: She opened her eyes . . .

MOTHER: You'll only wake her up again.

CUT TO *the Stephens' bedroom. Night.*
> [*Close-up of* FATHER.]

FATHER [*suddenly*]: Yes. Yes, of course.
> [*Pull back quickly, as* FATHER *stands up. He has been sitting on the chair in the corner of the bedroom.*]

That's where it is. [*Calling*] Sarah. [FATHER *turns and walks towards the door of the room.*] Why didn't I think – [*calling*] Sarah! [FATHER *pulls open the door of the room and walks on to the landing.*] I know where it is. I know where it is. I know where it's got to. [*He leans over the banisters.*] Sarah! I know where that photograph is.

CUT TO FILM: *Looking across a football pitch. Two school teams are playing a rough, hard match. The air is misty and the ground is muddy. There are only a scattered few spectators.*

The camera centres on Father, standing on the touch line, wrapped up to his ears in a heavy coat and scarf, shouting happily. He waves the boys on.

FATHER'S VOICE: There's a case in the attic.

CUT TO *the hall.*
> [FATHER *walks carefully down the last steps into the hall and rests a hand on the banisters.*]

FATHER: Sarah. [*He walks across the hall to the door of the front room. He pushes it open.*] Don't know why I didn't think . . .

>[FATHER *walks into the doorway and stops.*
>
>*The camera looks round the room, which is in chaos. A chair is lying on its side. The table is swept clear of flower vase and centre cloth.*]

[*Hesitantly*] Sarah.

>[FATHER *turns and walks quickly out of the room.*]

CUT TO *the kitchen.*

>[*Looking across the kitchen at the doorway and* FATHER, *who is looking into the room, which is in the same state of chaos as the front room, with broken china and cutlery scattered on the floor.* FATHER *looks at the mess for a moment and then turns away.*]

CUT TO *the back room.*

>[*Looking across the room, as the door opens and* FATHER *looks in. The room is undisturbed, neat and tidy.*]

FATHER [*calling*]: Sarah!

CUT TO *the front room.*

>[*The camera pushes slowly across the room, towards the armchair in the far corner. Almost hidden by the chair is a pair of legs.*
>
>*Cut to* FATHER, *as he crouches down beside the chair. With an enormous effort he pushes the chair away.*
>
>*Cut to a high shot, looking down at* FATHER, *kneeling beside* MOTHER'S *body, which is stretched out on the floor, in the corner of the room.*]

FATHER'S VOICE: Don't turn away.

FADE OUT

PART THREE

GLADLY, MY CROSS-EYED BEAR

First transmitted by Theatre 625 on B.B.C.-2 on
16 October 1966 with the following cast:

ALAN	Michael Bryant
FATHER	Maurice Denham
TERRY	Judi Dench
MRS HAYTER	Maryann Turner
DETECTIVE SERGEANT WILSON	Windsor Davis
POLICEMAN	Terry Leigh
Story Editor	James Brabazon
Designer	Richard Wilmot
Produced by	Michael Bakewell
Directed by	Christopher Morahan

FADE IN *the back room of the Stephens' house. Dawn.*

> [*The room is in semi-darkness. The curtains are drawn across the window and the only light switched on is a table lamp, standing on a small table beside* FATHER'S *chair.*
>
> FATHER *is sitting in his chair, slumped down into it with an ashtray on the arm of the chair. The ashtray is full of cigarette ends.*
>
> ALAN *is sitting on a small stool in front of the fire, stirring a cup of tea. He holds the cup and saucer in his hand*].

FATHER: Your mother – funny – she thought – she always said – I was jealous of you.

ALAN: How d'you mean? Jealous?

FATHER: The way you've got on.

ALAN: Me? Got on!

FATHER: 'Cause I did nothing with my life. Sat in an office, you know. One job.

ALAN: What've I done?

FATHER: You've done well.

ALAN: I wish I thought so.

FATHER: She was right about that. You've got on.

ALAN: Terry might – I don't know – have done something. She was – sort of special – once.

FATHER: We talked about you. Last night.

ALAN: She might've done – anything – if she'd had the luck. [ALAN *puts the spoon into the saucer.*]

FATHER: Sunday nights we mostly talked about you – and Terry.

ALAN: If she'd wanted to.

FATHER: She'll be here?

ALAN: Any minute now, Dad. [ALAN *looks at his wrist watch.*] Any minute.

> [*Silence.*]

SUPERIMPOSE TITLE: *Gladly, my cross-eyed bear*

FADE TITLE.

FATHER: Your mother was so excited about your job.

ALAN: Yes.

FATHER: Things looking up. Moving on.

ALAN: We talked about it. [ALAN *stands up and stretches. He pulls back one of the curtains. The cold, grey, early-morning light filters into the room, through the net curtains.*]

FATHER: She'll be cold. It looks cold – out there.

ALAN: Yes.

FATHER: Switch on another bar, Alan. Make sure the room's warm.

ALAN: Right. Yes, I will. [ALAN *walks across to the fire and crouches in front of it.*]

FATHER: She's very like your mother there. Did you know that?

ALAN: Terry? [ALAN *switches on the third bar of the electric fire.*]

FATHER: Your mother could never stand a cold room.

ALAN: A room Mum's been sitting in – next best thing to a furnace.

FATHER: Terry's the same.

[*Silence.*]

Will Terry be able to catch a train? This time in the morning? This early?

ALAN: I don't know, Dad. If she can't she'll take a taxi.

FATHER: Coming all this way?

ALAN: She said she'd get here as quickly as she could.

FATHER: Alan – look – you'll let her have it back, won't you? The money for the taxi.

ALAN: Yes.

FATHER: Terry can't afford to come half across London – in a taxi.

ALAN: No, Dad. All right.

FATHER: I've got no cash myself, otherwise . . .

[*Silence.*]

When was it you spoke to her?

ALAN: Twenty minutes – half-an-hour ago.

FATHER: She should be here – soon?

ALAN: Yes, she should.

FATHER: Poor old Terry. Getting her out of bed.

ALAN: Why don't you get a bit of rest, Dad. I can talk to Terry, when she gets here. You see her . . . [*he straightens up*] . . . a bit later. How about that? You can have a lie down . . .

FATHER: How long will she stay?

ALAN: What d'you mean?

FATHER: She's got her job to go to. So have you.

ALAN: I'll phone them a bit later. Tell them.

FATHER: Oh, yes. I suppose . . .

ALAN: Dad, I'm not going to work. I'm not going to leave you on your own today. There's no question of that!

FATHER: Yes, all right – but what about Terry? I mean, you can 'phone – and . . . [FATHER *gestures vaguely at* ALAN.] But Terry . . .

ALAN: I don't suppose Terry cares one way or the other about the job. She'd just as soon chuck it in, as not. There's always something else she can do.

FATHER: She changes her job, doesn't she? More often than people – when I was . . . [FATHER *shakes his head.*]

ALAN: The sort of work she does . . .

FATHER: She should do something better. She could – don't you think she could?

ALAN: If she wanted to.

FATHER: Why doesn't she want to?

ALAN: She's happy enough . . .

FATHER: No, she isn't happy. She isn't!

ALAN: You can't make her . . .

FATHER: What's the point – wasting her life – never doing – anything – never . . .

ALAN: I don't think it worries Terry all that much.

FATHER: It should worry her. Look at you.

ALAN: You can't compare . . .

FATHER: You're getting on. Your mother was proud of you – seeing you – make your way.

ALAN: Dad!

FATHER: She was always talking about you. She used to tell people . . .

ALAN: I wish half the things she told people – just half of them – were true.

FATHER: Your mother was proud of you.

ALAN: You can't compare Terry and me.

FATHER: If she tried . . .

ALAN: I've got a wife – and I've got two children. Terry . . .

FATHER [*simultaneously*]: Terry's got nothing! Why? Why is that?

ALAN: You don't know – Dad! You can't say . . . [ALAN *stops speaking abruptly and rubs a hand across his forehead.*] We don't want to quarrel, Dad. [ALAN *sits on the arm of the chair his* FATHER *is sitting in.*] Not today. Not about Terry.

[*Silence.*]

FATHER [*mumbling*]: Not quarrelling.

ALAN: Good.

FATHER [*quietly*]: I wanted her to have – Alan, I wanted to give her everything . . . [FATHER *takes* ALAN'S *hand and holds it tightly.*] Nothing. I gave her . . .

ALAN: You were married – how long were you married . . .

FATHER: . . . nothing.

ALAN: Come on, Dad. You can't sit here and – well, you can't sit here – not for the rest of your life!

FATHER: I loved her.

ALAN: Of course, you did. I know that.

FATHER: Do you?

ALAN: I saw you, didn't I? Thirty-odd years, I saw you together.

FATHER: Yes.

ALAN: You loved her.

[*Silence.*]

FATHER: When will she get here?

ALAN: As soon as she can.

FATHER: She knows, doesn't she? You told her?

ALAN: I told her.

FATHER: She should be here.

ALAN: She will be.

FATHER: I need her.

ALAN: Just as soon as she can get here.

[*Silence.*

ALAN *stands up and walks away from the chair.*]

FATHER: I'm sorry.

[ALAN *glances round at his* FATHER.]

You're here. I'm grateful. Truly I am.

ALAN: There's no need ... [ALAN *shrugs and looks down at the floor.*]

FATHER: But, Terry – I do need ...

ALAN [*abruptly*]: Yes.

FATHER: Now, her mother's ... [FATHER *chokes over the words and coughs.*]

ALAN: Easy, Dad. Take it easy.

FATHER: Now – I need her.

ALAN: I'll phone the flat. I'll make certain she's left. All right?

FATHER [*simply*]: Thank you.

[ALAN *nods abruptly and walks across the room to the door. He opens the door.*]

ALAN: And – er – drink some of your tea – before it's stone cold.

[ALAN *walks into the hall.*

A POLICEMAN *in uniform stands at the bottom of the stairs.*

ALAN *walks along the hall to the table beside the front door, where the telephone is kept.*]

Excuse me.

POLICEMAN: Certainly, sir.

[*The* POLICEMAN *moves a few steps along the hall, as* ALAN *picks up the receiver and dials a number. Waiting for an answer, he glances at the* POLICEMAN.]

ALAN: Will you be much longer?

POLICEMAN: Couldn't say.

ALAN: I don't suppose you'd tell me ... [ALAN *breaks off and half-turns away from the* POLICEMAN *as he speaks into the receiver.*] Hello. This is Alan Stephens. I'm sorry to get you up, yet again ... Oh, I see. Well, I don't feel quite as guilty about ... She has – already? Thanks. That's what I wanted to know ... It's just – my father's beginning to get a bit anxious and he asked me ... Yes – understandably ... She should be here any minute. Very likely, had some difficulty getting a taxi ... Hmm ... Thanks again. [ALAN *puts the receiver down and rests his hand on it for a moment, before he picks it up again and dials another number. As he waits for an answer,* ALAN *glances round at the* POLICEMAN.] Where's the detective sergeant?

POLICEMAN: He's in the front room, sir.

ALAN: If he wants to speak to me again ...

POLICEMAN: I expect he will.

ALAN: Yes. Well, I – sorry! [ALAN *speaks into the receiver again.*] Ellen – hi! It's Alan. Did I wake you up? ... As well as can be expected, I suppose. Rather better, really. At the moment, he's got everything pinned on Terry getting here. I don't know what magic he thinks she'll work – still! ... Would you? Thanks. There won't be anyone in the office yet. No – but when you do – tell her I won't be in today at all – possibly not tomorrow, either ... Oh, God! No, I'd better speak to him myself, if you'll cope with my secretary. Have you got his home number there? ... Thanks.

[*Silence.*]

Of course, that's it. No, I can remember now. Thanks. Look, what about the kids? ... I mean – what about telling them? ... Yes, well – I suppose it can wait. I don't know, it all seems ... [ALAN *shakes his head and rubs a hand across his forehead.*] Yes. See you later. 'Bye. [ALAN *puts the receiver down again and turns away from the telephone.*] Times like this, I wish I smoked – or maybe, bit my nails. Some nasty habit.

POLICEMAN: Yes, sir.

[ALAN *walks along the hall to the door of the back room. As he reaches it, he hesitates for a moment and looks at his watch. He thinks for a moment, then shrugs and opens the door. He walks into the room and shuts the door behind him.*]

ALAN: She's on her way. She should be here any minute, Dad. Really.

FATHER: Thank you.

ALAN: I wouldn't mind betting she's in a pretty terrible state herself. [ALAN *walks across to the window and looks out at the garden.*] Running round Chelsea, trying to find a taxi.

FATHER: As long as you're here.

ALAN: Getting some very odd looks from the neighbourhood coppers, I shouldn't wonder.

FATHER: It's just – with Terry . . .

ALAN [*abruptly*]: I know, Dad. Yes.
   [*Silence.*]

FATHER: Are they still here?

ALAN: Oh, yes.

FATHER: What are they doing?

ALAN: Honestly, Dad, I don't know.

FATHER [*irritably*]: They take their time.

ALAN: They'll get finished as quickly as they can. I suppose. They don't want to be hanging about, any more . . .

FATHER [*harshly*]: Everyone! Quickly as they can. That's what you think? Is it?
   [ALAN *turns and looks across the room at his* FATHER.] They – get through – they . . . [FATHER *stumbles into silence.*] I'm sorry.

ALAN [*quietly*]: That's all right, Dad.

FATHER: It's just . . .

ALAN: You're upset.

FATHER: . . . Terry – and them . . .

ALAN: It's natural.

FATHER: . . . and you say – all the time, you . . . [FATHER *breaks off abruptly and looks directly at* ALAN.] Yes, I am upset.

ALAN: I know.

FATHER: I don't know what's going to happen, do I?

ALAN: How d'you mean? Happen? [ALAN *gestures towards the front room.*] With them? Happen . . .

FATHER: Me! I don't know what I'm going to do.

ALAN: Well, you don't have to worry about that, do you?
[ALAN *walks forward, towards his* FATHER.]

FATHER: I have to worry. Yes!

ALAN: First of all, you're coming home with me. You'll stay – with me.

FATHER: I live here.

ALAN: Yes, I know. But, Dad – you can't – I mean, be reasonable – on your own? You can't stay here on your own.

FATHER: I live here.

ALAN: Ellen's going to put the kids in together. They always get a kick out of sleeping in the same room, so that's no problem. You are going to have ... [ALAN *stumbles slightly, hesitates, and then hurries on.*] ... have – little Sarah's room.

FATHER: No.

ALAN: We'll talk about it later.

FATHER: Can you put this house – this [*he stands up*] whole house – into one room?

ALAN [*grinning*]: You going to bring it all with you?

FATHER: I don't like your house.

ALAN: You'll want to sell some of – well, things you don't – need. You'll want to sell them, won't you?

FATHER: If I come and live with you and Ellen, I have to sell my home?

ALAN: You know I didn't mean ...

FATHER: If I can't keep ... [FATHER *turns, looking at the room around him.*] ... I've lived here – in God's name! If you want me to sell ... [FATHER *completes the turn, facing* ALAN *again.*] ... if you!

ALAN: All right!

[FATHER *turns away again and rests his hands on the mantelpiece.*]

FATHER: D'you know how long I've lived here – with your mother?

ALAN: Thirty-six years.

[*Silence.*]

Give or take a couple of months.

FATHER: Yes. [FATHER *rubs his hands along the tiled surface of the mantelpiece.*]

ALAN: Dad – there's no question ... [ALAN *rubs a hand across his forehead.*]

FATHER: I live here.

ALAN: We've got a home. You can share it. We want you to share it.

FATHER: You're going to Australia.

ALAN: Come with us.

[*Silence.*]

FATHER: Whatever I do – now ... [FATHER *shakes his head.*] I don't think you understand.

ALAN: I know it isn't the right time ...

FATHER [*violently*]: What I decide to do, now – it's the last time, Alan. Where I go – that – is where I'll die.

ALAN: Dad. Come on!

FATHER: You think I can live for ever?

ALAN: I don't think you need to worry about – well, something like that – now. I don't think you should have to worry ...

FATHER [*irritably*]: You don't think I should have to worry about anything. Yes, I know.

ALAN: No. I think you've got plenty of things ...

FATHER: All I have to do is let you look after me? You'll see I never have to worry again – worry about anything!

ALAN: I think you need a rest. I think you've earned a rest.

FATHER: Your mother said that.

[*Silence.*]

ALAN: She was right.

FATHER: How do you know? [FATHER *turns away from the mantelpiece, turning with his back to* ALAN.] People who do things – they earn themselves a rest. What have I ever done?

ALAN: I don't mean to make things worse for you, Dad.

FATHER: I've got old.

ALAN: I'm trying ...

FATHER: That – is my great achievement.

ALAN: I want to be as much – help – as I can.

FATHER: Old.

ALAN: I do think you ought to rest.

FATHER: I think I ought to die.

ALAN: Dad – for pity's sake!

FATHER: Have you got a better suggestion?

ALAN: I think it's [*he looks at his watch and taps the glass face*] altogether too early for reasonable people to be up and about, talking – about anything.

FATHER: You don't know what I'm talking about.

ALAN: You don't have to go upstairs. You can stay down here. Rest ... [ALAN *walks up to his* FATHER.]

FATHER: Funny – it's like you said. You don't even listen to what I say.

ALAN: I can make myself a cup of coffee and – well, I can sit in the kitchen. I don't mind.

FATHER: I'm talking. [FATHER *turns to face* ALAN.] I am talking.

ALAN: What?

FATHER [*desperately*]: I am here!

ALAN: Dad, I'm sorry. [ALAN *puts a hand on his* FATHER'S *arm.*] It's a habit. Talking to the children. Just – going on.
[*Silence.*]
[*Simply*] I'm sorry.

FATHER: Something I'm trying to tell you.

ALAN: Yes.

FATHER: I want to live here.

ALAN [*abruptly*]: It isn't possible, Dad.
[*Silence.*]
[*Quietly*] I know. Yes, you've lived here a long time. You want to go on living here.

FATHER: What would I do? Anywhere else? I wouldn't know ...

ALAN: You can't live here on your own.

FATHER: Terry can live here with me. Terry can look after me.

ALAN: Oh.

FATHER: She can run the house.

ALAN: Yes, of course.

FATHER: If she wants to go on working – well, she can get a job locally.

ALAN: Hmm.

FATHER: She won't be able to work much longer, anyway.

ALAN: She told you?

FATHER: Your mother – told me.

ALAN: You're going to talk to her – about this?

FATHER: She can make a home for herself.

ALAN: When she gets here?

FATHER: She needs a home.

[Silence.]

ALAN: Yes, I see.

FATHER: And then ... [FATHER turns and looks out of the window, at the garden.] ... I can stay here. I want to stay here. [FATHER rests a hand against the cold glass of the window.]

ALAN: Dad ...

FATHER: I know – here ...

ALAN [abruptly]: Don't ask her.

FATHER: What d'you say?

ALAN: Just – don't ... [ALAN shakes his head miserably, and turns away.]

FATHER: What're you talking about? What do you mean?

ALAN: I've asked you, Dad. Come and live with us. It's so simple.

FATHER: I know. Yes – you want to look after me – I know – thank you.

ALAN: No. Just – don't start – don't ...

FATHER: What? Start what? What're you trying to say?

ALAN: If Terry says – 'no'?

FATHER: Why should she?

ALAN: If she does?

[Silence.]

FATHER: She won't.

ALAN: You'll finish up – you know? On your own! That's how you'll finish up – and then, you'll blame us. Left you to die – old and alone.

FATHER: Oh, no.

ALAN [*vehemently*]: Yes!

FATHER: I won't give you the pleasure.

ALAN: You know Terry won't – you know ... [ALAN *gestures at his* FATHER, *with the flat of one hand outstretched towards him and his other hand on his hip.*] Dad! She's going to say – 'no'. Come on! You know she is.

FATHER: When I've asked her, when – if – that's what she says – all right – yes! Then, I'll know.

ALAN [*violently*]: Now! You know – and still, you're going to ask her.

FATHER: You know Terry so much better than I do?

ALAN: I know her. Yes. I've watched her. I've thought about her. Terry. Thirty years old – Terry. On her own – Terry – frightened sick – Terry – going out of her mind!

FATHER: Don't shout at me!

ALAN: Have you thought about her? [ALAN *clenches the fingers of his outstretched hand, drops his arm and turns away.*]

FATHER: She's my daughter.

ALAN: You may find she stopped – I don't know – about the age of sixteen – as far as she's concerned – Terry stopped being your daughter.

FATHER: Don't be ridiculous!

ALAN: You think people don't change – from three to thirty!

FATHER: You don't stop being somebody's daughter.

ALAN: On a piece of paper – yes – where it says – Teresa Anne Stephens – father – Edward Arnold Stephens. [ALAN *presses the fingers of one hand against his forehead.*] Here. No piece of paper. No daughter!

FATHER: You can't – stop – just because – you can't stop being someone's daughter.

ALAN: I told you yesterday – just ... [ALAN *slams his hands together.*] You didn't hear a word, did you? Felt – just like Terry – all the time – feelings. [*He walks towards his* FATHER.] Think! For once in your life. Look at things and then, think about them. Don't – bloody – don't – feel!

FATHER [*coldly*]: How many times do I have to tell you!

ALAN: You don't have to be alone. Nobody wants you to be alone.

FATHER: You're so certain Terry's going to say – 'no'.

ALAN: Yes.

FATHER: Why? How can you be so certain?

ALAN: I know Terry. This Terry!

FATHER: You're wrong.

ALAN: I am not wrong.

FATHER: You're jealous.

ALAN: What d'you mean?

FATHER: You know I'd rather live with Terry.
    [*Silence.*]

ALAN: Yes, I know that. You'd rather live with Terry, than – live with God – harp, wings and halo!
    [*Silence.*]
    [*Quietly*] I've always known that.

FATHER: She won't say – 'no'.
    [*There is a knock at the door of the room.
    Silence.*]

ALAN [*calling*]: Come in.
    [*The door is opened and* DETECTIVE SERGEANT
    WILSON *looks into the room.*]

WILSON: Mr Stephens. I wonder – can I have a word with you?

ALAN: Me?

WILSON: Er – yes. If you don't mind?

ALAN: No, I don't mind.
    [WILSON *steps back into the hall and leaves the door
    open.*]
    You talk to Terry as soon as she gets here. Tell me what you decide.

FATHER: I am – truly – if I've hurt you, Alan – I'm sorry.

ALAN: It's my fault. Making plans for people. It's always been a failing with me. Expecting everybody ...
    [*He simply stops talking, staring at his* FATHER.
    Silence.*]
    Anyway, you're probably right. I am jealous. [*He walks across to the doorway.*] You want to live with Terry? All

right. Why shouldn't you? I still think, it'd be simpler my way, but . . .

FATHER: It's more – practical – if Terry comes here.

[ALAN *stands in the doorway for a moment.*]

ALAN: Hmm. Try and get some rest. [ALAN *gestures at the chair.*] You look whacked.

FATHER: I don't think I could make the trip, all the way to Australia.

ALAN: Best thing that could happen to you. Have the time of your life.

FATHER: I'm too old.

[ALAN *shakes his head.*]

Here. I belong here. I know . . . [FATHER *puts his hand on his armchair.*]

ALAN: I'm not going to twist your arm, Dad. You do – just what you want to do.

FATHER: Someone has to look after Terry.

ALAN [*quietly*]: Oh, yes. [ALAN *turns away abruptly and steps into the hall. He pulls the door shut behind him and then stands for a moment, looking at the floor. Suddenly, he lifts his head and looks at* WILSON.] Yes. You wanted to speak to me?

WILSON: One or two things I want to clear up.

ALAN: Right.

WILSON: Where shall we go?

ALAN: The kitchen? [*He turns and steps towards the kitchen door. He pushes it open, glancing at his watch as he does so.*] Oh. Look, d'you mind – I ought to 'phone my boss – let him know I shan't be in today. I'd like to catch him at home.

WILSON: Fine. Yes. Go ahead.

[ALAN *steps back and lets* WILSON *walk into the kitchen.*]

ALAN: It won't take a minute.

WILSON: Don't worry.

ALAN: Thanks. [ALAN *turns and walks away along the hall. The door of the front room is open and he glances in, as he walks past. He picks up the receiver, hesitates for a moment and then dials a number. He glances over his shoulder at the door of the front room.*] Mr Thompson? [*He turns his head quickly and speaks into the receiver.*] Hello . . . Yes, this is Alan Stephens. I'm sorry to disturb you at such an ungodly hour . . . I'm afraid it is. I wanted to tell you myself. [*He twists the fingers of his free hand in the cable of the telephone as he talks.*] My mother – er – died – during the night . . . Yes, it is . . . Oh, yes – completely . . . He's – well, I suppose you could say he was – bearing up . . . I wanted to tell you about it and say – I thought, I'd come in tomorrow – if that's all right? . . . Oh, well – thank you. As a matter of fact, I think I'd rather – you know? [*He stands silently, listening, staring down at the floor.*] If there is anything – yes – of course, I'll be in touch. Thank you . . . Thank you.

> [*He puts the receiver down and presses both hands hard against it. Gradually, he relaxes and then straightens up and turns away from the telephone. He walks back along the hall to the kitchen, without looking into the front room this time.*
>
> WILSON *is sitting at the kitchen table, with a notebook open in front of him.*]

WILSON: All right?

ALAN: Oh, yes. [ALAN *picks up a chair from beside the kitchen door and carries it across to the kitchen table.*]

WILSON: I hope I didn't disturb anything important.

ALAN: How d'you mean?

WILSON: When you were talking to your father?

ALAN: Oh. Oh, no. We'd about finished, anyway.

WILSON: Always so many things to see to, at a time like this.

ALAN: I suppose so. Just now, I'd like him to get some rest. I don't suppose he will.

WILSON: What did the doctor say?

ALAN: Much what you'd expect, talking about a man my father's age.

WILSON: You'll have to watch him pretty carefully, these next few days.

ALAN: Yes. Well, that's more or less what the doctor said.

WILSON [*grinning*]: As a policeman, I make a very good doctor. [*He looks down at his notebook.*] Routine apology – I'm sorry this has to happen now. I'm sure you'd rather leave it.

ALAN: No. Not really. I think I'd rather talk about it to you, than ... [*He nods in the general direction of the back room.*] The facts – I mean, we're going to talk facts?

WILSON: That's right.

ALAN: Much less – frightening – than the – well, the implications.

WILSON: I should concentrate on the facts.

ALAN: Exactly.

WILSON: You saw your mother yesterday?

ALAN: Yes, I did. I came over in the afternoon.

WILSON: How did she seem?

ALAN: Before I can give you any kind of answer to that question, I'm afraid you'd have to know my mother – and that ...

WILSON: She was like herself?

ALAN: Very like herself. My sister was here, too.

WILSON: Oh, yes.

ALAN: My mother was always most like herself, when the whole family was gathered together.

WILSON: The whole family being you, your father, your sister – and your mother.

ALAN: Yes.

WILSON: You're expecting your sister now, aren't you?

ALAN: She should be here, more or less any minute.

WILSON: Right.

    [*Silence.*]

This whole thing – not what you would've expected?

ALAN: Just about the last thing, honestly. The very last.

WILSON: What time did you leave the house?

ALAN: Early evening. I was talking to my mother down here and then, I went up and said – you know – I was going – to my father.

WILSON: You don't know exactly when that was?

ALAN [*irritably*]: Does it matter?

WILSON: No. Not really. It has to go into my report.

ALAN: There's no crime. Suicide ... [ALAN *has difficulty with the word.*] ... it isn't a crime.

WILSON: No, sir.

ALAN: You carry out an investigation – well, Scotland Yard would be proud ...

> [WILSON *sits back on his chair, watching* ALAN, *who stammers into silence.*]

I'm sorry.

WILSON: You don't have to apologize.

ALAN: I'm not making things easy for you.

WILSON: You're being most cooperative. It's a question of the report – as you said yourself – the facts.

ALAN: Yes.

WILSON: It's a tragic business.

> [*Silence.*]

ALAN: It must've been just before six I left, last night. I was home in time to see – oh, what was it? The kids' programme – that comes on about six doesn't it?

WILSON: Yes, it does.

ALAN: I was home in time to see it.

WILSON: You live quite close?

ALAN: Ten minutes. Less, probably.

WILSON: You spoke to your mother, before you left?

ALAN: Yes, I did.

WILSON: Well?

ALAN [*wearily*]: She said – 'When will we see you again?' – Standard question. I said, I didn't know. Fairly soon – some time this week. Then, she said – 'When will I see the children?' That is also a standard question.

WILSON: Yes?

ALAN: It sort of went on like that. It usually does. She feels I neglect her. I feel ... [ALAN *shrugs and links his fingers in front of him.*]

WILSON: Would you like a cigarette?

ALAN: Thanks. I don't smoke.

> [WILSON *takes out a packet and opens it.*]

WILSON: You don't mind ...

ALAN: Make yourself at home. Things always get that bit more tense when Terry's around.

WILSON: Terry? Your sister?

ALAN: Short for Teresa. Yes – the family gathering is a pretty ugly sight.

WILSON: Your sister quarrels with your mother?

ALAN: Some things they don't agree about – you know?

WILSON: Such as?

ALAN: You'd do better, talking to her.

WILSON: Right.

ALAN: I didn't know she was going to be here. We none of us did. She just – looked in. It's sort of a habit with Terry – looking in. [ALAN *spreads his hands, fingers still linked.*] Time passes – nobody hears from her – and then, suddenly – she looks in. When I got here ... [ALAN *shakes his head.*] Situation normal. My mother – in the kitchen. She was making a cake – big celebration. My father – in the front room. He was watching TV. He was well out of it. My sister – she opened the door – and the atmosphere ... [ALAN *breaks his fingers apart and presses his hands, palms down, on the table in front of him.*]

WILSON: As a family, you don't get on very well together?

ALAN: As a family, we don't exist. We don't know each other. My mother and father – they live together. They probably even talk to each other, once in a while. Terry? Me? [ALAN *sits back in his chair.*] They don't know me. I left home – when was it? Ten – eleven years ago. I got married. They don't know my wife. They know – yes – what she looks like. They'd recognize the sound of her voice on the telephone. Know her? Ellen? Like they know the inside of Tutankhamen's tomb! [ALAN *pushes his hands deep into his trouser pockets.*] Why did she break the china? Why did my mother – she was the tidiest person in the whole world – bar none! You wouldn't see a crumb on the carpet – give my kids a rock cake in each hand and – on with the dance! When they'd finished – two minutes – you wouldn't see a crumb. Why – did she break the china? Why did she throw the knives – the forks ... [ALAN *gestures at the floor.*] Do you know?

WILSON: No, we don't.

ALAN: Collective – 'we'?

WILSON: Sorry. It's a habit. No – I don't.

ALAN: Are you going to call in another opinion?

WILSON: I'm going to talk to the Inspector.

ALAN: Will he know?

WILSON: He's had a lot of experience.

ALAN: If he does know – look, if he understands better than [*he presses his free hand against his chest*] we – understand. You'll tell me?

WILSON: Yes.

ALAN: I'd like to understand.

WILSON: Things would be a great deal easier ...

ALAN [*interrupting*]: All round? Yes – well, just for the moment – forget 'all round' – me. I want to know. [ALAN *stands up and walks to the gas stove.*] This is something I have to – you know? – live with – the rest of my life.

WILSON: Yes.

[ALAN *sweeps the kettle off the gas stove.*]

ALAN: I talked to her yesterday.

WILSON: Yes?

ALAN: Things – I said to her.

WILSON: What sort of things?

ALAN: I was angry. [ALAN *turns the tap on and puts the kettle under the flow of water.*] She made me angry and I said – things – to her – things I've thought – and – you know? – never said – wouldn't have said – God! Never in a thousand years, if I'd thought ...

[*Silence.*

ALAN *walks across to the gas stove and puts the kettle on to one of the front rings.*]

WILSON: It isn't likely, anything you might have said at that stage ...

ALAN [*abruptly*]: Have you got any matches?

WILSON: Yes, I have.

[WILSON *reaches into his trousers pocket and pulls out a box of matches, as* ALAN *turns to look at him.*]

ALAN: Something I didn't say?

[WILSON *throws the box of matches at* ALAN, *who catches it and waits for an answer.*

Silence.]

It's a fairly normal pattern, is it? All this – breaking up the happy home?

WILSON: There are patterns. I'm not greatly interested in them.

ALAN: You've seen it before?

WILSON: I've seen something like it – yes.

[ALAN *turns away and lights the gas under the kettle.*]

ALAN: I answer your questions. You don't answer mine?

WILSON: She was one person – one woman – Sarah Margaret Stephens . . .

ALAN: Yes.

WILSON: This is something she did. It's bound to be different from something – even something similar – any other – person – might do.

[ALAN *turns and looks at* WILSON.]

ALAN: It's different from anything she might do.

WILSON: She did it.

[ALAN *throws the box of matches back to* WILSON.]

ALAN: True.

WILSON: Using a method about as difficult – about as painful . . .

ALAN: Hmm.

WILSON: . . . as she possibly could.

ALAN: She could've gassed herself?

WILSON: Yes.

ALAN: No. Too dangerous – for Dad. She'd be dead and the gas – still turned on. I don't know – it seems like her.

WILSON: Sleeping pills?

ALAN: Now, that shows – really – that! [ALAN *shakes his head.*] She ought to be here – she ought to answer that one for herself!

WILSON: She didn't believe in sleeping pills?

ALAN: She didn't believe in aspirin. 'If God means you to have a headache . . .'

[*Silence.*]

[*Quietly*] Difficult – painful – I don't think she had any choice. Practical choice – given the circumstances. [*Suddenly,* ALAN *brings his hand up to his mouth and presses it hard against his lips.*]

[*Thickly*] She always said – one thing, she always said about me – I can hear – now – I can hear her saying it – 'You're so cold, Alan. Don't you feel anything any more?' A couple of weeks, I wouldn't come and see them, she'd say – 'Don't you know how much your father misses you?' The first thing she said – the first! – when I walked into the house – 'Hello, stranger.' The first thing – always. [ALAN *turns abruptly and walks across to the sink.*] No, I don't feel. Anything. Not any more. I taught myself – 'cause – feeling – what does feeling get you? [ALAN *turns at the sink and walks back across the kitchen, towards the gas stove.*] What's the first prize for feeling? Pain! I don't feel – love – I don't want to – feel – anything! Ever! All my life . . . [ALAN *stands in front of the gas stove, staring down at it. He shakes his head, violently.*]

[*Abruptly*] Sorry. I'm sorry! I don't know what started . . . [ALAN *turns his head and looks at* WILSON.]

WILSON: There's no need to apologize.

ALAN: Why should you have to listen . . . [ALAN *gestures vaguely.*] Pathetic! Really, I am sorry. Where's the tea-pot? [ALAN *walks across to the cupboard and opens it.*]

WILSON: You talked to your mother, before you went home?

ALAN: Yes, I did. I told her I'd made up my mind to take the job. Ah! [ALAN *reaches into the cupboard and takes out a teapot.*]

WILSON: I don't think you told me about that?

ALAN: The job? I don't think you asked me. [ALAN *looks at* WILSON *and smiles.*] I'm going to Australia. I'm taking my family with me. We shall be away some years, as far as it's possible to estimate.

WILSON: Years?

ALAN: The firm pays for a trip home every two years. The actual time I shall stay out there . . . [ALAN *carries the teapot across to the gas stove.*] Difficult to say.

WILSON: You told your mother . . .

ALAN: We'd been talking about it most of the afternoon. Naturally, everyone had a great deal to say – advice to give. Families always have a great deal of free advice to offer.

WILSON: Was she upset at the idea?

ALAN: On the contrary, she wanted me to take the job. I mentioned it at teatime and she was the first to say – you know?

WILSON: No. What did she say?

[*Silence.*]

ALAN: 'You mustn't think about us, Alan. Your father and I can manage quite well. We've got the house. We've got enough money. The only thing that matters – really – is your career.' [ALAN *turns and smiles at* WILSON.] Word for word, as she said it, if you want to write it down?

WILSON: What did your father say?

ALAN: I don't remember. Not very much. Is it important? Dad hasn't a lot to say for himself, at the best of times – when he's talking about the old days – picnics – day-trips to the seaside – the sun always shining – and happiness – you could buy it in packets – three for a penny! When it comes to talking about my job – well, he doesn't really know anything about it. I did talk to him – a bit later on. [ALAN *pours boiling water into the teapot.*] He thought I should take the job, too.

WILSON: The last thing you said to your mother . . .

ALAN: Why is that so important? I don't see why the last thing . . .

WILSON: It helps us to know the state of mind . . .

ALAN: Entirely calm.

[*Silence.*]

WILSON: That doesn't make it any easier for us to understand, why – a few hours later – she took her own life. Does it?

[ALAN *rolls the boiling water round the teapot.*]

ALAN: 'Mind how you go.' I started the car and then, I waved to her, out of the window. She said – 'Mind how you go.'

[*Silence.*]

How does that help? [ALAN *walks across the kitchen to the sink and empties the boiling water out of the teapot.*]

WILSON: Perhaps, if you told me what she said before that?

ALAN [*harshly*]: 'Take the job. Go to Australia. I hope I never see any of you again.' [ALAN *hurls the teapot into the sink and it smashes.*] I didn't kill my mother. I didn't make her – I didn't . . .

WILSON: Of course you didn't.

ALAN: 'Bloody children.' That's the only time I ever heard her swear.

WILSON: She didn't want you to take the job?

ALAN: She didn't want me to take my – children away from her. [ALAN *turns and looks at* WILSON.]

WILSON [*quietly*]: I see.

ALAN [*harshly*]: Oh, no! In thirty-five years, you couldn't see.

WILSON: No.

ALAN: Whatever I say! The customer is always right. Is that your motto? It's the first time I knew that. I always thought the police had the answers – and the public . . . [ALAN *cannot finish the sentence and gestures at* WILSON.]

WILSON: I don't want to argue with you, sir. Where would that get me?

ALAN: Maybe, thrown out of the house?

WILSON: I'll leave soon enough, sir. When I've finished making the necessary inquiries.

ALAN: You're taking God's own time about it!

WILSON: There are some aspects . . .

ALAN: Aspects? What aspects? Aspects of what!

WILSON: Why don't you sit down, sir?

ALAN: I don't want to sit down, sir!

[*Silence.*]

WILSON: Yes, I suppose it is taking rather a long time. [WILSON *shuts his notebook.*] Treading carefully, you always take that bit longer than usual.

ALAN: Treading carefully! Are you – treading carefully?

WILSON: Yes, sir.

ALAN: I'd hate to be around ... [ALAN *breaks off, steps across to the chair, and sits on it, facing* WILSON.] What's it like, when you don't 'tread carefully'?

WILSON: I think your mother killed herself. I think the evidence points conclusively to that, as a fact.

[*Silence.*]

But – when I make my report to the Inspector, he is going to say – 'Are you sure, Wilson – absolutely – certain?'

ALAN: I don't understand what you mean.

WILSON: No. [WILSON *pushes his chair back and stands up.*] I'd like to have a word with your father, before I go.

ALAN: Now, just a minute. [ALAN *stands up quickly and catches hold of* WILSON'S *arm.*] Something here – look – something – I don't know what ...

WILSON: Nothing. [WILSON *pulls his arm free from* ALAN'S *hand.*] It won't take more than a couple of minutes – with your father.

[*Silence.*]

ALAN: D'you mind, if I'm there, too?

WILSON: I don't mind at all.

[ALAN *steps past* WILSON *and opens the kitchen door.*]

ALAN: I'm sorry I – used you ... [ALAN *looks over his shoulder, back at* WILSON.] ... took advantage ...

WILSON [*formally*]: You don't have to apologize, sir.

ALAN: You could hardly get up and walk out.

WILSON: As I said, at the beginning ...

ALAN [*abruptly*]: I know. Yes.

WILSON: I should apologize to you.

ALAN: My mother was a very simple person. She was easily hurt. Unfortunately, she spent most of her life, asking – to be hurt. In the end, perhaps – one of us ...

[*Silence.*]

That's a question, isn't it? One of us.

[ALAN *turns away and walks into the hall across to the door of the back room.* WILSON *follows him.*]

WILSON: Mr Stephens.

[ALAN *turns.*]

A question without an answer. A question it isn't – really, is it? – worth pursuing?

ALAN: Funny – how easy it is to apologize to you.

WILSON: You don't have to apologize to me.

ALAN: How difficult . . . [ALAN *stops speaking and stares at* WILSON, *for a moment.*] Just a form of words?

WILSON: For your own benefit. It doesn't mean anything.

ALAN: No.

[ALAN *turns away and opens the door of the back room.* FATHER *is sitting in the armchair.*]

[*Quietly*] Dad.

[*Silence.*

ALAN *glances back over his shoulder at* WILSON.]

WILSON: Don't wake him. I'll call back this afternoon.

FATHER [*harshly*]: I'm not asleep. What is it? What do you want?

ALAN: Sorry, Dad. [ALAN *steps forward into the room.*] I thought you were having a rest.

FATHER: Is Terry here?

ALAN: Not yet.

FATHER: Where is she?

ALAN: I don't know, Dad. She'll be here.

[*Silence.*

FATHER *turns his head and looks at* WILSON, *who is still standing in the doorway.*]

FATHER: What do you want?

WILSON: I'd like to talk to you for a moment, Mr Stephens. If you feel up to it.

[FATHER *turns his head and looks at* ALAN, *then he pushes forward in his chair and stands up. He turns to face* WILSON.]

FATHER: What is it? What do you want to know?

[WILSON *walks forward, into the centre of the room.*]

WILSON: First, I want to apologize for the time I've taken, rummaging around.

FATHER: You have your job to do.

WILSON: I'm afraid, it must seem to you, I've been pretty slow doing it.

FATHER: I haven't thought about it.

WILSON: One or two things – bothered me at first. I think everything's clear enough now.

FATHER: Is it?

WILSON: I won't have to take up any more of your time.

FATHER: It makes no difference to me.

[WILSON *walks across the room, closer to* FATHER.]

WILSON: Just the one thing I'd like to ask.

FATHER: Yes?

WILSON: When you found Mrs Stephens, you didn't find any sort of note, she might've left for you, for your son?

FATHER: She left nothing.

WILSON: It's often the case . . .

FATHER: Nothing.

[*Silence.*]

WILSON: Thank you, Mr Stephens. [WILSON *glances at* ALAN *and nods.*]

ALAN: Well, then.

FATHER: She killed herself?

[*Silence.*]

WILSON: All the indications . . .

FATHER: Why?

[*The front doorbell rings.*]

ALAN: I'll go. [ALAN *turns and walks quickly across the room, towards the door.*]

FATHER: You say – everything's clear enough – do you know – why?

WILSON: Well, Mr Stephens – no, I don't. It isn't likely . . .

[ALAN *walks out of the room.*]

. . . anyone can tell you, with absolute certainty . . .

[ALAN *shuts the door behind him and walks towards the front door. He opens the door and* TERRY *walks into the hall. She is wearing a raincoat buttoned up to the neck and a scarf pulled round her head and tied at the back. She is wearing no make-up at all.*]

ALAN: Where've you been? For pity's sake! I thought you said . . .

TERRY: Shut up! Will you? Just – shut up!

ALAN: I've heard nothing – you know? – since I got here – five – six hours ago – nothing but – 'Where's Terry? When will Terry get here?'

TERRY: You phone up in the middle of the night . . .

ALAN: All through the night! [ALAN *shuts the door.*] I phoned you ten times.

TERRY: You tell me – 'Come running!'

ALAN: What happened to you?

TERRY: You don't tell me how! What d'you think? It's easy – this time of the morning?

ALAN: Why didn't you speak to me?

TERRY: I didn't want to speak to you.

ALAN: He's going out of his mind!

TERRY: People just don't cooperate – six o'clock in the morning.

ALAN: 'I need Terry.'

TERRY: As fast as I could! I promise you . . .

ALAN: Every ten seconds – 'Where is she?'

TERRY: It's true?

[*Silence.*]

ALAN: Yes.

TERRY: She's – dead?

ALAN: Yes.

[TERRY *shakes her head.*]

TERRY: Killed herself?

ALAN: Cut her wrists.

TERRY: No.

ALAN: He found her.

[*Silence.*]

TERRY: Where is she?

ALAN: She's at the hospital – [*quickly*] the mortuary.

[TERRY *lurches sideways against the wall and brings her*

hands up to her mouth. She retches. ALAN *steps close to her and puts his hands round her shoulders. She lifts her face out of her hands and they look at each other.*]

TERRY: It's true?

[ALAN *nods his head.*]

[*Mumbling*] Didn't believe it.

ALAN: I know.

TERRY: Couldn't – believe . . .

ALAN: All the way from the house, when I was coming over here – Dad phoned me . . .

[TERRY *nods her head, staring up into* ALAN'S *face.*]

'It isn't true.' That's all I could think. 'It can't be true.' I said it – out loud – once, at least. I said – 'It isn't true.'

[*Silence.*]

TERRY: The taxi driver – you know? 'What are you doing? Running about the streets – this time of the morning?' I said . . . [TERRY *brings a hand up to her mouth again.*]

[*Mumbling*] . . . and he – sort of – helped me – into the taxi – as if I was sick – as if . . .

ALAN: I told Thompson – you know?

TERRY: Yes.

ALAN: He said – oh, I don't know – something about – 'tragic – poor old Alan'. I wanted to say . . .

TERRY: 'It isn't me.'

ALAN: 'She's dead.'

TERRY: 'I'm alive.'

ALAN: Oh, yes!

TERRY [*stumbling*]: And – 'You're alive, too – and she's dead – and – why?'

ALAN: When Thompson said . . . [ALAN *shakes his head.*] I thought – yes – she is dead.

TERRY: The taxi driver . . . [TERRY *nods, with fierce agreement.*] . . . when I told him.

ALAN: Now – she is dead.

TERRY: 'Cause I've told someone – and they believed me.

ALAN: Now.

[TERRY *and* ALAN *huddle against the wall, close together. The door of the back room opens and* WILSON *walks out*

214

into the hall. ALAN *steps away from* TERRY, *who turns her back to* WILSON, *as he walks towards them, rubbing her eyes with her fingers.*]

WILSON: Is this your sister?

ALAN: Yes, it is.

[TERRY *turns to face* WILSON, *standing straight.*]

This is Detective Sergeant Wilson.

[*Silence.*]

WILSON: You have my deepest sympathy.

[TERRY *nods once, abruptly.*]

Look, I won't worry you any more at the moment, but I would like to talk to you at some point – er – Miss Stephens.

TERRY: Yes.

WILSON: I could call back, or . . .

TERRY: I don't know where the police station is, but I'm sure . . .

ALAN: I can run you round there, Terry.

WILSON: It might be better – at the station.

TERRY: I'd rather.

WILSON: Right.

[*Silence.*]

I'll see you a bit later, then.

[WILSON *nods at* TERRY *and walks past, on his way to the front door.* ALAN *follows him.*]

FATHER'S VOICE [*calling*]: Terry? Is that you, Terry?

[WILSON *opens the front door.*]

WILSON: Don't worry about me.

TERRY: Yes, Dad.

FATHER'S VOICE: Terry. Come here.

ALAN [*urgently*]: Terry.

[ALAN *steps away from the front door, towards* TERRY, *as she turns towards the back room.*]

I want to talk to you.

FATHER'S VOICE: Terry!

[TERRY *walks quickly towards the back room, leaving* ALAN, *stranded, halfway between her and* WILSON.]

WILSON: 'Bye for now.

[ALAN *turns quickly back, to face* WILSON.]

ALAN: Oh, yes. I'm sorry.

[WILSON *pulls the door shut behind him, as* ALAN *steps towards him.*

Silence.

ALAN *turns and walks towards the back room.*

TERRY *and her* FATHER *are standing close together, but not actually touching, as* ALAN *arrives in the doorway.*]

ALAN: I told you, didn't I? As soon as she could get here.

[TERRY *starts to untie her scarf and pull off her coat.*]

Here. Let me.

[ALAN *walks forward and takes* TERRY'S *coat off. He takes the scarf out of her hands.* TERRY *looks round at* ALAN *and slants her head slightly, questioningly.*]

FATHER: Alan says, I have to go and live with him.

[TERRY *turns her head sharply to look at her* FATHER *again.*]

I want to live here. I want to go on – living here.

ALAN: Terry.

TERRY: How can you?

ALAN: We'll talk about it later.

FATHER: I want to talk about it – now!

ALAN: We've got plenty of time, haven't we, Terry?

TERRY: Talk about – what?

FATHER: Terry . . .

ALAN: Give her a chance, Dad. She's only just got here.

FATHER: I want to live here!

TERRY: Why did she – kill herself? Why did – Mum . . .
[*Silence.*]

ALAN: We don't know.

TERRY: You were here. You [*she steps closer to her* FATHER] were here. What happened?

ALAN: He doesn't know. How can he know?

TERRY: He was here!

FATHER: I was upstairs.

TERRY: And you didn't know – what? – she was dying!

ALAN: For pity's sake!

TERRY: You didn't know? What were you doing?

ALAN [*harshly*]: Leave it!

TERRY: How is it possible? A woman – cuts . . . [TERRY *turns her hands over and looks down at her wrists.*] . . . and you were . . . [TERRY *looks up at the ceiling.*] You were there – just – up there – and you . . . [TERRY *shuts her eyes tight and clenches her teeth.*]

ALAN: She was on her own . . .

FATHER: She liked to be on her own, in the evening. She always stayed down, after I went up to bed.

TERRY: She liked to be on her own? Mum!

ALAN: Yes. She always stayed . . .

TERRY: Yes! All right. She stayed down here on her own. Right. You went off to bed – and she . . . [TERRY *turns to face* ALAN.] That means – that – is supposed to mean, she liked! – being on her own? No one – there isn't anyone hated being on her own, more – Mum?

FATHER: 'You go up.' She always told me.

TERRY: S'pposing she hadn't? Would you've stayed down here with her? Would you?

FATHER: 'I've got a few things to do. I'll potter down here.'

TERRY: What happened? What did you say?

ALAN: Terry!

TERRY: Suddenly – she . . . [TERRY *slaps her hands together.*] You know what it means? All right, Mum hasn't seen the inside of a church – how long? Since she got married?

FATHER: Since after you were born.

TERRY: She believed. I mean – hell-fire and damnation!

FATHER: I was upstairs. I was waiting for her to come to bed.

TERRY: Waiting?

ALAN: Just because you feel . . .

TERRY: Meaning, you wanted her to come to bed?

ALAN: . . . maybe, you had more than something to do with it.

TERRY: Nothing! I had nothing to do with it.

ALAN: Leave him alone.

TERRY: If anyone knows . . .

ALAN: Nobody knows.

TERRY: He was upstairs.

ALAN: Where were you?

TERRY: Should I have been here?

FATHER: Why did she break so many things – favourite things?

TERRY: What? She did what?

FATHER: Nearly the whole tea service.

[TERRY *looks questioningly at* ALAN.]

ALAN: Go easy on him, Terry.

FATHER: Smashed to pieces.

ALAN: Don't take him through it all again.

TERRY: Mum broke something?

FATHER: She broke a vase in the front room. It isn't like her.

TERRY: No.

FATHER: The photographs – all the photographs – the children – you – Alan.

TERRY: She must've made a noise, doing that.

FATHER: I found them on the floor.

TERRY: One hell of a noise!

FATHER: I couldn't believe it. I came down and everything – I looked in all the rooms – and everything – broken.

TERRY: Where were you, Dad? Ten years – twenty?

ALAN: Terry, no!

TERRY [*harshly*]: It could've been you. It could've been me – dying – you know?

FATHER: I thought, then – I thought . . .

TERRY: What did she do?

FATHER: . . . funny – what's been going on?

TERRY: You could let her – leave her!

FATHER: I didn't hear anything, I thought.

TERRY: Thirty, forty years back?

[*Silence.*]

FATHER: What do you mean?

TERRY: Was it so much better?

FATHER: I don't know what you mean.

TERRY: Thirty years ago. What did you do?

FATHER: I don't understand . . .

TERRY [*violently*]: Escape!

ALAN: Enough. All right, that's enough! Come on, Dad. [ALAN *steps forward and takes hold of his* FATHER'S *arm.*]

FATHER: What does she mean?

TERRY: You know what I mean.

ALAN: You've been sitting around all night. I think it's time you went upstairs and had a bit of a rest.

FATHER: I don't – know . . .

TERRY: Yes! [TERRY *steps in between* ALAN *and her* FATHER.] You do. You do know!

ALAN [*wearily*]: Leave him alone.

TERRY: He isn't [*she pulls* ALAN'S *hand off her* FATHER'S *arm*] one of your kids. He doesn't need – you.

FATHER [*simply*]: Terry, look after me.

TERRY: What did Mum do to you? How could you – Dad, in the name of heaven!

FATHER: Stay with me. [FATHER *takes hold of one of* TERRY'S *hands.*]

TERRY: You let her die. [TERRY *pulls her hand away.*]

ALAN: Shut up!

TERRY: Killed – her.

FATHER: You can have the house.

ALAN: Terry.

FATHER: You can do anything you like with it.

ALAN: What's the matter with you? [ALAN *walks towards* TERRY.]

TERRY: Why didn't he – couldn't he . . .

[ALAN *takes hold of* TERRY *by her shoulders.*]
. . . stop her?

ALAN: He was upstairs.

TERRY: '. . . and a million miles away . . .'

ALAN: She knew he was up there.

TERRY: 'Captain, aren't thou sleeping . . .'
[ALAN *shakes* TERRY *into silence.*]

ALAN: He was thinking about you – all he ever thinks about.

TERRY: Kids. That – is all he ever thinks about. You – me

– when we were kids – Michael – and little Sarah –
some kids – any kids! You don't have to be afraid of kids.
What can they do? Tell them – what can they say? What
do they know? Tell them anything! They'll believe you.
Look at their faces – laugh at them – believing. There's a
man on the moon and it's made of cheese. There's gold
at the end of the rainbow and it turns to ashes. There's a
river – and on the other side . . . [TERRY *shrugs* ALAN'S
hands off her shoulders.] Tell them – knights on white horses
– tell them – pain – goes away, 'cause Daddy's here.

ALAN: He knows you're pregnant.

TERRY: He should worry!

ALAN: He does.

TERRY: One more kid.

ALAN: He worries himself sick.

TERRY: Yes, I can see. [TERRY *pushes past* ALAN *and walks
towards her* FATHER, *who is watching them, as if they were
strangers.*] You don't get your hands on him.

ALAN: He doesn't know what you're talking about.

FATHER: I don't understand . . .

    [TERRY *holds her hand up in front of her* FATHER'S
    face.]

TERRY: How many fingers am I holding up?

    [*Silence.*
      Suddenly, FATHER *slaps her hand away.*]

  [*Laughing*] Yes!

ALAN: You bitch!

TERRY: It's a game. Isn't it a game, Dad? We all play it.
When things get rough and you just don't want to know
– when people get nasty – and you want out!

ALAN: Listen to yourself!

TERRY: The great 'let's pretend' game! Let's pretend it
isn't happening. Let's pretend it's twenty years ago –
and the world was young!

ALAN: No wonder Mum couldn't stand the sight of you.

TERRY: Let's pretend . . . [TERRY *turns sharply to face*
ALAN.] She loves me.

ALAN: She can't stand to have you in the house.

TERRY: Loves me!

FATHER: She's dead.

[*Silence.*]

ALAN: The last thing she said to me . . .

TERRY: Don't tell me!

ALAN: 'If Terry has to behave . . .'

TERRY: I don't want to hear!

ALAN: 'Why does she come and see us?'

FATHER: Your Mother's dead.

ALAN: 'I don't want her in the house. If I had my way . . .'

TERRY: She didn't say that.

ALAN: Yes.

TERRY: Love!

ALAN: 'If it wasn't for her father . . .'

TERRY: She didn't say . . .

FATHER [*simultaneously*]: Anything she said – what does it matter now?

ALAN: '. . . I wouldn't open the door to her.'

TERRY: She didn't mean . . .

ALAN: Yes!

FATHER: She's dead.

ALAN: Seeing you – hearing you – I don't blame her!

FATHER [*harshly*]: Your mother's dead!

[*Silence.*]

FATHER: Leave her rest.

TERRY: No. [TERRY *turns to face her* FATHER.] She didn't die, did she? Just – die! Of old age – an accident – looking the wrong way – and pow! She killed herself.

ALAN: Playing dramas – melodramas.

TERRY: Facts.

ALAN: Tearing at everyone in reach, because you want to scream.

TERRY: We'll let her rest, soon enough. We'll burn her – throw her ashes on to the wind – and then – we'll let her rest. Ten days, we'll forget her – for an hour. Ten weeks – we'll forget her for a day – and ten years . . .

[*Silence.*]

As if she never was.

FATHER: We'll bury her. We won't ... [FATHER *gestures vaguely. He cannot find the word.*]

ALAN: Yes, Dad.

FATHER: She wanted to be buried.

TERRY: She didn't want to die.

FATHER: We talked about it. She wanted to be buried.

TERRY: Just in case.

ALAN: I'll see to it, Dad. Don't worry.

TERRY: Tomorrow – next week – some time in the future – some unspecified time – they might open all the graves – and everybody ... [TERRY *stretched her arms wide.*] Everybody up!

ALAN: I'll make the arrangements.

TERRY: There'll be some funny-looking people about then!

ALAN: Shut up.

TERRY: That's Mum. Each way – two bob each way! Never to win – 'cause you can't win.

ALAN: Get hold of yourself!

TERRY [*harshly*]: I didn't have time. I didn't tell her ...

ALAN: Terry!

TERRY: I was here – and I didn't say ... [TERRY *turns away in misery and leans her face against the cold glass of the window.*] I wanted to say ...

ALAN: I thank God, I haven't got your – mind – your – imagination.

> [TERRY *puts her hands up to her mouth and presses them hard against her lips.*]

Once – d'you know? The thing in all the world – the one thing I really wanted – was that – mind – that – whatever it is – way of thinking – seeing – that you have – you know?

TERRY: Oh, yes.

ALAN: The way you could – make up – oh, God! The world you lived in – secret world – I wanted to be part of that world ...

TERRY: Games.

ALAN: I wanted to be part of it so very much. Just for a moment.

TERRY: Just games.

ALAN: I never had a dream – you know? The whole of my life.

TERRY: How lucky can you get?

ALAN: You could see things – I remember – sitting in a train with you – looking out of the window.

TERRY: Oh, God!

ALAN: Looking at the same things and I knew, you were seeing – gold.

TERRY: Trees and fields.

ALAN: Horses – and men on horses.

TERRY: I wanted your teddy-bear.

ALAN: Running with the train. I could see you – waving to them.

TERRY: The old one, with the cross-eyes.

ALAN: And the train – sort of coach – some great ceremonial coach.

TERRY: You had him tucked up in bed with you, every night.

ALAN: I wanted to be you. I wanted to see the things you could see.

TERRY: I would've given anything . . .

ALAN: I wanted to think – and to dream.

TERRY: What was his name?

ALAN: Like the princess – and going half across the world – with that man.

TERRY: You gave him a special name.

ALAN: D'you remember that story?
     [*Silence.*]
  Do you?

TERRY: Yes.

ALAN: I could see that story, when you told it to me. I could see the princess . . .

TERRY: I remember.

ALAN: I could see the man.

TERRY: Dad told me that story. [TERRY *looks past* ALAN'S *shoulder at her* FATHER.] Dad – made it up for me. One night, when I was frightened.

ALAN: Dad? [ALAN *turns and looks across the room at his* FATHER.]

TERRY: He always told me stories.

ALAN: That story?

TERRY: When you'd gone to sleep.

ALAN: The princess?

TERRY: Every story I ever knew.

ALAN: I thought you made it up. I always thought . . .

TERRY: Dad told me.

[*Silence.*]

FATHER [*suddenly*]: I didn't lie to you! Did I say – did I ever tell you – 'Anything – I can do anything!' Did I say that?

ALAN: Easy, Dad. [ALAN *steps towards his* FATHER.]

FATHER: Your mother said . . .

[ALAN *puts his hand on his* FATHER'S *shoulders.*]

ALAN: It's all right.

FATHER [*harshly*]: Get out of my way! [FATHER *pushes past* ALAN, *shrugging his hands off, and stands in front of* TERRY.] When did I say to you – tell me! When did I ever pretend – your mother said . . . [FATHER *shakes his head angrily.*] Why should you blame me?

TERRY: What did Mum say?

FATHER: My fault. She said it was my fault.

TERRY: What did she mean? What was she talking about?

FATHER: You.

TERRY: Your fault?

FATHER: I lied to you. I made you think – it would be all right – everything – would be all right, as long as you told me – 'cause I could make . . . [FATHER *clenches his fists and shuts his eyes, in a desperate effort to speak the words.*]

ALAN: Mum said – what – was your fault?

FATHER [*violently*]: I let Terry think I could keep her safe. I wouldn't let anyone hurt her.

TERRY: Yes.

FATHER: I never said that.

TERRY: Over and over.

FATHER: No.

TERRY: Yes, you did.

FATHER: You were frightened of the dark.

TERRY: I believed you.

FATHER: I had to say something.

TERRY [*violently*]: I believed you.

FATHER: I said – I didn't think – anything.

TERRY: To keep me quiet!

FATHER: Comfort you.

TERRY: You didn't have to say that.

FATHER: You were crying.

TERRY: 'I'll keep you safe.'

FATHER: It was the middle of the night.

TERRY: 'Daddy won't let them hurt his baby.'

FATHER: Your mother said . . .

TERRY: You wanted to believe it. You [*she steps close to her* FATHER] wanted to believe – you – only you, in all the world – could keep me safe.

FATHER: I wanted to stop you crying.

TERRY: You didn't have to say that.

FATHER: Your mother . . .

ALAN: She's dead.

TERRY: She was never more alive.

ALAN: You – both of you – make me sick.

TERRY: Tell us the sad, sad story of your life.

ALAN: You were born when I was five. End – of sad story.

TERRY: And I thought you loved your baby sister!

ALAN: The first time I wanted you to – I don't know what I wanted – exactly.

TERRY: You wanted to kill me.

ALAN: No. I was six years old.

TERRY: That makes any difference!

ALAN: I didn't want to kill you.

TERRY: Just – put me away?

ALAN: Yes.

TERRY: Finished with her, now. Play with me?

ALAN: One thing I'd done – I was four – I don't remember – something like. I put my hand on a light bulb. Everyone told me, all the time – 'Don't play with the light, Alan.

Leave the light alone. Don't touch it, Alan. You'll burn yourself.' One time, I touched it – and I burnt myself – and I cried – and everyone said – 'What a silly thing to do.'

TERRY: Sounds pretty silly.

ALAN: The first time I thought – 'Go away Terry. Don't be here any more.' The first time [*he shakes his head and half-smiles*] I thought – 'I hate you.'

TERRY: Six years old?

ALAN: I switched on a lamp – that lamp! [ALAN *points across the room at the table lamp, which stands on the small table beside* FATHER'S *chair.*] I let the bulb get hot. I knew it wasn't hot, when you switched it on.

TERRY [*quietly*]: No.

ALAN: I waited. When it was hot . . .

TERRY [*shuddering*]: Oh, no.

ALAN: . . . I put my hand on it. I held tight on to it with my fingers.

FATHER [*quietly*]: Yes.

ALAN: And then . . . [ALAN *turns his hand over and looks at the palm.*] . . . I was only a baby, really. I let go.

[TERRY *reaches out and touches the palm of* ALAN'S *hand, gently.*]

I loved you.

TERRY: Really? Did you do that?

ALAN: Could I make it up?

[TERRY *stretches her fingers round* ALAN'S *hand and grips it.*]

Could I – imagine – something like that?

FATHER: I remember.

ALAN: You found me.

TERRY: 'Cause you loved me?

ALAN: Oh, no. I hated you.

[*Silence.*]

TERRY: Why shouldn't you hate me? I was always a spoiled brat, anyway.

ALAN: You were my sister. Everyone told me – 'You must love your baby sister.'

TERRY: That's enough to put you off God.

ALAN: I knew they were right. You were very little.

TERRY: And you were very big? Six years old!

ALAN: There was no one I could ask.

TERRY: Dad?

> [ALAN *turns his head and looks at his* FATHER. *who is watching the scene, blankly.*]

Well, you can't blame me, 'cause they were all as thick as Nelson's column. What about Mum?

ALAN [*quietly*]: She would have switched on the lamp. She'd have known what I was trying to do. [ALAN *turns his head and looks at* TERRY *again.*] You never have understood about her.

TERRY [*harshly*]: You made it all up! [TERRY *shakes her head angrily.*] The whole bit! Just for my benefit. You made it all up!

FATHER: No, it's true.

TERRY: And I believed – my God!

ALAN [*calmly*]: I didn't make it up.

TERRY: It just happens – I mean – to fit so . . . [TERRY *jerks two spreadeagled fingers up at* ALAN.] Get stuffed!

ALAN: I remembered . . .

TERRY: With bread crumbs and parsley sauce!

ALAN: . . . and I told you.

TERRY: What do you mean?

ALAN: I thought you'd be interested.

TERRY: Mum would've switched on the lamp! [TERRY *spreads her arms wide in protest.*] What sort of – how can you . . . [TERRY *swings one arm round in front of her and points a finger at* ALAN.] You – are the one supposed to – what is it – love – our late, lamented mother! Everyone knows I couldn't stand the sight . . . [TERRY *chokes on the words and retches.*] How can you say – a thing like that – about her?

ALAN: I think it's true.

TERRY: It's no more true, than Father Christmas.

ALAN: I thought about Mum.

TERRY: What do you think I was doing?

ALAN: Oh, no!

TERRY: Every day of my stupid life.

ALAN: You never – thought about her.

TERRY: And then, when I come here – specially . . .

ALAN: Felt – about her.

TERRY: I don't say any . . . [TERRY *stops abruptly. She looks at* ALAN *and slants her head at him, questioningly.*]

ALAN: Like Dad. You felt – oh, sure! – great oceans of feeling!

TERRY: What're you talking about?

ALAN: I don't – feel – things. It's so long now – I don't think I can.

    [*Silence.*]

[*Quietly*] Hmm.

TERRY [*viciously*]: And that puts you 'one up', does it? Thinking – as done by the best – the very best people. 'I absolutely never go anywhere these days – without thinking' – says the Right Hon. . . .

ALAN: All the shouting . . .

TERRY: Somehow, I have – if you'll pardon the expression – the distinct feeling . . .

ALAN: . . . the screaming!

TERRY: . . . you're trying to tell me something.

ALAN: 'Who's to blame?'

TERRY: Unfortunately, the message just isn't getting through.

ALAN: 'Why – did she kill herself?'

TERRY [*cold*]: Do you know?

    [ALAN *shakes his head.*]

ALAN: I'm thinking about it.

TERRY: If you come up with an answer . . .

ALAN: Will you accept your share of the responsibility?

TERRY [*abruptly*]: I wasn't here.

ALAN: There was no one . . .

TERRY: Yes!

ALAN: She was quite alone.

TERRY: He – was here.

ALAN: She sent him away.

[*Silence.*]

FATHER: 'I've got a few things to do. I'll potter down here.'

ALAN: What did she say to you?

TERRY: 'Don't come and see us again.'

ALAN: 'Take the job. Go to Australia. I hope I never see any of you again.'

[*Silence.*]

FATHER: I don't want to go to Australia.

ALAN: She's here now.

FATHER: I want to stay – as I am. Here. I want to go on – living here.

TERRY: There's no accounting for tastes. [TERRY *looks round for her coat and sees it, lying across the back of one of the armchairs.*]

ALAN: Ask her.

FATHER: Terry . . .

[FATHER *stops speaking abruptly, as* TERRY *walks across to the chair. He looks at* ALAN.]

ALAN: Dad's got something he wants to say to you.

[TERRY *picks up her coat.*]

TERRY: I'm going home.

ALAN: You have to ask her.

[TERRY *looks at her* FATHER.]

FATHER [*hesitantly*]: Stay here. Terry – please, don't go away.

[*Silence.*]

TERRY: All right. [TERRY *drops her coat across the chair again.*] I'll phone the office.

ALAN: That isn't what he means.

FATHER: Stay with me.

[TERRY *looks questioningly at* ALAN.]

ALAN: Ask him.

FATHER: You need a home.

TERRY [*quietly*]: I've got a home.

FATHER: Yes, but a real home – with a garden.

TERRY: The way the damp keeps getting through the bedroom wall, I'd be able to grow . . . [TERRY *runs out of words and she stops, staring at her* FATHER.] What are you talking about, Dad?

FATHER: I'm really no trouble. I'll look after myself. That isn't the point. It's just [*he puts his arm round* TERRY'S *shoulder*] knowing you're somewhere – close – knowing I can find you.

TERRY: He wants me to stay here? [TERRY *pulls away from her* FATHER.] You want me to live here? Live [*she looks round at the room*] here!

ALAN: Easy, Terry. Think.

TERRY: He's got to be – you can't be . . . [TERRY *cuts off, staring at her* FATHER.]

[*Quietly*] Serious. Yes – you are.

FATHER: It could be – like . . .

TERRY: No. I mean – [*violently*] no!

FATHER: The good days, Terry – all – the good days.

TERRY: I hate this house.

ALAN: You've made your point.

TERRY: I couldn't live here – if you paid me, I wouldn't live here!

FATHER: We can start – all over – start – again.

TERRY: Terry. I'm Terry! You want [*she gestures towards the wall of the front room*] Sarah. [*Viciously*] Start again!

ALAN: He's villain, is he? Mister Villain! Black hat – and moustache.

TERRY: He makes me feel . . . [TERRY *shudders.*]

ALAN: He asks you – 'Look after me' . . .

TERRY: I feel . . .

ALAN: Suddenly, he – is the big villain.

TERRY: . . . dirty!

ALAN: He's your father.

TERRY: You look after him.

ALAN: He doesn't want me.

TERRY: He can't have me.

[*Silence.*]

ALAN: I told him.

[ALAN *turns to look at his* FATHER, *who is still standing at the window, looking out at the garden.*]

TERRY: He should have listened to you.

FATHER: Your mother told me. [FATHER *turns and looks across the room at* ALAN *and* TERRY.] I should have listened to her.

TERRY: Yes.

FATHER: 'Make them – love them – give them' [*he shakes his head*] 'everything!'

TERRY: When? When was that? When did you give me – us – when . . .

FATHER: 'They'll go away. You'll never see them again.' I should have listened to her.

TERRY: The whole bit! [TERRY *slaps her hands together.*] 'How sharper than a serpent's tooth it is . . .' I've seen it, Dad – it's great. Turns out sad in the end. Still, all the best things do. [TERRY *sweeps up her coat.*] Now – I'm going.

FATHER: You go away now. You let him take me to Australia. You'll never see me again.

[*Silence.*]

TERRY: I trusted you.

ALAN: Your fault, not his.

[TERRY *looks over her shoulder at* ALAN.]

TERRY: He said – 'Trust me.'

ALAN: You do everything you're told to do?

TERRY: I – wasn't even six.

ALAN: A little man says – 'Trust me' – he's asking . . .

TERRY: I didn't know he was a little man.

ALAN: . . . he isn't promising.

TERRY: How could I know?

ALAN: You know now.

TERRY: What difference does that make?

ALAN: Forgive him.

TERRY: Easy for you – to say . . .

ALAN: Think about it.

TERRY [*irritably*]: Take up Pelmanism?

ALAN [*calmly*]: Stop making snide remarks.

TERRY: It's the way I was brought up. You're quick – or you're dead.

ALAN: Try.

TERRY: All the time – me – do something – try something – don't do . . . [TERRY *pulls her coat up and hugs it against her stomach.*] Some of the time – you – all of you – aren't you supposed . . . [TERRY *shakes her head, wearily.*]

ALAN: Who can get close enough?

TERRY: You want to see the scars?

ALAN: Relax.

TERRY: You tell me something often enough – I'm a very good pupil. I believe it. My mother told me . . . [TERRY *laughs quietly, shrugs and turns in a tight matador's circle, trailing her coat round her feet.*]

[*Reciting*] 'I never should, play with the gipsies in the wood . . .' [TERRY *completes the circle and looks up at* ALAN.]

[*Angrily*] I'm thinking.

ALAN: Yes, I know.

TERRY: Suppose you don't go to Australia?

ALAN: I'm going.

TERRY: You said it wasn't decided. You said you had the weekend to make up your mind.

ALAN: The weekend's over.

TERRY: If you didn't go, maybe Dad wouldn't mind so much.

ALAN: Ask him.

TERRY: Dad? [TERRY *puts her hand on her* FATHER'S *arm.*]

FATHER [*harshly*]: I belong here.

TERRY: He minds. [TERRY *lets go of his arm.*]

FATHER: This is my home. Why shouldn't I live here?

TERRY: Right. You're right! You live here. No problem. [TERRY *turns away and picks up her coat.*] Now – can I go home?

FATHER: No, you can't.

TERRY: It was sort of a rhetorical question, Dad.

FATHER: You can't just – walk out.

TERRY: I wasn't really asking.

FATHER: I need you.

TERRY: More – telling!

FATHER: You've got to stay here with me.

TERRY: No 'got to' about it.

FATHER: Someone's got to.

TERRY: Dad – he's on his knees – he's begging you. Look at him.

FATHER: You're my daughter.

TERRY: He needs you.

FATHER [*shouting*]: I – need you.

TERRY: Once in your life – Dad! For someone else?

FATHER: We could have a wonderful life, Terry.

TERRY: We could have nothing!

FATHER: I know about the – baby. Your mother told me . . .

TERRY: It's my baby.

FATHER: I can help you.

TERRY: No.

FATHER: Have you got any money? You'll need a lot of money.

TERRY: Somehow, Dad – on my own . . .

FATHER: We could have a wonderful life.

TERRY [*shouting*]: Let me alone!
      [*Silence.*]
    Please, Dad. All my life, you've hung on to me. Let go?

FATHER: It was your mother – made you go away, Terry.

TERRY: No.

FATHER: Now – surely you can come home?

TERRY: It wasn't Mum.

ALAN: Dad.

FATHER: Anything you want – anything – I can give you.

ALAN: Don't beg her.

TERRY: You, Dad – I had to – needed to get away – from you.

FATHER: We'll have the house repainted.

TERRY: I can't come back and let you – I can't Dad – please!

FATHER: All the rooms – re-decorated.

TERRY: Let you do to me, what you did to Mum?

ALAN: Listen to her.

TERRY: Let you kill me?
[*Silence.*]
FATHER [*angrily*]: What d'you mean? What're you saying?
TERRY: Let me go.
FATHER: You said – about your mother – said something – what was it?
TERRY: Don't shout at me. I mean – who are you – shouting at me!
FATHER: I'm your father.
TERRY: You're an old man I've known all my life.
FATHER: Don't speak to me like that!
TERRY: I don't even like you very much.
FATHER: Show some respect . . .
TERRY [*harshly*]: I don't respect you.
FATHER: My father – I remember my father . . .
ALAN: Leave him alone.
FATHER: He wouldn't have stood for you – talking to him – talking like that.
TERRY: Your father's dead – like my mother. A fat lot of difference it makes, what either one of them would've stood for.
ALAN: Go away.
TERRY: I want to go. He said – he [*she points at her* FATHER] told me . . .
ALAN: All my life, I've watched you two – all my miserable life! Now – can't you – today – for a moment – think . . .
TERRY: If you say that – honestly – once more!
ALAN: Last night – what happened last night.
FATHER: I don't need you to tell me . . .
    [ALAN *picks up a straight-backed chair and slams it sideways at the wall.*
    Silence.]
ALAN: Think about that!
FATHER: What the dickens! What are you doing? What do you think . . . [FATHER *walks across and picks up the chair.*] You want to behave like that, you go and do it in your own house. [FATHER *sets the chair upright again, with an effort.*]

TERRY: Go and live with him, Dad.

FATHER: The two of you – I don't understand.

ALAN: You don't think!

FATHER: You think I'm such an old – fool – why don't you – both of you – go away – leave me alone. I'll get along. I can manage. I've managed before.

TERRY: He doesn't want to.

FATHER: Go on. Both of you!

TERRY: Dad – if I could – if it was – oh, God! if it was possible – if it could work!

FATHER: I can manage.

TERRY: Once upon a time ... [TERRY *stops and half-laughs.*] Here we go. There was a lovely princess ...

FATHER: You were glad enough – there was a time, Terry – you wanted nothing more than I should tell you that story – over and over again.

TERRY: Yes – there was a time – and it's gone – and ... [*Silence.*]
I'm going too.

FATHER: Yes. Better if you do.

ALAN [*quietly*]: All my life ...

TERRY: It's no good.

FATHER: I'll live with Alan. I'll go to Australia. I'll never see you again.

ALAN: You two – there was something – I mean – you had something ...

TERRY: Maybe, we didn't deserve it.

FATHER: One day, you'll be sorry.

TERRY: Maybe, it was a mistake.

FATHER: I hope – you'll be sorry.

TERRY: Maybe, it was meant for – two other people – quite different people.

ALAN: I would've given anything!

FATHER [*violently*]: You will be sorry!

TERRY: Yes, I will. [TERRY *touches the chair.*] That was great – you know?

ALAN: It was stupid. Trying to do things your way.

TERRY: Oh, no.

ALAN: All I did was frighten him.

TERRY: It was great. [TERRY *takes hold of* ALAN'S *hand and turns it over.*] You didn't make it up?

    [ALAN *shakes his head.*]

I never did anything – half ... [TERRY *bends down and kisses the palm of* ALAN'S *hand.*]

FATHER: I don't want to stay here, any more.

ALAN: Yes, all right.

FATHER: If we're going, I want to go.

TERRY: Couple of things I'd like to pick up. In my room.

ALAN: Okay.

FATHER: There's a case in the attic.

ALAN: I'll come back this evening.

FATHER: I want it. I want to look at it.

ALAN: It can wait. Surely?

FATHER: No. The photograph – I'm quite certain the photograph's in that case.

ALAN [*blankly*]: Photograph?

FATHER: I thought – quite suddenly – last night, 'I know where it is. It's in that old case.'

ALAN: Dad, I don't know what you're talking about.

FATHER: The school photograph.

ALAN: Oh, God!

FATHER: I want to show it to Gordon.

ALAN: It's not that important, Dad. It can wait till ...

FATHER: I shan't come back here again.

    [*Silence.*]

ALAN: Where is it?

FATHER: The case is in the attic.

TERRY: With three trunks, five boxes – and the dust of ages! Good luck.

FATHER: I'm absolutely certain ...

ALAN: I'll fetch it down.

TERRY: What do you want to take with you, Dad?

    [FATHER *looks blankly at* TERRY.]

[*Grinning*] Apart from your toothbrush?

FATHER: I don't know. [FATHER *looks round at* ALAN, *desperately.*] Alan, what shall I need?

ALAN: Not much. For the moment, anyway.

TERRY: I'll run up and put a few things into a suitcase.

ALAN: Just the basic essentials.

TERRY: Right. [TERRY *walks briskly across the room, towards the door.*]

FATHER: Are you going?

TERRY: Upstairs, Dad. Just upstairs.

FATHER: You won't ... [FATHER *gestures vaguely in the direction of the front door.*] ... without saying – 'Good-bye'?

TERRY: Do I ever?

FATHER: I tried to understand – things – you said.

TERRY: I know.

[*The front doorbell rings.*]

ALAN: I'll go.

FATHER: I tried to help you.

TERRY: Yes.

[ALAN *walks across towards the door and opens it.*]

FATHER: Your mother said ...

[ALAN *walks out of the back room and towards the front door.*]

TERRY'S VOICE: Whatever she said – I don't blame you.

[ALAN *opens the front door.*

MRS HAYTER *is standing on the doorstep.*]

MRS HAYTER [*quietly*]: Alan, I was just wondering – would your father like to come and have his breakfast with me?

ALAN: Oh, well – I don't know.

MRS HAYTER: The children have gone to school already. It's quiet. There's no one ...

ALAN: It's very kind of you, Mrs Hayter.

MRS HAYTER: Nothing of the sort. Your mother was a good neighbour to me. Many's the time ...

ALAN: As a matter of fact, I don't think we'll be here much longer.

MRS HAYTER: Are you taking him home with you?

ALAN: Yes, I am.

MRS HAYTER: That's the best thing. Much the best.

ALAN: I think so.

MRS HAYTER: After all, you've got your own life, haven't you?

ALAN: Well, it isn't so much that . . .

MRS HAYTER: But you have!

[MRS HAYTER *stops speaking abruptly, looking past* ALAN, *away along the hall.* ALAN *turns and looks over his shoulder.*]

FATHER: There's a bulb upstairs, Alan. You'll need a bulb.

MRS HAYTER: Hello, Mr Stephens.

FATHER: I know where it is.

TERRY: I'll help him look.

[FATHER *and* TERRY *turn and begin to walk up the stairs together.*]

ALAN: I won't be a minute.

FATHER: You mother always kept a bulb handy – just in case.

ALAN: My wife's bound to have something ready . . .

MRS HAYTER: He looks so old, doesn't he? [MRS HAYTER *turns her head and looks at* ALAN *again.*] I'm sorry, Alan – what did you say?

ALAN: It's kind of you to offer . . .

MRS HAYTER: It's no more than your mother's done for me. Many a time.

ALAN: I'd rather get him home . . .

MRS HAYTER: Tired, I suppose. He's been up all night, has he?

ALAN: We all of us . . .

MRS HAYTER: I didn't know your sister was here.

ALAN: She got here a little while ago.

MRS HAYTER: We were talking about her . . . [MRS HAYTER *shakes her head and half-smiles at* ALAN.] Just yesterday, your poor mother . . .

ALAN: Perhaps, I could phone you, Mrs Hayter?

MRS HAYTER [*quickly*]: If there's anything you need? Of course. You must. I've got a key to the back door. Your mother left me a key. We often – you know?

ALAN: She was always talking about you.

MRS HAYTER: I shall miss her.

ALAN: Honestly, I don't know what she would have done without you.

FATHER'S VOICE: Alan!

MRS HAYTER: She was more – much more than just a neighbour.

ALAN: Yes, of course.

FATHER'S VOICE: Come along, Alan.

ALAN: I think I'd better go and see what it is he wants.

MRS HAYTER: He'll miss her, too.

FATHER'S VOICE: Terry's found the bulb.

MRS HAYTER: I don't suppose he's taken it in. Not yet. Not properly.

ALAN: No.

MRS HAYTER: Your mother used to say . . .

FATHER'S VOICE: Alan! What're you doing down there?

ALAN: I'm sorry, Mrs Hayter.

MRS HAYTER: No, you go along. I know what he gets like.

ALAN [*coldly*]: Yes.

MRS HAYTER: If you want anything, you know where I am.

ALAN: You're very kind. [ALAN *starts to shut the door.*]

MRS HAYTER: If you want to leave my telephone number with – with anyone . . .

ALAN: Thanks.

MRS HAYTER: I'll leave you to get on.

> [ALAN *watches her, as she walks off the step, and then shuts the door.*]

FATHER'S VOICE: We're waiting for you, Alan.

ALAN [*irritably*]: All right! Give us a chance! [*He walks quickly up the stairs to the landing.*]

TERRY: What did she want?

ALAN: Just – being helpful.

TERRY: That'll be the day.

> [FATHER *carries a chair out of the bedroom and puts it down on the landing, under the trap door into the attic.*]

ALAN: This is ridiculous!

FATHER: Think you can manage, Alan?

> [ALAN *walks across to the chair and places it centrally under the trap door.*]

ALAN [*quietly*]: I can manage.

TERRY: Where's your spirit of adventure!

ALAN: You want to go clambering . . .

TERRY: That's man's work!

FATHER: I've got the bulb. Terry found it.

[ALAN *climbs up on to the chair.*]

ALAN: Good for Terry! [ALAN *reaches up to his full height and pushes the trap door up and open, letting it swing back on its hinges.*] Right then. [ALAN *brings down a hand and reaches for the bulb.*]

FATHER: Here you are. Here you are!

[FATHER *puts the bulb into* ALAN's *hand and* ALAN *lifts it again. He puts the bulb down on the floor of the attic. He rests his hands on the edge of the trap door and prepares to lift himself up, into the attic. Gathering his strength, he looks down and sees* TERRY, *grinning up at him.*]

ALAN: It's all right for you!

[TERRY *laughs, and then, reluctantly,* ALAN *laughs, too.*]

FATHER: What the dickens are you two laughing at?

ALAN: I don't know. [ALAN *prepares for the lift, takes a deep breath and then raises himself bodily through the trap door.*]

TERRY: Tara!

[ALAN *scrambles into a sitting position, on the edge of the trap door.*]

FATHER'S VOICE: Careful, Alan.

ALAN [*bitterly*]: I'll be careful. [ALAN *reaches for the electric light bulb.*]

FATHER'S VOICE: Mind how you go.

[ALAN *hesitates, reaching across the width of the trap door, and looking down.*]

TERRY'S VOICE: Don't drop it!

[ALAN *straightens up and sits back into the shadows of the attic, with the bulb in his hand. He stands up and searches along a sloping beam for the light socket.*]

FATHER'S VOICE: Shall we switch the light on?

ALAN: No. [ALAN *finds the socket and fixes the bulb into it.*] Now you can switch it on.

[*The light switches on and* ALAN *looks around the sloping* attic. *The beams have not been covered and moving about has to be done with extreme caution.*]

FATHER'S VOICE: It's a brown case.

ALAN [*irritably*]: Hang on!

[*The attic is crowded with boxes and trunks, books and toys and every possible kind of junk.*]

FATHER'S VOICE: Can you see it?

ALAN: No, I can't. [*He steps carefully across to the boxes and trunks.*]

TERRY'S VOICE [*laughing*]: Shall I come up?

[ALAN *pulls a box to one side and then moves a trunk.*] Shall I?

ALAN: No!

FATHER'S VOICE: It shouldn't be difficult to find.

ALAN [*quietly*]: Oh, God! [ALAN *rests his hands on the boxes and lowers his head on to his chest.*]

FATHER'S VOICE: I think your mother put it with other cases. If you can find them?

TERRY'S VOICE: Alan.

ALAN: Yes, I've found them. [ALAN *straightens up again.*]

FATHER'S VOICE: Is it there?

ALAN: I can't see. If you'll both of you – just shut up for a minute!

[*Silence.*

ALAN *reaches in amongst the boxes and pulls out a case. He lifts it up on to the top of the trunks and looks at it.*]
A brown leather case – 'bout medium size?

FATHER'S VOICE: Have you found it?

ALAN: With a wonky catch?

FATHER'S VOICE: Let's have a look at it?

[ALAN *lifts the case off the trunks in a broad, sweeping movement. He lowers it through the trap door towards the upstretched hands of* FATHER *and* TERRY.]

ALAN: Careful with it.

FATHER: You watch what you're doing.

[FATHER *and* TERRY *catch the case and lower it to the floor. They laugh with relief and* FATHER *starts to open the case at once.*]

241

ALAN: Wait for me.

> [ALAN *lowers himself through the trap door and* TERRY *steadies the chair as he puts his feet on it.*]

Thanks.

> [FATHER *opens the case. It is full of papers and letters, bits of books, photographs and junk.*]

FATHER: I don't remember [*he looks up at* ALAN] all this.

ALAN: It is the right case?

FATHER: I'm sure it is. Only, I don't . . . [FATHER *looks down at the case again and begins to sort through the contents.*] . . . remember . . .

> [TERRY *turns abruptly and walks across the landing, into her bedroom.*]

ALAN: You think it's here?

FATHER: I'm sure it is.

> [ALAN *glances across the top of* FATHER'S *head at the door of* TERRY'S *bedroom, as she pushes it shut behind her.*]

ALAN: We'll take it into your room.

FATHER: I'm all right here. I'll find it. [FATHER *begins to search more energetically through the case.*] Oh, yes.

> [ALAN *walks round him carefully and pushes open the door of* TERRY'S *bedroom.*]

It's bound to be here. Somewhere.

CUT TO *Terry's bedroom.*

> [TERRY *is standing at the window of her bedroom.* ALAN *stands in the doorway.*]

FATHER'S VOICE: I'll find it.

ALAN: Can I come in?

> [TERRY *nods without turning round to look at him, as he walks into the room.*]

TERRY [*mumbling*]: Shut the door.

> [ALAN *pushes the door shut quietly.*]

[*Desperately*] He's an old man. He really is – an old man.

[TERRY *turns to face* ALAN.]

ALAN: Yes, he is.

TERRY: I didn't know – talking to him – the things I said to him . . . [TERRY *shakes her head in misery.*] An old man!

[ALAN *walks across the room to* TERRY *and stands close to her. She lifts her head and looks up at him for a moment and then steps close to him, presses herself against him.*]

[*Quietly*] Put your arms round me?

[ALAN *puts his arms round her, one round her waist, the other across her back.*]

Hold tight.

ALAN [*gently*]: Easy, baby.

TERRY: I'm going to break – in pieces – small pieces.

ALAN: No, no.

TERRY: Hmm.

ALAN: You're safe. I've got you – safe.

TERRY: God will punish me.

ALAN: 'Cause you were beastly to – an old man?

TERRY: How could I say – [*urgently*] Alan! [TERRY *puts her arms round* ALAN *and presses her face hard against his chest.*]

ALAN: It's all right.

TERRY [*mumbling*]: Shaking – I'm – shaking. I can't stop . . .

ALAN [*firmly*]: It's all right.

TERRY: . . . shaking.

ALAN: Nobody's going to punish you. I won't let them.

TERRY: My stomach – I think . . . [TERRY *gulps and struggles away from* ALAN.] Sick.

ALAN [*calmly*]: You can't be sick.

TERRY [*moaning*]: Hmm.

ALAN: You can't be sick here and you can't get to the bathroom. [ALAN *puts his hands palms down on* TERRY'S *shoulders.*] You can't get past him.

[*Gradually* TERRY *stops shaking and lets her arms sink to her sides again. She nods her head.*]

All right?

TERRY: All right.

[ALAN *takes his hands off her shoulders and steps back.*]

Don't go away.

ALAN: Come and sit down.

[TERRY *walks forward and* ALAN *gestures at the bed.*

TERRY *sits sideways on the edge of the bed.* ALAN *leans back against the wall.*]

Sorry, I haven't got a cigarette for you.

TERRY: 'S all right.

[*Silence.*]

What are we going to do about him?

ALAN: I'm going to take him with me. I'm going to look after him – and – when we go to Australia – I'm going to take him with me.

TERRY [*hesitantly*]: He doesn't – er – want to go to Australia.

ALAN: No. Put it another way, he doesn't want to live with me.

TERRY: I can't, Alan. Live here – and . . . [TERRY *shakes her head and pulls her upper lip back between her teeth.*]

ALAN: Of course, you can't.

TERRY: Hmm.

ALAN: He'll survive.

TERRY: Perhaps, I ought to . . . [TERRY *looks up at* ALAN.] Should I?

ALAN: No. [ALAN *steps across and sits next to her on the bed.*] For pity's sake! What would you do with him? Look, baby – we've got it all set up – we can work him in and never notice.

TERRY: He – wants me – to look after him.

ALAN [*casually*]: He can't have everything.

TERRY: Honestly, if I thought . . .

ALAN: Ellen's potty about him. I can't think why. He's got the kids.

TERRY [*urgently*]: Don't let him – little Sarah – don't . . .

ALAN: No.

TERRY: He'll promise – and she might . . .

ALAN: Ellen puts little Sarah to bed. Ellen tells the stories, she'll see . . .

TERRY: It's only 'cause he – loves – wants to love . . .

ALAN: Little Sarah has an infinite capacity for being loved. He'll do very well with her.

TERRY: As long – just as long . . .

ALAN: She thinks he's funny. She thinks he's sweet. He's very old and she can't understand half the things he says to her. I don't think she'll come to any great harm.

TERRY [*abruptly*]: Couldn't you stay here? I mean, not [*she gestures at the room and the house around them*] here – just – [*laughing*] here!

[ALAN *stands up and turns away from* TERRY.]

ALAN: I have to take that job. I have to go . . .

TERRY: But, you said . . .

ALAN [*harshly*]: I know what I said!

[*Silence.*]

ALAN *walks across to the window and rests his hands on the sill, looking out at the playground across the road.*]

I know what I said.

TERRY: Ellen?

ALAN: No! [ALAN *turns to face* TERRY *across the end of the bed.*] You all have a pretty wild picture of Ellen, don't you?

TERRY: I hardly know her.

ALAN: Pushing me into things. Making me . . . [ALAN *breaks off and takes hold of the rail across the end of the bed.*] A pretty wild . . .

[*Silence.*]

TERRY: She thinks you ought to take this job? She thinks you ought to go to Australia?

ALAN: Yes, she does.

TERRY: She isn't going to change her mind?

ALAN: No.

TERRY: Not even – now – and . . .

ALAN [*coldly*]: No.

TERRY: If you talked to her – if you explained . . .

ALAN: I don't want to go – I live – I've always lived here – near here! You think – I . . . [ALAN *leans forward across the end of the bed.*] You are the one always did – the – un- expected – wanted – the adventures. You – round the world in eighty days! I – just . . . [ALAN *pushes himself backwards against the window.*] Home – a quiet home – and knowing – every day – where I belong – where – I'm going.

245

TERRY: That doesn't make sense.

ALAN: No, it doesn't, does it? I'm going to Australia – off – into the wild, blue . . . [ALAN *turns abruptly and looks out of the window again.*]

TERRY: You don't have to go.

ALAN: Simple! Just like that. 'You don't have to go!'

TERRY: If you feel . . .

ALAN [*violently*]: I have to go!

TERRY: . . . like that about it.

ALAN: Feel! [ALAN *turns and looks at* TERRY.] Yes.

TERRY [*coldly*]: What?

ALAN: In language you'll understand – a situation you'll understand – I go to Australia – I take Ellen and the kids – Dad – to Australia – and . . . [ALAN *grips the rail at the end of the bed*] 'start a new life'! – or I don't have – Ellen and the kids.

TERRY: Oh, God!

ALAN: Right!

[TERRY *nods her head.*]

Got it in one. I [*he forces the words singly out of his mouth*] fell in love.

TERRY: You had to tell Ellen, of course!

ALAN: No. I didn't – have to. I did.

TERRY [*nodding*]: A situation I understand.

ALAN: Hmm.

TERRY: Is it that girl – what's her name? The girl I met that time – must be all of two years ago, isn't it? I let you borrow my room – where I was living . . . [*Suddenly, desperately,* TERRY *puts her hands up to her head.*] Everything gets . . .

ALAN: No, it isn't.

[TERRY *stands up and steps across to the wall.*]

TERRY: . . . so confused – sort of run together.

ALAN: It isn't her.

TERRY: Funny, I thought you'd be – faithful – you know? If you ever decided . . .

ALAN: Her name was Pat.

TERRY: That's right.

ALAN: I haven't seen her – oh! Ten – eleven months.

TERRY: I didn't take to her.

ALAN: It isn't Pat.

[TERRY *turns and presses her face against the wall.*]

TERRY [*murmuring*]: Things seem to happen – the same things – over and over. Names and places – and time – all piled on top of each other – one on top ... [TERRY *pushes herself away from the wall and faces* ALAN.] 'Give her up, or I'll take the children away'?

ALAN: No.

TERRY: Something like.

ALAN: Nothing like.

TERRY: 'Take us all to Australia ...' [TERRY *hits* ALAN *hard on the chest.*] You have to take an old man on a one-way trip to his grave, 'cause you ... [TERRY *hits* ALAN *again on the chest.*] ... and your wife – can't ... [TERRY *turns away and stumbles across the room to the wall.*] 'Cause you go chasing – and you – oh, God! You would, wouldn't you? You get caught.

[TERRY *rests a hand against the wall and leans sideways against it.*

Silence.]

ALAN: Try and understand.

[TERRY *turns to face* ALAN *again.*]

TERRY: I'm sorry – I hit you.

[ALAN *shrugs and shakes his head.*]

Suddenly, it seemed the only thing I could do.

ALAN: Yes, I know.

TERRY: It's like that – really? Is it?

ALAN: How d'you mean?

TERRY: If you stay here?

ALAN: I'll see her again? Oh, yes.

TERRY: You couldn't – think – about it?

ALAN: I love her.

TERRY: How do you feel about Ellen? [*Before* ALAN *can answer* TERRY *holds up a hand.*] Unfair. Forget I said it. I know how you feel about Ellen. I've been told.

ALAN: What? What d'you mean?

TERRY: It's not the first time, sweetie. [TERRY *reaches for the bed and takes a step sideways, towards it.*] You're not – you may feel – unique – I'm sorry, you're not. [TERRY *sits on the bed, almost falls across it.*] I have had the honour – many times over – to be a person – the person – selected by husbands for the special privilege of being told ... [TERRY *turns her head and looks at* ALAN.] You haven't got a cigarette?

[ALAN *shakes his head.*]

Hmmm. How they feel about their wives – in similar – really, very similar – circumstances. You are not unique.
[*Silence.*]

Well, now. We have a problem, don't we? We have a pretty problem, Moriarty. What are we going to do?

ALAN: I'm sorry I had to tell you.

TERRY: It couldn't happen to a nicer girl.

ALAN: I wasn't going to.

[TERRY *stands up.*]

TERRY: I'll ask Dad.

ALAN: What?

TERRY: He'll give me a cigarette. [TERRY *walks towards the door.*]

ALAN: No. Leave him alone.

TERRY [*harshly*]: I need – a cigarette.

[ALAN *catches hold of her and pulls her away from the door.*]

ALAN: Bite your nails. Suck your thumb! He's happy. Leave him alone!

TERRY: You go to Australia, sweetie. You and Ellen – little Sarah – Michael – all of you. I'll look after Dad.

ALAN: You'll do what?

TERRY: He wants to live here? Right. He can live here. I'll move in with him.

ALAN: No, you won't.

TERRY: How much longer can he live, anyway?

ALAN: You couldn't begin to look after him.

TERRY: He wants me to. Surely, that's more than half the battle, isn't it?

ALAN: Leave you two together, under one roof!

TERRY: I'll learn. Anyway – I'll have other things to think about.

ALAN: You'll fight like cat and dog.

TERRY: You'd be surprised, sweetie. I lived for a year with a man I really hated – but – hated! All right, we hardly spoke – but we didn't fight. I got on with my life. He got on with his.

ALAN: This is ridiculous!

TERRY: He's lived here – in this house – for thirty years.

ALAN: Longer than that.

TERRY: You can't ask him to leave it – just like that! Walk out and never see it again.

ALAN: It's the best thing he can do.

TERRY: How do you know that!

ALAN: It's obvious. You think – just because she's dead – she won't be here – everywhere? The longer he stays here, the longer he takes to get over – losing her.

TERRY: How long has he got anyway?

ALAN: Too long to spend it – sitting round this house – mourning her.

TERRY: If he wants to . . .

ALAN: He doesn't know what he wants!

TERRY: You do?

ALAN: If he's going to go on, yes, I do know.

TERRY: Suppose he wants to stop? Suppose he – just wants . . . [TERRY *clasps her hands across her stomach.*]

ALAN: He can't, can he? Just stop!

TERRY: People do.

ALAN: He's got five years – maybe more. I hope – many more.

TERRY: God, I don't.

ALAN: Away from this house . . .

TERRY: For his sake.

ALAN: . . . somewhere new . . .

TERRY [*quietly*]: Suddenly, you sound like Mum.

ALAN: . . . things to interest him.

TERRY: Suddenly – quite suddenly . . .

ALAN: You think he [*he points at the door of the room*] would

still be here, if it wasn't for Mum? What do you think
has kept him going, all these years?

TERRY: Why does he have to – keep going?

ALAN: Don't be stupid!

TERRY: No, tell me. Why?

ALAN: He's alive.

TERRY: So was Mum. She was the one . . .

ALAN: Shut up, Terry!

TERRY: . . . always said – everyone has to keep going.

ALAN: Shut up!

TERRY: She wouldn't let God rest – on the seventh day!

ALAN: Here. In this house – on her own – she . . . [ALAN
turns away sharply.] You want him – I mean – leave him –
here – and a month, two months . . .

TERRY: I'll be here.

ALAN: Will you?

TERRY: Let him stay.

ALAN: No.

TERRY: Let me have him.

ALAN: How long will it last? I mean [*he turns to face*
TERRY] how long will you stay here, stay with him?
How long have you stayed – anywhere? Three years
with your husband? Suppose Dad lives longer than three
years? What happens to him, when you decide to leave?
He – is an old man. You said that yourself.

TERRY: He should be allowed to rest.

ALAN: All right. I leave him here – with you – and I go
to Australia. Six months later – maybe three months –
I get a telegram – 'Come and get him.'

TERRY: Oh, no.

ALAN: How do you know?

TERRY: I'll stay with him.

ALAN: How can you say that?

TERRY: I swear to you . . .

ALAN: What does that mean?

TERRY: I mean it, Alan. Please – believe me?

ALAN: The world is littered with people who believed you –
believed you'd stay with them. Where are you?

TERRY: That's not fair.

ALAN: It's true.

TERRY: I will – I promise, I will ...

ALAN: I can't take the chance.

TERRY: I promise.

ALAN: 'To love, honour and obey' – what is it? 'Till death do us part.' Are you dead? Is he – is Leonard dead?

TERRY: It was a mistake.

ALAN: Yes.

TERRY: I could make a home for Dad.

ALAN: As long as it suited you – just that long – and no longer.

TERRY [*quietly*]: You're certain, aren't you? Really? Deep down – where it counts – where the dirt settles thick – you're certain. [TERRY *lurches forward and crouches beside the bed, almost kneeling.*] Serves me right, I suppose. Why should you believe me? Do I believe myself? Ah!

ALAN: You going to do that packing, or shall I?

TERRY: I suppose ... [*She looks up at* ALAN, *who is standing beside her.*] You know? What I'm trying to do is get in good with God. Yes, I think that's what I'm trying to do.

ALAN: Make up your mind, will you?

TERRY: I have this problem with God. I mean, I don't believe in him – but – at the same time – I just know he's up there, watching me – waiting to go ...

ALAN: Pow?

TERRY: Right. You're right!

[ALAN *reaches down and puts his hand under* TERRY'S *arm.*]

Leave me alone. I'm all right. I'm happy – down here.

ALAN: I think we've wasted enough time.

TERRY: I thought we were talking. Is that what we were doing? Wasting time?

ALAN: I'd like to get packed and out of here, as soon as possible.

TERRY: Just doesn't seem worth – you know – going to all the trouble of being – good ... [TERRY *laughs.*] Whatever that means. If he isn't there – and it is all one great big con trick! The whole God bit! Know what I mean?

ALAN [*irritably*]: Come on! [ALAN *pulls* TERRY *up on to her feet.*]

TERRY: Ooops! [TERRY *steadies herself holding on to* ALAN'S *arms.*]

ALAN: Now. Pull yourself together!

TERRY: You're right. Of course, you're right. Big brother's always right.

ALAN: You want to stay here awhile? On your own?

TERRY: I'd leave him. Hmm. When I wanted to go – oh, I don't know – somewhere new – on my own. I'd go. You'd be lucky to get a telegram.

ALAN: I don't think you would.

TERRY: Yes, you do.

ALAN: No.

TERRY: You're right. I'm telling you and I should know. Shouldn't I know? I'm me. Who is supposed to know better than me, what I'm likely to do?

ALAN: Honestly, Terry . . .

TERRY: Honestly, Alan . . . [TERRY *squeezes* ALAN'S *arms.*] . . . that's the kind of girl I am. Ask anyone.

ALAN: I think you'd make Dad a wonderful home.

TERRY: Anyone who knows me – 'cause not many people do. I see to that.

ALAN: It's just – with the baby – and all that to think about.

TERRY: My baby?

ALAN: You'll have more than enough to do.

TERRY: Yes. Suppose – Alan, have you thought . . . [TERRY *shakes her head violently.*] No. People don't, do they? Mothers. They don't go off and . . . [TERRY *steps very close to* ALAN *and whispers to him.*] Only, you see – if I'm that sort of girl – and I am. Suppose, when I've got the baby, I go off one day – just – go – and leave her. Suppose I do that?

ALAN: You won't. Don't be silly. Of course, you won't.

TERRY: You think I'll go off and leave Dad.

ALAN: You're going to make a wonderful mother.

TERRY [*abruptly*]: Wonderful home! Wonderful mother!

D'you know, Alan – everything in your world's just bloody wonderful! Aren't you lucky?

ALAN: Terry – look – just now – talking just now, I said a lot of things – I'm sorry – I didn't mean them.

TERRY: Not to worry, sweetie. That's called – talking to people. I know you don't mean what you say. No one – means what they say. The number of people who've said – 'I love you' – I can't count them. I know they don't mean it. Goodness yes! [TERRY *gently pushes* ALAN *to one side and walks across to the window.*] The hours I've spent . . . [TERRY *glances back over her shoulder, at* ALAN.] Go on, if you're in a hurry. Don't wait for me.

[ALAN *shakes his head.*]

I used to stand at this window – night and day – by the hour. D'you know? Yes, you know. [TERRY *presses a hand against the glass, takes it away and looks at the misty print.*] Funny – I was never on my own, then. I never felt – on my own.

ALAN: I'll go and see how Dad's getting on.

TERRY: You hurt me. Saying all those things.

ALAN: I'm sorry.

TERRY: Yes, I know. Still – you said them. I've got them – in my head. Just saying you're sorry – that doesn't take them away.

ALAN: You couldn't look after him, love.

TERRY: I could try.

ALAN: Yes, of course.

TERRY: You won't even let me try.

ALAN: There isn't time.

TERRY [*violently*]: There's never time! For things you could do – good things – if only people wouldn't always . . .

[*Silence.*]

ALAN: Always?

TERRY: I don't know. Something about people – and rushing – always having to rush – home – to the pictures – to the office – into bed – out of bed . . .

[*Silence.*]

Back to their wives. [*Abruptly*] Sorry. That wasn't fair.

ALAN: 'S all right.

TERRY: I can't really – think. Not now. 'Cause every time I start, it works round to something about you – something beastly – 'cause you hurt me.

ALAN: Hmm.

TERRY: I think the most super things, you know? Only, there's never anyone to tell – or – only the wrong – one. I've given up telling the – wrong ones. They don't understand – and . . . [TERRY *laughs*] I think it frightens them.

ALAN: It's a kind of magic.

[TERRY *turns and looks at* ALAN.]

TERRY: Is it?

ALAN: Oh, yes. I used to listen to you for hours. All I can remember – really remember from – [*grinning*] my childhood – is listening to you talk.

TERRY: I was always so much younger than you.

ALAN: 'Bout the time you were five, I started listening. I never really stopped.

TERRY: I didn't know.

ALAN: You used to make up poems.

TERRY: Oh, God! No.

ALAN: Yes, you did.

TERRY [*laughing*]: Oh, I know. I know I did.

ALAN: I keep hoping little Sarah might . . . [ALAN *shrugs*.] I don't know – some of it might show – in her. I'd like to be able – to listen – again. [ALAN *walks towards* TERRY.] I didn't mean to hurt you.

[*As he reaches her,* TERRY *puts up a hand and rests it against his chest, so he doesn't get too close to her.*]

TERRY: I know. Matter of fact, you didn't say anything I haven't said to myself – ten thousand times.

ALAN: It's not the same.

TERRY: It's a bit of a shock, when you find someone else – knows.

ALAN: I had no right to say them.

TERRY: You don't want Dad . . . [TERRY *pats* ALAN *on the chest and eases past him, back along the side of the bed.*] . . . falling into the wrong hands.

ALAN: I don't want you making promises, because you feel
sorry for him.

TERRY: Oh, no.

ALAN: And then, not able to keep them.

TERRY: I don't feel sorry for him.

ALAN: It would hurt you . . .

   [TERRY *runs a hand along the cover of the bed.*]

TERRY: We ought to make this bed. Look at it!

ALAN: If you made promises and then, broke them . . .

TERRY: I know all about that.

ALAN: . . . again.

TERRY: What you said – that was true.

ALAN: I think it might hurt . . .

TERRY: I don't think I could stand it. [TERRY *looks over her
shoulder at* ALAN.] No, you're right. Thank you.

ALAN: That's why – I said . . .

TERRY: 'I must be cruel . . .'

ALAN: I love you.

   [*Silence.*]

TERRY: I love you, too.

FATHER'S VOICE: Alan.

ALAN: I think he's found it.

FATHER'S VOICE: I've found it.

TERRY: That'll make all the difference to our lives, won't
it? [TERRY *rubs at her eyes pushing the eye-lids upwards.*]

ALAN: It's just what we need, isn't it? A photograph of me
– and ten other roughs – in shirt, shorts and football
boots! [ALAN *walks across the room to* TERRY *and puts an
arm round her shoulder.*]

TERRY: I don't know how we've survived so long without
it.

FATHER'S VOICE: Alan. Where are you?

ALAN [*calling*]: Here I am, Dad. [ALAN *reaches forward and
opens the door.*] Coming.

FATHER'S VOICE: I've found it.

ALAN: I knew you would.

   [ALAN *lets* TERRY *walk out of the room first and then
follows her.*

FATHER *is still on his knees in front of the case and the landing is covered with papers and photographs.*]

ALAN: What have you been doing?

FATHER: Give us a hand.

[FATHER *reaches a hand towards* ALAN, *who helps him to his feet.*]

ALAN: Look at this mess!

FATHER: Here it is! [FATHER *holds out the photograph which is a carefully posed group of schoolboys in shirts, shorts and football boots. The boy in the centre of the group is holding a football, which has been painted white for the occasion.*] I knew I'd find it again, if I went on looking for it long enough.

ALAN: That's it. That [*he tilts the photograph so* TERRY *can look at it too*] is definitely the photograph.

FATHER: You see? [FATHER *points at the photograph, picking out one particular boy.*] There you are, Alan.

TERRY: Handsome. Very handsome indeed.

ALAN: Thank you.

FATHER: The first eleven – when was it?

ALAN: Nineteen-forty-seven.

TERRY: I was twelve years old.

ALAN: And looking every day of it.

FATHER: Gordon. [FATHER *points at the boy in the centre of the group.*] That's Gordon, isn't it?

ALAN: Yes, it is.

TERRY: He looks pretty pleased with himself.

ALAN: Of course, everyone knew he was going to be captain, but – oh! – the day they told us.

FATHER: I don't think Gordon believed me.

ALAN: I went away into a small, dark corner . . .

TERRY: Did you cry? Actually cry?

FATHER: When I told him about the photograph, I don't think he believed that I still had it.

ALAN [*stiffly*]: I was seventeen years old.

FATHER: I'd like him to see it.

ALAN [*grinning*]: Yes, I actually cried.

[TERRY *takes the photograph out of* FATHER'S *hand and looks at the picture of* ALAN *more closely.*]

FATHER: I'd like to show it to Gordon.

ALAN: Yes, of course.

TERRY: The trouble is, you just don't look the type.

ALAN: Oh, I don't know. I look as tough as the next man.
[ALAN *takes the photograph away from* TERRY *and looks at it.*]
Who is the next man?

TERRY: Crying.

FATHER: He'd like to see it, wouldn't he?
    [ALAN *looks at* TERRY *for a moment without speaking.*
    He nods his head and grins at her.]

ALAN: No.

FATHER: Wouldn't he?

ALAN: Sorry, Dad. What . . .

FATHER: He'd like to see it. Gordon – wouldn't he?

ALAN: You show it to him, he'll very likely try and steal it
from you. This [*he gives the photograph back to* FATHER]
was his finest hour.

FATHER: I'll take it with me.

ALAN: Right. Well, I think we ought to be getting along.
[ALAN *looks at his watch.*] Ellen's expecting me – good
grief! She's been expecting us for the last hour.

TERRY: Ellen's a good wife. She knows how to wait.

FATHER: Have I got everything?

ALAN: You haven't got anything. Terry, you push those few
things into a case, will you? [ALAN *crouches down and starts*
to pick up all the papers and photographs.] I'll clear up out
here.

FATHER: What shall I do?

ALAN: Hold on to that photograph, if you really want to
take it with you.

TERRY: Dad – suppose you didn't have to go?
    [ALAN *turns sharply, still on his knees, and looks up at*
    TERRY.]

FATHER: The kitchen's in a terrible mess, Alan.

TERRY: Dad.

FATHER: We ought to do something about that. I mean,
we can't just leave it.

TERRY: Suppose you didn't have to go away?

[FATHER *turns his head and looks at* TERRY.]

Suppose you could stay here?

FATHER: I can't.

TERRY: Suppose you could?

FATHER: I'm going with Alan. I'm going to live with Alan.

TERRY: If I stay with you . . .

FATHER: We're going to Australia.

TERRY . . . you don't have to.

FATHER: Ellen's expecting us.

TERRY: You can live here.

FATHER [*harshly*]: I don't want to.

[*Silence.*]

Alan, we ought to do something about the kitchen.

ALAN: I'll talk to Mrs Hayter.

FATHER: Would she come in, d'you think – and – just clear up some of the mess?

ALAN: I'm sure she will.

FATHER: I don't like to go – leaving . . . [FATHER *shuffles a step closer to* ALAN, *away from* TERRY.] You know how your mother . . .

ALAN: Yes, I know. [ALAN *turns and starts gathering the papers together again. He pushes them all into the case.*]

FATHER: I'll give you a hand, shall I? Alan?

ALAN: All right. Just . . .

[FATHER *kneels down beside* ALAN, *with some difficulty.*] . . . don't lose that photograph again. Tell you what. Here. Give it to me. [ALAN *takes the photograph away from his* FATHER *and props it up against the banisters.*]

FATHER: Off you go, Terry. Quick as you can. [FATHER *doesn't look round at* TERRY, *even when he is speaking to her. He concentrates on the business of gathering up the photographs.*] We don't want to keep Ellen waiting any longer than we have to.

[TERRY *turns and walks quickly into the main bedroom.*] I can't tell you the things I found in that case, Alan. Things were lost years ago.

ALAN: It's funny the way things turn up. [ALAN *gathers together a bundle of papers and pushes them into the case.*]

FATHER: We should go through it together.

ALAN: Yes.

FATHER: You'll be amazed – the things there are tucked away in there.

ALAN: I'm sure. [ALAN *moves across the landing on his knees, to gather the papers farthest away from the case.*]

FATHER: I made a bit of a mess, I'm afraid.

ALAN: We'll soon have it cleared up.

FATHER: Ellen won't make a fuss, will she?

[ALAN *looks round at his* FATHER.]

ALAN: How d'you mean?

FATHER: Go to a lot of trouble. Put herself out – you know what I mean?

ALAN: She just has to move a few toys out of your room and put them in Michael's. No trouble at all.

FATHER: I don't want to be a bother. [FATHER *sits back on his heels, looking at a photograph he has found on the floor, a photograph of* ALAN *in school uniform.*] Funny – seeing that photograph again – brought it all back.

ALAN: Yes?

FATHER: Those Saturday afternoons. My goodness it used to get cold sometimes.

ALAN: It certainly did. [ALAN *sits back on his heels and looks at his* FATHER.] I could never understand . . . [ALAN *shakes his head abruptly stops and scrambles back to the case. He puts some more papers into it.*]

FATHER: Other things.

ALAN: Hmm?

FATHER: Things we did together. Yesterday I was trying to remember . . .

[*Silence.*

ALAN *sits back again and surveys the landing. It is almost clear of clutter.*]

Then I saw the photograph – and everything.

[ALAN *stands up and walks across the landing to gather up the last remaining photographs.*]

We used to walk – d'you remember? – when you were quite small, we used to walk to the end of the road together?

ALAN: Did we?

FATHER: There was a river. Quite a small river.

ALAN: How old was I? [ALAN *takes the photograph from his* FATHER, *puts it with the others he has and crouches down beside the case again.*]

FATHER: You thought it was great adventure.

ALAN: The end of the road?

FATHER: It isn't there now. It was a long time ago.

ALAN: Riverdale Avenue?

FATHER: It was all fields then.

ALAN: I can remember when they built those houses.

[ALAN *shuts the case and stands up again.*]

FATHER: Your mother and I used to take you – in your pram. You were just a baby.

ALAN: We used to play there. Fast as they put them up, we tried to pull them down.

FATHER: It was all fields – and open . . .

ALAN: We got chased off there, more times . . .

[*Smiling,* ALAN *turns to look at his* FATHER, *who has sunk down on to his heels, his hands in his lap.*]

Dad? [ALAN *steps across to him and crouches beside his* FATHER.] What's the matter, Dad? What is it?

FATHER: I didn't know.

ALAN [*gently*]: What do you mean? Didn't know what?

FATHER: She was going – to . . . [FATHER *stares into* ALAN's *face.*] I didn't know.

ALAN [*quickly*]: Of course, you didn't.

FATHER: I was up here. I was – thinking – you know?

ALAN: Yes, I know.

FATHER: There must have been – some noise . . . [FATHER *shakes his head slowly.*] I didn't hear . . .

ALAN: Try not to think about it.

FATHER [*moaning*]: Mmmm.

ALAN: It doesn't help . . .

FATHER: If she'd called me . . .

ALAN: . . . thinking about it.

TERRY'S VOICE [*quietly*]: Maybe, she did.

[ALAN *turns his head sharply and looks at* TERRY, *across the top of his* FATHER'S *head.*]

TERRY [*simply*]: She called me. Just – I wasn't listening.
[TERRY *is standing in the main bedroom doorway, holding a small suitcase in one hand.*]

FATHER [*quietly*]: Things – your mother and I – things that weren't – there were some things [*he leans closer to* ALAN, *speaking almost into his ear*] were never easy – and she couldn't – talk about them, you see? Talk to me – about them. But it was all so long ago – before you . . .

[*Silence.*]

[*Blankly*] Before you were born.

ALAN: Easy, Dad. Easy.

TERRY: Let him say it.

[ALAN *turns his head again and looks at* TERRY.]

He wants to say it – to you – to someone. You can listen, can't you?

FATHER [*whispering*]: I didn't mean to hurt her. I didn't know – I mean – you don't think. I – didn't think.

ALAN: Hurt her?

FATHER: That first night – I wanted . . . [*Suddenly* FATHER *pushes himself upright.*]

[*Loudly*] I loved her. I wanted so much . . .

[TERRY *steps across the landing towards her* FATHER *and stands close behind him.*]

[*Harshly*]: I didn't think – about her – just . . .

[*Silence.*]

. . . what I – wanted.

[ALAN *looks up at* TERRY, *who shakes her head.*]

And always – after that – always! – She never – never once in all the years – the years and – years! – Looked at me. Asked me . . .

ALAN: Come on, Dad.

TERRY: She's let go of us.

ALAN: Come on home.

TERRY: Why shouldn't we – just – walk away?

FATHER: It was all so very long ago.

[ALAN *helps his* FATHER *up on to his feet.*]

You don't think ... [FATHER *grips* ALAN'S *coat.*] It couldn't have been – all these years – it couldn't have been – why?

ALAN: No.

FATHER: It couldn't, could it?

ALAN [*firmly*]: No, it couldn't.

     [FATHER *lets go of* ALAN'S *coat.*]

We should be getting along, I think.

FATHER: I'll just ... [FATHER *checks in mid-sentence and looks at* ALAN.] If there's time, I'll just go to the bathroom?

ALAN: We'll wait for you downstairs.

FATHER: Yes, all right.

     [FATHER *walks away along the landing, towards the bathroom.* ALAN *looks at* TERRY.]

ALAN: After you.

     [TERRY *walks across the landing and down the stairs.* ALAN *follows her, picking up the photograph as he goes.*]

ALAN: I'll fetch your coat.

TERRY: Thanks.

     [ALAN *walks briskly into the back room, glances round, sees* TERRY'S *coat and walks across to pick it up. He hesitates for a moment, holding the coat in his hands, and then turns and walks back out of the room.*

     TERRY *is standing with her back to the door of the front room, which is now closed.*]

ALAN: You going to put it on?

     [TERRY *nods.*]

What a fantastic memory Dad's got.

     [*He holds the coat up and* TERRY *turns to slip her arms into the sleeves.*]

TERRY: Hmm.

ALAN: He was just telling me – seeing all the photographs – and guff – and everything.

TERRY: Some things he remembers.

ALAN: He was saying about you and him – how you used to walk down to the end of the road. [ALAN *straightens the coat on her shoulders.*] There we are.

TERRY: Thanks.

ALAN: Riverdale Avenue. When it was just fields down there.

TERRY: That was a while ago.

ALAN: You used to stand and look at the river. You thought it was a great adventure.

[*Silence.*]

TERRY [*suddenly*]: Yes. That's right. Yes, we did. I must've been two – or three at the most. Does he remember that?

ALAN: He was just talking about it. [ALAN *takes his own coat off the banisters.*]

TERRY [*hesitantly*]: I'm sorry – just now – getting at Dad – trying to make him . . . [TERRY *shrugs.*]

ALAN: Not to worry.

TERRY: I wanted him to stay here – suddenly – more than anything in the world.

[ALAN *pulls his coat straight.*]

ALAN: Once Dad makes up his mind . . .

FATHER'S VOICE: Is my coat down there, Alan?

ALAN: Yes, Dad. I've got it. [ALAN *walks along the hall.*] Mum gave Gladly to little Sarah.

TERRY: What?

ALAN: Gladly. She found him one day, playing round the house.

TERRY: That was his name. Oh, yes!

[ALAN *takes his* FATHER'S *coat off the hall stand.*]

ALAN: Your name for him. I called him – Teddy – as far as I can remember.

TERRY: Does she love him?

ALAN: Loves him to death. Sleeps with her every night.

TERRY: When she's finished with him, perhaps . . .

ALAN: If there's anything left of him, by then.

FATHER'S VOICE: Have you spoken to Mrs Hayter, Alan?

ALAN: I'll phone her, Dad. Soon as we get home.

CUT TO FILM: *Looking across the road, through the empty swings, slides and roundabouts, at the Stephens' house.*

The front door opens and Alan walks out of the house, followed by his Father and, last of all, Terry. Terry pulls the front door shut behind her and the three of them walk along the garden path to the front gate. Alan pulls the gate open and steps back to let his Father walk out, on to the pavement and across to Alan's car, which is parked at the curb.

Terry follows her Father and then Alan, who walks quickly round the front of the car to unlock the driver's door. He gets into the car and reaches across to unlock the front and rear passenger doors. As he starts the engine, Terry helps her Father into the car and shuts the door after him. Terry climbs quickly into the back of the car and shuts the door. Alan glances briefly over his shoulder to check that she is settled and then drives off.

Looking across the road, through the empty swings, slides and roundabouts, at the front of the Stephens' house.

FADE OUT

PART FOUR

THE INNOCENT MUST SUFFER

First transmitted by Theatre 625 on B.B.C.-2 on 23 October 1966 with the following cast:

MOTHER	Margery Mason
FATHER	Maurice Denham
ALAN	Michael Bryant
TERRY	Judi Dench
GORDON	Emrys James
MRS HAYTER	Maryann Turner

Story Editor	James Brabazon
Designer	Richard Wilmot
Produced by	Michael Bakewell
Directed by	Christopher Morahan

FADE IN *the back room of the Stephens' house.*

> [*A white, freshly laundered, freshly ironed table cloth crackles out of its folds and spreads across a square wooden dining table.*
>
> *Pull back as* MOTHER *reaches in, across the table, arranging it symmetrically, folds to the edges of the table. Even when the cloth is settled, the folds lift slightly from the surface of the table.*
>
> MOTHER *walks out of the back room into the hall. She stops at the bottom of the stairs and rests a hand on the banisters.*]

MOTHER: Ted?

> [*Silence.*]

Time you were getting up.

> [*She walks away towards the kitchen.* MRS HAYTER *is sitting at the kitchen table, drinking a cup of tea.* Two-way Family Favourites *murmurs in the background.*]

MRS HAYTER: Are the children coming to see their Nanna today?

MOTHER: No. [MOTHER *opens the kitchen drawer and starts to take out cutlery for the table.*]

MRS HAYTER: Aren't they? Really? Well! But it must be – surely, isn't it . . .

MOTHER: I saw them last week. Alan had to go out. I baby-sat for them.

MRS HAYTER: Oh, yes. But that's not the same thing at all, is it? Baby-sitting.

MOTHER: Little Sarah came down to see me.

MRS HAYTER: She's a scamp.

MOTHER: No, it isn't the same. [MOTHER *shuts the drawer.*]

MRS HAYTER: I think it's mean of her.

MOTHER: Alan's coming to see us. Pour yourself another cup of tea.

MRS HAYTER: I'm all right. Thanks.

267

MOTHER: I won't be a moment. [MOTHER *walks out into the hall.*]

MRS HAYTER: Alan isn't the children.

[MOTHER *crosses to the back room, walks across to the table, and standing on the near side, puts the cutlery down in the centre.*

CUT TO *black. A high-pitched, grating screaming noise.*

CUT TO *the back room again.*

MOTHER *is now standing on the far side of the table. The table is laid. She stares at the two places, mats, knives, forks and spoons, as if she has never seen them before.*]

SUPERIMPOSE TITLE: *The innocent must suffer*
[*Slowly,* MOTHER *lifts a hand and presses it against her forehead.*]

FADE TITLE.

[*Suddenly, briskly,* MOTHER *rubs the hand across her forehead, presses the fingers into her eyes for a moment and then walks round the table towards the door, 'pulling herself together'. She stands in the doorway and looks up at the banisters.*]

MOTHER: Buck up, Ted. Dinner'll be spoiled.
[*Silence.*]

CUT TO *the kitchen.*

MRS HAYTER: I don't know how you can face cooking a joint – every blessed Sunday.

MOTHER: Ted wouldn't know it was Sunday, if he didn't have his joint.

MRS HAYTER: Two veg – and gravy, I suppose?

MOTHER: If a thing's worth doing ... [MOTHER *opens the oven and takes out the joint.*]

MRS HAYTER: One thing about Dick – he doesn't expect much of a lunch – Sunday.

MOTHER: We've always made a point of Sunday dinner.

MRS HAYTER: Even now – when it's just . . .

MOTHER: I suppose it's silly, really.

MRS HAYTER: I think it's marvellous.

[MOTHER *puts the joint on to a serving dish and back into the oven.*]

I just hope your husband knows how lucky he is.

MOTHER: Oh, no. I don't think . . . [MOTHER *pours most of the fat out of the baking tin into a small bowl and then puts the baking tin on the stove.*]

MRS HAYTER: If I went to this much trouble – Sunday – I can tell you – there'd be prayers said in my house.

[MOTHER *walks to the kitchen door.*]

'Thank you, Jill – for a lovely meal!' They'd hear about it for a week.

MOTHER [*calling*]: I'm making the gravy.

[*Silence.*

MOTHER *turns and walks back to the stove.*]

You'll excuse me – getting on?

MRS HAYTER: Oh, yes. Don't worry about me.

[MOTHER *pours boiling water from the potato saucepan into the fat in the baking tray and starts to make the gravy.*]

Matter of fact, I should be getting back home. See what those children of mine are getting up to.

MOTHER: I like to eat early, when Alan's coming to see us.

MRS HAYTER: D'you notice how quiet it is? [MRS HAYTER *stands up, walks to the back door and opens it.*]

MOTHER: Gives me a chance to get things cleared away.

MRS HAYTER: That's a bad sign – when you can't hear anything. [MRS HAYTER *shuts the back door.*] Dick's as bad as they are. Between them, they can just as likely burn the house down. Thanks for the cup of tea.

MOTHER: You're welcome.

MRS HAYTER [*grinning*]: Better make myself scarce, anyway – before your husband comes down.

MOTHER: He takes longer and longer every day. I don't

know! All the morning – just ... [MOTHER *shakes her head and stops speaking as suddenly as she began.*]

MRS HAYTER: How is he?

MOTHER: Bored. I should think he'd be bored. I know I'd be bored – with nothing to do all day. Bored to tears!

MRS HAYTER: Makes a lot of extra work for you.

MOTHER: I don't mind that. If he'd just – take an interest in something. He hardly even goes out any more.

MRS HAYTER: Poor old chap.

[MOTHER *looks round at her, sharply.*]

Doesn't seem fair, does it? All the time in the world – and nothing to do with it. I'll see you a bit later, I expect. [MRS HAYTER *walks across to the kitchen door and looks back.*] Unless you'd like an extra mouth to help with all that super food? Eggs and bacon – that's the order of the day in my house! [MRS HAYTER *turns and walks out of the kitchen.*] 'Bye, now.

[MOTHER *pours the gravy into a gravy boat.*]

MRS HAYTER'S VOICE: Hello, Mr Stephens. How are you this morning?

FATHER'S VOICE: Fine, thank you. Yes, I'm fine.

MRS HAYTER'S VOICE: Just in time for your lunch.

[*The sound of the front door being shut.*]

MOTHER [*calling*]: I'm dishing up. You go and sit down.

FATHER'S VOICE: Can I help?

MOTHER: No. I can manage.

CUT TO *the back room.*

[*Close shot of the joint and the hands holding the carving knife and fork. The fork is pushed through a slice of meat and the meat is lifted, balanced on the knife and put down on to a plate in front of the carver. Pull back to show* MOTHER *carving the joint.*]

FATHER: If that's for me, that's more than enough.

MOTHER: It's the only meal you'll get today. [MOTHER *puts the carving knife and fork down and picks up a serving spoon.*] Make the most of it. [MOTHER *puts a helping of potatoes on to the plate.*]

FATHER: Now – don't give me too much!

[MOTHER *picks up a second serving spoon and puts some cabbage on to the plate. She passes the plate to* FATHER.]

MOTHER: It isn't hot.

FATHER: Is there any gravy?

MOTHER [*quietly*]: Yes. [MOTHER *passes the gravy boat to* FATHER.]

FATHER: Thanks. [FATHER *pours gravy liberally over the food on his plate.*]

MOTHER: You start. Don't wait.

[FATHER *cuts a piece of meat, pushes his fork through it and carefully assembles a mouthful of food on his fork.* MOTHER *watches him prepare the mouthful of meat, potatoes and cabbage.* FATHER *brings the fork up to his mouth. He chews the food carefully, looking at* MOTHER *across the table as he does so.*

CUT TO *the table.* MOTHER'S *food is hardly touched.* FATHER'S *plate is almost cleared.*]

FATHER'S VOICE: Did you say Alan was coming round this afternoon?

MOTHER'S VOICE: Yes.

FATHER'S VOICE: Bringing the children?

MOTHER'S VOICE: No.

[*Pull back to include* MOTHER *as she pushes her chair back and stands up.*]

MOTHER: I'll fetch your pudding. [MOTHER *picks up her own plate in one hand.*]

FATHER: Is that all you're going to eat?

MOTHER: I don't feel very hungry. [MOTHER *picks up the serving dish with her other hand.*]

FATHER: Mind how you go with that knife.

MOTHER: I made apple charlotte. Is that all right?

FATHER: Did Alan tell you – when he thought he might get here?

MOTHER: After lunch sometime. I don't know exactly. Why?

FATHER: There's a thing I want to watch this afternoon – on television.

MOTHER: I don't suppose he'll mind. Probably sit down and watch it with you. [MOTHER *turns and walks across to the door.*] Shall I make some custard?

FATHER: I like a bit of custard with apple charlotte.

CUT TO *the kitchen.*

[*Close shot of a saucepan and a spoon, stirring the mixture of milk and custard powder as it thickens.*]

FATHER'S VOICE: Funny we haven't heard from Terry lately.

MOTHER'S VOICE: We'll hear from her. When there's something she wants.

FATHER'S VOICE: It's a long time.

MOTHER'S VOICE: No news is good news.

FATHER'S VOICE: I miss her.

[*The custard thickens and* MOTHER *picks it up, turns and pours the custard into a bowl.*]

MOTHER'S VOICE: Yes.

[*Silence.*]

FATHER'S VOICE: Thought I'd show willing. I brought my plate out.

MOTHER'S VOICE: Right. Well – now you're here, you can take this in for me.

[*Pull back as* MOTHER *lifts the bowl and holds it out to* FATHER. *They look at each other across the bowl for a moment and then* FATHER *takes it.*]

CUT TO *the back room.*

[*Close shot of* FATHER'S *jacket, which he has placed carefully across the back of an armchair, as* FATHER *reaches into the inside pocket and takes out his cigarette case.*]

FATHER'S VOICE: Sure you won't have one?

MOTHER'S VOICE: Quite sure.

[*Pull back as* FATHER *selects a cigarette and puts it carefully into his mouth. The table is cluttered with the debris of the meal.* MOTHER *is sitting at the table.*]

MOTHER: I'll make you a cup of tea – while I clear up.

FATHER: No. Thanks all the same. I'd rather . . . [FATHER

puts his cigarette case away in his jacket and takes out his lighter.]
Much rather – you had a bit of a rest. You must have
been on your feet all morning – getting that meal ready.
[FATHER *turns to look at* MOTHER.]

MOTHER: I'd like to get cleared up, before Alan arrives.

FATHER: What difference does it make – a few dishes on
the table – what possible . . . [FATHER *lights his cigarette.*]

MOTHER: You sit there – smoke your cigarette – and I'll
just potter.

FATHER [*angrily*]: You – sit there. You need the rest.

MOTHER: I like the place to look nice.

FATHER: By the time he's had dinner – they always eat
late, you know that – helped Ellen with the dishes –
played with the children . . . [FATHER *walks back to the
table and sits down again.*] You've got plenty of time to
have – well, just a bit of a rest. Surely!

MOTHER: Yes. All right.

FATHER: I'm not suggesting you should put your feet up.
Just [*he gestures at her with the hand holding the lighter*] sit
there. Relax.

> [FATHER *puts his hand down and turns the lighter end
> over end on the table in front of him.*
> *Silence.*
> MOTHER *reaches out and gathers a couple of dishes into
> a pile.*]

What did Mrs Hayter have to say for herself?

MOTHER: Nothing much.

FATHER: Took long enough about it.

MOTHER: She asked how you were.

> [FATHER *taps the lighter rhythmically on the table.*]

FATHER: That's nice of her.

MOTHER: Oh, she is – really – quite nice. [MOTHER *reaches
out and gathers another dish into her pile.*] Talks rather a lot.
Still . . .

> [*Silence.*]

FATHER: There's not much in the papers today.

MOTHER: I haven't looked.

FATHER: I shouldn't bother. [FATHER *looks for an ashtray.*]

MOTHER: No, no – stay where you are. I'll get it. [MOTHER *gets up and walks across to the mantelpiece. She picks up an ashtray and carries it back to the table. She puts it down in front of* FATHER *and then picks up the pile of dishes.*]

[*Hesitantly*] I'll just – take these things out – and put the kettle on?

FATHER [*angrily*]: Yes. Yes, all right.

CUT TO *the kitchen.*

[*Looking down at the sink and the washing bowl in it, as* MOTHER *runs hot water into the bowl. The front doorbell rings.*]

FATHER'S VOICE: I'll go – shall I?

[*Pull back as* MOTHER *squeezes some washing-up liquid into the bowl. The sound of the front door being opened.*]

Hello, stranger.

TERRY'S VOICE: Hello, Dad.

[*Lift to look into* MOTHER'S *face, as she turns her back to the sink, hearing the sound of* TERRY'S *voice.*]

FATHER'S VOICE: This is a surprise. I didn't know . . .

[*The voices drop into an inaudible murmur as* MOTHER *reaches up and pushes at her hair, trying to tuck some loose ends away. She drops her hands to her waist and pulls at her apron.*]

. . . your mother doesn't know . . .

[MOTHER *walks across to the kitchen table and picks up a pile of dirty dishes. She turns and carries them back to the sink.*]

[*Calling*] Mother. Got a surprise for you out here.

MOTHER: What d'you say? [MOTHER *puts the dishes into the water.*]

FATHER'S VOICE: Look who's here. [FATHER *opens the kitchen door and walks in.*]

MOTHER: I can't hear a word . . .

FATHER: Look who it is.

MOTHER: What are you talking about?

[*Brushing a hand across her forehead,* MOTHER *turns to face him, as* TERRY *walks into the kitchen.*]

TERRY: Hello.

MOTHER: Oh.

FATHER: I knew you'd be surprised.

MOTHER: Hello, stranger.

TERRY: How are you?

MOTHER: As well as can be expected, I suppose.

FATHER: Didn't know Terry was coming by today, did you?

MOTHER: Are you going to start drying-up or aren't you? [*Close shot of* MOTHER.] Have you had anything to eat?

TERRY: Thanks. Yes, I have.

MOTHER: Have you?

TERRY: I had a sandwich – you know?

FATHER: That's not enough.

MOTHER: 'Bout all you ever eat.

TERRY: I usually manage a couple of meals a day.

MOTHER: You're looking tired.

TERRY: Thanks.

FATHER: Haven't you been well? [FATHER *fills the kettle at the cold water tap.*]

TERRY: I'm in excellent health.

MOTHER: Doesn't look like it. [MOTHER *turns back to the sink and gets on with the washing-up.*]

TERRY: Thirty last month. Did you know that?

MOTHER: Yes, of course.

TERRY: I thought – since I didn't get a birthday card.

MOTHER: We didn't know where to send it, did we?

FATHER: Let me do it. [FATHER *takes the tea towel from* TERRY.]

MOTHER: Your present's here – waiting for you.

TERRY: Oh, that's nice. What is it?

FATHER: Wait and see.

MOTHER: Where are you living now?

TERRY: Ah?

FATHER: It's well hidden.

TERRY: Rather proud of that. Sorry, Dad – what did you say?

FATHER: There's no point pulling the house to pieces, because you won't find it.

TERRY: Oh, no! I'll bet it's hidden in the same place it's always hidden.

MOTHER: It isn't hidden. Don't be ridiculous! It's in the back room. The kettle's boiling.

FATHER: Oh, yes. [FATHER *puts the tea towel down and walks across to the gas stove.*]

MOTHER: Milk? Sugar?

TERRY: Yes. [TERRY *looks round for the sugar.*]

FATHER: I'll get them.

TERRY: Must be about five hundred years old, I think. Tall! I can't see the top.

FATHER: Disappears in the clouds?

TERRY [*laughing*]: Well, no – not exactly. My bedroom's in the basement and the window cuts it off.

　　[FATHER *puts the sugar bowl down beside* TERRY's *cup.*]

FATHER [*firmly*]: Disappears in the clouds. You climb up it . . .

MOTHER: What's the matter, Terry?

TERRY: Nothing. Why? What d'you mean?

MOTHER: You're white as a sheet.

TERRY: Am I? [TERRY *puts her hands to her cheeks.*]

MOTHER: Ted – get the girl a chair.

FATHER: Here. [FATHER *pulls forward the chair, which stands back against the wall by the door.*] Come on, love.

　　[MOTHER *takes the tea towel away from* FATHER *and dries her hands on it vigorously.*]

MOTHER: Well, that's done. You go and sit down, Ted.

FATHER: Have we finished?

MOTHER: I'll do the rest. Isn't there something you wanted to watch this afternoon?

FATHER: I thought Alan was coming to see us.

MOTHER: He said he might.

TERRY: That'll be jolly.

MOTHER: If he can get away.

FATHER: There's a film on this afternoon.

MOTHER: Certainly won't be here for a while yet. If he gets here at all.

TERRY: Ellen being difficult?

MOTHER: You might as well watch some of it – while you've got the chance.

[FATHER *puts a hand on* TERRY'S *shoulder.*]

FATHER: You're sure you're all right?

TERRY: Oh, yes. I felt – suddenly – felt it was hot in here – you know?

FATHER: Does get hot.

MOTHER: It looked like you were going to pass out.

FATHER: You don't get enough to eat.

TERRY: Oh, yes – I do! I'm a pig – an absolute pig. I never stop eating.

FATHER: This girl you're living with – is she a sensible girl? More sensible than you?

TERRY: Jess? Oh, yes. She's more sensible than God.

MOTHER: Jess? What sort of name is that?

[FATHER *straightens up, turns and walks across to the refrigerator.*]

TERRY: Short for Jessica. Like Terry – short for Teresa?

MOTHER: Yes.

TERRY: I think we make a good pair.

MOTHER: How did we ever start calling you Terry?

[FATHER *puts the bottle of milk down on the table, next to* TERRY'S *cup of coffee.*]

Ted! Really! Put it in a jug.

FATHER: Terry doesn't mind.

MOTHER: I mind.

FATHER [*abruptly*]: All right You put it in a jug.

[*Silence.*]

Sit there and have a rest. [FATHER *turns and walks out of the kitchen.*] I'll leave the door open, shall I?

TERRY: Thanks, Dad.

[*Silence.*

FATHER *walks away towards the front room.* TERRY *turns and looks up at* MOTHER.]

MOTHER: How d'you think he's looking?

277

TERRY: Much the same.

MOTHER: Do you? [MOTHER *shakes her head, picks up the bottle of milk and carries it back to the refrigerator.*] You never did look at other people.

TERRY: Older. He looks older.

MOTHER: He is older.

TERRY: Tired.

MOTHER: Doesn't know what to do with himself.

TERRY [*coldly*]: Gets under your feet?

[MOTHER *shuts the refrigerator and turns to look at* TERRY.]

MOTHER: Yes. Yes, he does.

TERRY: Perhaps you should put him in a home?

MOTHER: That's what I can expect, isn't it?

TERRY: Old people's home.

MOTHER: I know.

TERRY: You won't get old.

MOTHER: Soon as your father's gone.

TERRY: I'll be dead and buried, before you get old.

MOTHER: I can just see you. Alan – Ellen – and you. 'Well, then – now he's dead, what are we going to do with her? She can't stay here with us.'

TERRY: Ellen?

MOTHER: 'I've got no room for her.'

TERRY: Me.

MOTHER: 'Much better put her away.'

TERRY [*laughing*]: Dear God!

MOTHER: 'Put her into a home.'

TERRY: Who'd have you? It's not easy – getting into one of those places. I've been trying for years. Seems like it might be the ideal place for me.

MOTHER: I'm serious.

TERRY: No, you're not. I hope you're not. It makes a very sick joke. If it's for real – eeech! I may just throw up. [TERRY *drinks some of her coffee.*]

MOTHER: Don't talk like that.

TERRY: Sorry, Mother. I'm so sorry. I may be – just a little bit sick.

MOTHER: I thought you were going to be.

TERRY: Sick?

[*Silence.*]

So did I.

MOTHER: What's the matter with you?

TERRY: Nothing.

MOTHER: Don't be silly, child. Obviously ...

TERRY [*abruptly*]: I'm perfectly all right.

MOTHER: ... something's the matter. [MOTHER *walks across the kitchen and shuts the door.*] Are you pregnant?

TERRY: No.

MOTHER: You've put on a lot of weight.

TERRY: Yes!

MOTHER: Have you seen a doctor?

TERRY: Not recently.

MOTHER: Have you got a doctor?

TERRY: No. Not at the moment. The last time I went out with him, he suggested a couple of things I didn't altogether fancy, so I haven't been out with him again.

MOTHER: Terry, why don't you stay the night? Go down and see Doctor Parker in the morning.

TERRY: If I want to see a doctor, I'll find one of my own. Thanks all the same.

MOTHER: Doctor Parker knows you better than anyone.

TERRY [*grinning*]: I wouldn't say that.

MOTHER: Go and see him.

TERRY: I don't want to see him.

MOTHER: Go and see – someone.

TERRY: I think I'll go and watch some telly. [TERRY *pushes her cup away and stands up.*]

MOTHER: If you haven't seen a doctor, how can you be certain ...

TERRY [*harshly*]: 'Cause I know about things like that. I mean, yes, it may have come as a lovely surprise to you – Alan. 'Goodness, doctor, is that mine?' I know – 'cause I have to know. Not having the luxury of a husband, I might have to do something about it. Can we have the door open again?

[*Silence.*

MOTHER *turns away and opens the door.*]

Thank you.

[*The front doorbell rings.*]

Shall I go?

MOTHER: If you don't mind. I just want to get the cake into the oven.

TERRY: Oh, no – come on! You're not going to bake a cake! Just because I've come to tea?

MOTHER: No. I'm making it for your father. I bake a cake for him every Sunday.

TERRY: Does he eat it?

[*The front doorbell rings again.*]

MOTHER: Hurry up with you, before it wakes your father.

TERRY: Yes, yes. On my way . . . [TERRY *walks out of the kitchen. She turns in the doorway and looks at her* MOTHER *for a moment.*]

MOTHER: Go along.

TERRY: That serious conversation – what would we talk about?

[TERRY *turns and walks away along the hall.* MOTHER *rests her hands on the gas stove.*]

FATHER'S VOICE: . . . answer the door?

TERRY'S VOICE: Yes, Dad.

[*The high-pitched, grating noise screams into the front of* MOTHER'S *mind. She lifts one hand to her forehead.*]

FATHER'S VOICE: . . . expected to do everything . . .

[MOTHER *lowers her head forward on to her chest. The noise throbs in her mind and drives her down towards the blackness. Suddenly, she jerks her head up and shakes it, trying to clear it.*]

MOTHER: Is that you, Alan?

ALAN'S VOICE: Yes, it is.

MOTHER: Just putting a cake in the oven.

[MOTHER *crouches down, opens the oven door, and checks the temperature. She walks across to the kitchen table. She weighs out flour and sieves it into a mixing bowl. She works efficiently, automatically. She lifts her head and looks for the baking powder.*

CUT TO *black. The screaming noise.*

CUT TO *a second mixing bowl – looking down into it, as* MOTHER *creams the cake mixture with a wooden spoon. Pull back to show* MOTHER *working the mixture and swing to show* ALAN, *standing in the kitchen doorway.*]

ALAN: The kids send their love. [ALAN *walks across to the kitchen table and looks into the bowl. He dips a finger into the cake mix and puts it into his mouth.*] Tastes good.

MOTHER: It'll taste better – cooked. [*She transfers the cake mix to a lined baking tin, carefully.*] When am I going to see them?

ALAN: When are you coming over?

MOTHER: I thought they might come with you – this afternoon.

ALAN: You knew damn' well ... [*He stops abruptly and watches his* MOTHER *silently for a moment.*] I told you.

MOTHER: I thought you might change your mind. I thought Ellen ...

ALAN: It isn't a question of changing ... [*He turns away and walks across to the sink.*] I was telling Dad – I thought I'd come over next weekend – give him a hand with the garden.

MOTHER: What did he say?

ALAN: He said he could manage it himself – perfectly well – he said.

MOTHER: He can't.

ALAN: No.

MOTHER: He's hardly looked at the garden in – oh, I don't know how long.

ALAN: It shows.

MOTHER [*abruptly*]: It's not his fault.

ALAN: I didn't say ...

MOTHER: When you get to be his age, you see if you feel like digging ...

ALAN: I don't expect I shall. I know he doesn't. That's why I said . . .

MOTHER: Shut the door, Alan. I want to talk to you.
    [*Silence.*
        ALAN *walks across the kitchen and pulls the door shut.*]

ALAN: What's it all about? What's the big secret?

MOTHER: I'll just . . . [*She picks up the baking tin.*] Hang on a minute, will you? I'll just put the cake . . . [MOTHER *carries the baking tin across to the oven and opens the oven door.*]

ALAN: Making a lot of fuss, aren't you?

MOTHER: Hmm?

ALAN: I don't expect she'll eat it, anyway.
    [MOTHER *puts the cake carefully into the oven and shuts the door.*]

MOTHER: I'm not making the cake . . .

ALAN: The weight she's putting on!

MOTHER: Yes, I know. [*She straightens up and turns to face* ALAN.]

ALAN: A glass of lemon juice – three times a day – and a piece of toast.

MOTHER: How d'you think she's looking?

ALAN: Like Dad. Do her the world of good to get out in the sunshine a bit more often.

MOTHER: She doesn't look well, does she?

ALAN: She looks like three weeks of late nights and an overdose of joie de vivre. You making a cup of tea?

MOTHER: I just made Terry a cup of coffee.

ALAN: I hope she enjoyed it.
    [MOTHER *walks back to the kitchen table and starts to clear up.*]

MOTHER: The kettle's still hot.

ALAN: If I put it on – it won't take . . . [*He walks across to the gas stove. He takes out the gas lighter.*] Have you had this thing fixed? Or is it still likely to blow the house up?

MOTHER: Hold it downwards.

ALAN: The marvels of . . .
    [*He lights the gas and shifts the kettle on to the centre of the flame.*

Silence.]

I think she's looking pretty ropey, as a matter of honest fact.

MOTHER: I thought she was going to faint – one time.

ALAN: Did you get a chance to ask her . . .

MOTHER: I think she's pregnant.

ALAN: Oh. [*He turns and looks at his* MOTHER.] That's a thought. Not particularly original . . .

MOTHER: She says – no, she isn't.

ALAN: You said . . .

MOTHER: Are you pregnant? Yes, I did.

ALAN: Was Dad here?

MOTHER: Don't be stupid!

ALAN: She said – flatly . . . [*He stops and half-laughs.*] If you'll pardon the expression!

MOTHER: I want you to talk to her.

ALAN: I was talking to her. Just now. You said – you wanted . . .

MOTHER: I want you to ask her.

ALAN: Thanks.

MOTHER: She might tell you.

ALAN: She might not!

MOTHER: More likely you – than . . .

ALAN: What're you going to do about it? Always supposing she is.

MOTHER: I don't know.

ALAN: Give it some thought. You're not often wrong, are you?

MOTHER: I'll make some sandwiches for tea.

ALAN: You want me to lead up to it? Sort of box clever?

MOTHER: What?

ALAN: Or maybe – just ask – straight out?

MOTHER: If she is . . .

ALAN: You think that's why she's here?

MOTHER: If she wants to tell me . . .

ALAN: She won't find it easy. Did she tell you she was coming?

MOTHER: Of course she didn't. Does she ever?

ALAN: Where've you hidden the teapot?

MOTHER: Use the small one, will you? It's in the cupboard.
[ALAN *opens the cupboard above the kitchen table and looks for the small teapot.*

MOTHER *goes on cutting bread and buttering it.*]

ALAN: Who else is coming?

MOTHER: Hmm?

ALAN: You're making sandwiches enough for two small armies.

MOTHER: Have the children gone out to tea?

ALAN: Yes, they have. Some sort of party. One of their friends.

MOTHER: They've got a lot of friends.

ALAN: More than we had? Yes. It's the mothers, really. Put the kids down in a garden somewhere, stuff them all full of jelly and cake – and forget about them. Makes the weekend a bit shorter.

MOTHER [*abruptly*]: If she wants to come home – Alan – tell her . . .

ALAN: You tell her.

MOTHER: I thought – perhaps . . .

ALAN: You think she's going to believe me? Oh, no. Some things . . .

MOTHER: I've always relied . . .

ALAN [*harshly*]: Yes, I know.
    [*Silence.*]
    She going to stay for supper?
    [MOTHER *shakes her head.*]
    Ask her. Make her stay. Talk to her.

MOTHER: How can I – make her stay? You know what she's like.

ALAN: Make an effort. Some sort of special – effort. Try – and talk to her. Maybe that's why she's here.

MOTHER: If she wants – to stay here – really – if she wants to – she only has to ask. Alan – tell her?
    [ALAN *shakes his head firmly.*]

ALAN: You – tell her. [*He pours himself a cup of tea.*] There's usually a reason – when she comes to see you. Maybe this time . . .

MOTHER: Her father was saying – if she wanted to spend her holiday with us this year . . .

ALAN: What did you say?

MOTHER: I said she was welcome. Of course, she is. She might find it boring.

ALAN [*laughing*]: I don't know why I bother. You know what you want? Really? You and Terry? [*He points at his* MOTHER *with his tea cup.*] One of those blokes – interpreters – you know? Stands around telling everybody what the last bloke's just said – only they couldn't understand, 'cause he was speaking . . . [*He shrugs and drinks some of his tea.*]

MOTHER: I don't know what you're talking about.

ALAN: D'you want a cup of tea?

MOTHER [*automatically*]: No, thanks. I've just had one.

ALAN: Plenty in the pot.

MOTHER: No.

ALAN: Suppose it was Michael – or little Sarah! You want little Sarah to come on holiday with you.

MOTHER: I can just see Ellen . . .

ALAN: What're you going to say? 'You're quite welcome – of course – you may find it just that bit boring.' Is that what you're going to say?

MOTHER: Terry isn't – little Sarah!

ALAN: It makes no difference.

MOTHER: Sarah – little Sarah's three – three and a half . . .

ALAN: Terry's thirty? All right!

MOTHER: She's a woman. A grown woman.

ALAN: You want her to do something – it has to sound – well, like she might enjoy herself. Like you want her.

MOTHER: If I didn't want her . . .

ALAN: You wouldn't bloody ask her! Yes, I know. It isn't enough.

MOTHER: I'm not going to beg her.

ALAN: Yes, you are.

MOTHER: Why should I?

ALAN: Because . . . [*He stops abruptly, staring at his* MOTHER, *close to her.*]

285

[*Quietly*] Who gets most out of it? Who's asking – [*violently*] who – is giving?

MOTHER [*coldly*]: I don't – Alan – I just . . . [*She breaks off abruptly and brings a hand up to her chest.*] Giving! Everything – I've given – d'you hear?

ALAN: If she thought for a moment – maybe – she was doing you a favour.

MOTHER [*harshly*]: What?

ALAN: Instead of doing what's right – what's only right! What's 'expected'!

MOTHER: You don't know . . .

ALAN [*violently*]: Yes! We know what's expected.

MOTHER: Do you? Sometimes, you wouldn't think . . .

ALAN: It doesn't necessarily make any difference. Knowing.

MOTHER: No!

ALAN: If we had any idea – if we behaved like other children – if . . .

MOTHER: Your father and I . . .

ALAN: You never see us. You never see your grandchildren.

MOTHER: I'm glad you think it's funny.

ALAN: I think it's pathetic!

[MOTHER *hears the noise, low in the background, pushing through the sound of* ALAN's *voice.*]

Why do you want to see us? In God's name! What have you got to say to us? Me? I bore you. My children – right. That's different. Yes. I grant you. But me – it's always – 'Alan, I never see you. Your father . . .' [*He puts the tea cup down on the table.*] If you never saw me again – but little Sarah . . .

MOTHER [*harshly*]: Don't call her – don't . . . [*She turns away and steps neatly, precisely, towards the sink. She grips the edge.*]

ALAN: What d'you say?

MOTHER [*mumbling*]: Nothing.

ALAN: 'Bout Sarah . . .

MOTHER [*violently*]: Of course, I want to see you – we – want to see you . . .

ALAN: We haven't got a thing to say to each other, have we? How many evenings have we sat in there – how many?

MOTHER: What does it matter? [*She turns to face* ALAN.] Talking! It isn't talking – just . . .
  [*The noise throbs in the front of her mind.*]
  It's being – not being . . .
  [*She reaches a hand out to* ALAN *and he steps forward to take hold of it.*]

ALAN: What is it? What's the matter?

MOTHER: I don't know what he thinks about, Alan. I don't know what . . .
  [*The noise begins to subside and* MOTHER *runs her fingers across her forehead.*]
  In his mind . . . I don't know . . .

ALAN: Dad?

MOTHER: He doesn't talk – sometimes – hours – and he doesn't . . . [MOTHER *shakes her head and wrings her two hands together, linking them together across her stomach, looking at* ALAN.]

ALAN: Come and see us. Spend the evening . . . [*He hesitates in mid-sentence and turns away.*]

MOTHER: He doesn't like going out now. He never did – much – now . . .

ALAN: You can't just – sit . . . [*He gestures vaguely with one hand.*]

MOTHER: We do.
  [ALAN *stands at the kitchen table.*
    Silence.]
  Go – please – go and talk to Terry.

ALAN: Yes. [*He turns his head and looks at his* MOTHER.] I'll fetch her down.

MOTHER: Tea won't be ready for a while yet.
  [*Silence.*
      ALAN *nods his head and turns away. He opens the kitchen door and walks out into the hall.*]
  Don't – er – shut the door.
  [*She stares across the kitchen at the doorway.*

CUT TO *black. Silence.*

[CUT BACK TO *the kitchen.* FATHER *is standing in the doorway, looking at* MOTHER.]

FATHER: When are we going to have tea?

MOTHER'S VOICE [*abruptly*]: When it's ready. [*She walks across to the gas stove and lights the gas.*]

FATHER: Haven't you put the kettle on?

MOTHER: It won't take a minute.

FATHER: What've you done with the kids?

MOTHER: Upstairs, I think.

FATHER: Are they?

MOTHER: Talking. Yes.

FATHER: I'll give them a shout.

MOTHER: There's plenty of time.

[*She puts the kettle on to the centre of the gas ring.*
Looking along the kitchen table, past the plate of sandwiches, out into the hall at FATHER.]

FATHER [*calling*]: Tea's made.

[MOTHER *juggles with the sandwiches, arranging them more elegantly.*]

MOTHER: Leave them alone.

FATHER: What d'you say?

MOTHER: If they want to talk. [*She walks across to the gas stove and picks up the kettle.*]

FATHER'S VOICE [*calling*]: Come on, you two!

MOTHER [*harshly*]: Leave them alone. [MOTHER *pours boiling water into a large teapot.*]

FATHER'S VOICE: What are they doing up there?

MOTHER: Talking.

[FATHER *is standing in the doorway, as* MOTHER *carries the teapot across to the sink.*]

FATHER: They can talk down here. Can't they talk down here?

MOTHER: Yes, of course.

FATHER: I don't see them that often . . .

MOTHER: Just – for a moment . . .

FATHER: What?

MOTHER: Nothing.
> [*Silence.*
>> MOTHER *turns and looks along the kitchen at* FATHER.]
Nothing.

CUT TO *the front room.*
> [MOTHER *walks briskly into the room carrying a tray.*]
FATHER'S VOICE: Your mother's poured out.
> [MOTHER *puts the tray down on the table and starts to spread teapot and sugar bowl, milk jug and slop basin in a circle around her place at the table.*]

CUT TO *the hall.*
> [MOTHER *walks out of the front room. She glances at* FATHER, *who is standing at the bottom of the stairs.*]
MOTHER: You sit down. Don't wait for them. [*She walks along the hall towards the kitchen.*]
FATHER: Don't let it get cold.
> [MOTHER *walks into the kitchen.*]

CUT TO *the front room.*
> [*Centre on the tea table, fully laid and adorned with cake and sandwiches, jelly and small cakes. Pull back as* MOTHER *reaches for her chair.*]
FATHER'S VOICE: Alan. Terry. D'you hear?
MOTHER: Ted. Come and sit down. [MOTHER *glances at the doorway as* FATHER *walks into the room.*]
FATHER: Once they get talking . . .
MOTHER: Here they come.
FATHER: About time. [FATHER *turns to walk out into the hall again.*]
MOTHER: Sit down. For goodness' sake!
> [*As* FATHER *turns and walks round the table to his chair,* TERRY *and* ALAN *walk into the room.*]
ALAN: What's all the shouting about?
MOTHER: Sit down both of you.
TERRY: Are we expecting royalty?
FATHER: What have you been talking about?

TERRY: A feast – fit for a king. [TERRY *pulls her chair back and sits down on it.*]

ALAN: Or queen – as the case may be!

TERRY: Right. You're right.

FATHER: Terry?

[MOTHER *picks up the teapot and starts to pour out.*]

MOTHER: Put your own sugar. Terry.

[TERRY *reaches forward and picks up one of the cups. She passes it to her* FATHER.]

FATHER: It's a long time since we've sat down, all of us together – and had tea.

ALAN: Yes, it is.

TERRY: Thought at least, we'd have the fatted calf.

MOTHER: We didn't know you were coming, did we?

[TERRY *picks up another cup and passes it to* ALAN.]

ALAN: Thanks.

FATHER: Feels like old times.

TERRY: Honestly, did we sit down to tea – like this? All of us. When we lived at home?

MOTHER: Yes, of course we did.

[*Close shot of* MOTHER.]

FATHER: New job, Alan? What new job?

ALAN: It's by way of being promotion, as a matter of fact.

FATHER: Promotion! That's good.

MOTHER: It's about time.

FATHER: They must be pleased with you.

ALAN: Yes, I think they are.

FATHER: That's good. Isn't it, Mother? That's very good!

MOTHER: Will it be more money?

ALAN: It would be. Really quite a lot more money.

TERRY: But you're not going to take it.

ALAN: Let's have the jam back. If you've finished with it?

[TERRY *picks up the jam dish and holds it in her hands.*]

TERRY [*carefully*]: You're not going to take the job?

ALAN: I'm thinking about it. Jam?

[TERRY *passes the jam dish to* ALAN.]

[*Politely*] Thanks.

FATHER: You're not going to take it?

ALAN: I don't know.

FATHER: They'll expect you to take it, won't they? If it's a promotion?

ALAN: What they expect and what they get – those are two very different things, Dad.

TERRY: Tara!

MOTHER: Be quiet, Terry!

FATHER: I don't understand, Alan. If it's a promotion and if it's more money, why aren't you going to take it?

TERRY: In a nutshell, Dad. That puts it in a sweet, crunchy nutshell. I can't wait to hear the answer.

MOTHER: You listen to me, young lady. You're not too old . . .

TERRY [laughing]: To go across your knee? Oh, come on! Not too old – maybe – twice again too large.

MOTHER: You can still be sent out of the room.

TERRY [harshly]: You send me out of the room, sweetie, you send me out of the house.

FATHER: Don't speak to your mother like that.

TERRY: Goodness, is this my mother? I quite forgot. I thought it was my older sister. Lawks!

MOTHER: You think you're very clever, don't you?

TERRY: Sometimes – yes. I think I get by.

ALAN [laughing]: In a fairly large crowd.

FATHER [persistently]: Why aren't you going to take the job?

ALAN: Dad, look – I haven't decided what to do. Not yet.

TERRY: It means moving away from London?

[Silence.]

ALAN: Yes, it does.

TERRY: Lock, stock and barrel! If I can refer to darling Ellen . . .

MOTHER: Is that what it means?

ALAN: Yes.

MOTHER: You mustn't think about us, Alan.

[The noise and the sound of her own words reverberates in MOTHER'S mind.]

Your father and I can manage quite well. We've got the

house. We've got enough money. The only thing that matters – really – is your career.

[*The words are distorted, almost obliterated by the noise.*]

We've tried to give you every possible chance, if this is the right thing for you to do – well, then – you must do it. That's all there is to it.

[*The noise scrambles the words.*]

After all, we're getting on now . . .

TERRY: Mrs Stephens, wife and mother . . .

[MOTHER *stares at* TERRY'S *mouth opening and shutting, hardly able to distinguish the words.*]

. . . I present you with the Jesus of Nazareth award for suffering humanity. May God bless you and all who sail . . .

[MOTHER *slaps* TERRY *hard across the face. Silence.*]

MOTHER: You have a filthy mouth.

TERRY [*gasping*]: I'd better go and wash it.

[MOTHER *presses her hand to her forehead.*]

MOTHER: How dare you speak like that in this house!

[FATHER *pushes back his chair and stands up.*]

Oh, yes. That's right!

TERRY: What – pray tell me, mother dear – is so special about this house?

[FATHER *walks round the table and* MOTHER *watches him. He walks behind* ALAN, *who half-rises to speak to him.*]

MOTHER: I might've known . . .

[FATHER *keeps as far as possible away from* MOTHER.]

TERRY: You think he is here? You think he is going to be offended, because your daughter . . .

MOTHER [*to* FATHER, *viciously*]: Coward!

TERRY: Why doesn't he strike me dead?

[MOTHER *turns her head and looks at* TERRY.]

MOTHER: I will not have you making your cheap jokes . . .

TERRY: If they're so shocking, why doesn't he reach down – pow! – and strike me dead?

[FATHER *opens the door of the room and walks out into the hall.*]

MOTHER: You think you're so important?

TERRY: I think anyone, who needs – something – I don't know – anything. God knows . . .

MOTHER: Your friends think that's funny, I suppose.

TERRY: Once and for all, the friends I've got – I haven't got any – you could butter on that piece of bread, eat and you still wouldn't choke on them.

ALAN: Terry, be quiet.

TERRY: Sweetie, I've only just got started.

MOTHER: You don't make me laugh.

TERRY: Five elephants and a camel, stuck in a phone box, wouldn't make you laugh.

MOTHER: If you can't control your tongue . . .

TERRY: You wouldn't let him take that job . . .

MOTHER: . . . I think it's better, if you don't come and see us any more.

ALAN: Mother, no.

[*The front doorbell rings.*]

MOTHER: Answer the door.

ALAN: Both of you . . .

TERRY: Truce.

[ALAN *turns and walks across to the door. He goes out.*]

MOTHER: Don't come and see us again.

TERRY: I won't.

[*Silence.*

MOTHER *begins to clear the table. Automatically,* TERRY *helps her.*]

MOTHER: I can manage.

[TERRY *puts the plate down and turns away from the table.*]

TERRY: I'll give you the address. In case you need – er – in case anything happens and you want to get in touch.

MOTHER: Thank you.

TERRY: I'm on the phone.

MOTHER: You might as well leave the number.

TERRY: I thought I would.

MOTHER: When is it due?

TERRY: Four – five months.

MOTHER: You ought to have a doctor look at you.

TERRY: I go to the hospital.

MOTHER: Hmm.

TERRY: They're very good. I'm going to have it in hospital.

MOTHER: They'll make you. If it's the first. [MOTHER *looks round at* TERRY.] It is the first?

TERRY: First I've had. Yes.

MOTHER: If you're anything like me, you'll have a rough time.

TERRY: That – seems to be the general opinion.

[*Silence.*]

MOTHER: Do you want to have it?

TERRY: Yes.

MOTHER: I didn't really – mean ... [*She shrugs.*] If you want to come and see us ...

TERRY: You meant it. Anyway I don't want to. I've only got five months – at the most – five. I have to learn a great many things. Looking after myself – living on my own ...

MOTHER: I thought you said – er – Jessica. Isn't that her name? Isn't she living with you?

TERRY: For the moment. Yes. Just – for the moment.

MOTHER: Till – the baby?

TERRY: No.

[*Silence.*]

MOTHER: Do you want me to tell your father?

TERRY: You do what you want to do.

MOTHER: No. It's up to you.

TERRY: I'd rather – rather you didn't – if that's possible?

[MOTHER *nods her head.*]

MOTHER: You'll drop us a line.

TERRY: Not – not for a while.

MOTHER: When ...

TERRY: Yes. Oh, yes. D'you have anything without tips? [TERRY *holds up a packet of tipped cigarettes.*] Smoked my last – on the train.

[*The chime of an ice-cream van tinkles outside in the street.*]

MOTHER: Oh, I must get ... [MOTHER *stops and shrugs.*] No need. No, I don't have to get any ice cream.

[TERRY *breaks the tip off one of the cigarettes and drops the tip into the grate.*]

Have you thought about – all the things? You'll need a great many ...

TERRY: I've thought. I've read. I've asked.

MOTHER: You've – told a lot of people?

TERRY: No one. It isn't something ... [TERRY *shrugs and puts the cigarette into her mouth.*] Anyway, I have to go on working. No – a few theoretical ...

MOTHER: I always thought ...

TERRY: Have you got a match?

[*Silence.*

MOTHER *walks across to the fireplace and picks up a box of matches, which is lying on the mantelpiece.*]

MOTHER: If it had teeth, it would've bitten you.

TERRY: I'm really very frightened.

MOTHER: There's no need.

[MOTHER *strikes a match and lights* TERRY'S *cigarette, as* ALAN *walks back into the room.*]

ALAN: Gordon.

TERRY: I'll go and say good-bye to Dad.

ALAN: I've just palmed Gordon off on to him.

TERRY: He'll have to get out then, won't he?

ALAN: Put it a bit more graciously.

TERRY: What is he? Some sort of tender plant?

ALAN: Aren't we all?

TERRY: I'll tell him – 'daughter-talk'.

ALAN: That'll put the fear of God ...

TERRY: What would we do without you?

ALAN: What?

TERRY: 'A very present help in time of trouble.' [TERRY *pats* ALAN'S *face gently.*]

ALAN: I suppose you know what you're talking about.

TERRY: What makes you think that?

[TERRY *walks out of the room.* ALAN *walks across and shuts the door. He turns and looks at his* MOTHER.]

295

ALAN: She is pregnant.

MOTHER: Hmm. [MOTHER *walks across to the window.*]

ALAN: Makes a difference.

MOTHER: What?

ALAN: She isn't – you know – responsible . . .

MOTHER: For what she says?

ALAN: She doesn't mean . . . [ALAN *walks towards his* MOTHER.] She never did – half the things she says . . .

MOTHER: She can be very hurtful.

ALAN: She doesn't think.

MOTHER: Stands at this window – hours at a time.

ALAN: Dad? [ALAN *stands beside his* MOTHER.]

MOTHER: Looks out. I think . . . [*She turns and looks at* ALAN.] You're going to take the job?

ALAN: I don't know.

MOTHER: You're going to take it. [MOTHER *walks past him to the table, and continues clearing the tea things.*]

ALAN [*quietly*]: I haven't made up my mind.

MOTHER: You might have told me about it.

ALAN: I haven't known myself . . .

MOTHER: 'Stead of – blurting it . . . [MOTHER *stops speaking and stares down at the table.*]

ALAN: What's the matter? [ALAN *walks across to his* MOTHER.]

MOTHER: You might have told me.
   [*Silence.*]
   Talked it over . . .

ALAN: I was going to.

MOTHER: When are you going?

ALAN: I don't know – if . . .

MOTHER: When?

ALAN: Soon.

MOTHER: Where?

ALAN [*abruptly*]: Australia.

MOTHER: How long have you known?

ALAN: Not long.

MOTHER: How long? Long enough to phone? Long enough . . .

ALAN: I didn't want to tell you on the phone.

MOTHER: Didn't want to tell me. Frightened ...

ALAN: Oh, for ...

MOTHER: ... to tell me.

ALAN: ... pity's sake!

MOTHER: Talked it over with Ellen?

ALAN: Yes.

MOTHER: She wants to go.

ALAN: Can we – look – if we're going to talk – you know – leave Ellen ...

MOTHER: Found time to talk about it – to Ellen?

ALAN: Leave her out of it!

MOTHER: Tom Rutherford. You remember Tom?

ALAN: What?

MOTHER: He went to Canada. D'you remember him?

ALAN: No. Yes. I think so. I don't honestly ...

MOTHER: You went to the same school. He was round here ...

ALAN: All right! I remember him. What about – Tom Rutherford?

MOTHER: He went to Canada. He took his mother and father with him.

ALAN: You want to go to Australia?

MOTHER: I'm not saying ...

ALAN: Just – some people – children – know how to behave?

MOTHER: Paid for everything.

ALAN: Is he married? Does he have children?

MOTHER: Yes. He's married.

ALAN: Children?

MOTHER: I don't know.

ALAN: His wife – gets on with his mother? Put them in the same room ...

MOTHER: It isn't every woman ...

ALAN: ... they won't scratch each other's eyes out?

MOTHER: The way Ellen treats me ...

ALAN: The way you treat Ellen ...

MOTHER: Since the day you got married ...

ALAN: She's tried to take me away from you.

MOTHER: It isn't funny!

ALAN: She's tried to come between . . .

MOTHER: You make a joke . . .

ALAN [*harshly*]: It is a joke!

MOTHER: She's never tried . . .

ALAN: She breaks her heart – trying!

MOTHER: She never comes to see me. She never even phones me.

ALAN: Why? Have you thought? I mean, what happens when she phones?

MOTHER: Of course, you take her side.

ALAN: What do you say to her?

MOTHER: You've always taken her side.

ALAN: She's my wife. I love her.

MOTHER: You're supposed – to . . .

    [*Silence.*]

I'm your mother.

ALAN: 'I thought you were all dead.' Like – 'Hello, stranger' – when I walk into the house. Every week the same. 'Hello, stranger.' It could be a year!

MOTHER: You don't come and see us every week. If you did – if you made the effort.

ALAN: It still wouldn't be enough. Every week – I ought to come and see you twice a week – twice a week – I ought to come and see you . . .

MOTHER: When I was a girl . . .

ALAN: If I lived at home!

MOTHER: . . . my sister . . .

ALAN: Every day. Yes, I know. Your mother despised her.

MOTHER: You don't know that.

ALAN: You – despise me. I can't do enough – I'm always wrong – yes, I know. You despise me – hanging about. Worrying what'll happen to you.

MOTHER: Don't worry . . .

ALAN: I ought to be off on my own.

MOTHER: For all the good . . .

ALAN: If I thought – honestly – half the things you say – if I thought you meant them, I would have taken the first job – five years ago – I would have gone to Newcastle and – happy – you know? – laughing. Just – let you get on with it.

MOTHER: Five years ago?

ALAN: They've been after me – wanting me to move away from London . . .

MOTHER: Newcastle?

ALAN: That was one job. There've been others.

MOTHER: Why didn't you take them? One of them?

ALAN: It's a long trip – every other Sunday – back to London.

MOTHER: No.

ALAN: I'm hardly ever home as it is – given a train journey . . .

MOTHER: You're like your father.

ALAN: . . . I'll never see – what d'you mean?

MOTHER: You've got a job you can do. It's not good enough for you, but you can do it. You've done it now for how long – six – seven years. Your father worked twenty years – the same job. He could have been promoted. He could've got better jobs – any number of them. He didn't want a better job. He knew the job. He stayed where he was. He was – frightened . . .

ALAN: Dad?

MOTHER: Change – frightened him.

ALAN: It was a job and jobs were hard to get.

MOTHER: What do you know about it?

ALAN: It was money every week – for you – for us!

MOTHER: The idea – a new job – new people round him . . .

ALAN: We didn't ask much.

MOTHER: Responsibility!

ALAN: Just – all there was – more next week – and twice as much on Sundays.

MOTHER: Your father . . .

ALAN: Stayed where he was, 'cause it was safe? Yes. 'Cause – end of the week – so much money. Enough.

MOTHER: My fault. You're blaming . . .

ALAN: No.

MOTHER: I didn't stop him.

ALAN: You didn't push.

MOTHER: You don't know.

ALAN: Change frightens you. Strangers – in the house – they worry you. Dad – and Terry – me – you can cope. Strangers . . .

MOTHER: You might as well be strangers. You and Terry – for all I see of you.

ALAN: I'm going to take this job.

MOTHER [*hesitantly*]: You said – just now, you said . . .

ALAN: I've made up my mind.

[*Silence.*]

MOTHER: It was all a lie. I've always known. You don't really – any more than Terry – you don't care what happens to us. Your father – me – you don't care. You'll go off to Australia and we'll never see you again – and that's what you want – that's what you've always wanted. Like Terry – only you haven't got the courage – you couldn't say – 'I'm the only person matters to me and you'll have to lump it.' You – let us think we could rely on you – let us think you'd always be there, if we needed help – and now – first chance you get – first real chance! – you're off – and it was all – lies.

ALAN: I should – years ago – when I got married – I should've gone – like Terry – yes – gone away and let you – at least, let you hate me – given you some reason to – hate . . .

[*Silence.*]

All I ever did was fail you – 'cause how can anyone – I mean – it isn't possible to satisfy – to be the thing – it just isn't possible!

MOTHER: You think you know – what do you know! Self – you know – all the time – all your life. The same as Terry. The same as your father – self! Looking at yourself, thinking about yourself – loving yourself. Everyone else – they can go hang – as far as you're concerned. The devil take . . . [MOTHER *breaks off and faces* ALAN.] What do you know about me? What could you – you! – just a

300

baby – eating and sleeping and keeping warm. You couldn't even do that for yourself. I did it. I fed you. I put you to bed and when you couldn't sleep . . .

ALAN: I know – yes – you were the perfect mother.

MOTHER: I looked after you.

ALAN: You didn't have any choice, did you?

MOTHER: Nights I sat with you!

ALAN: You couldn't let us starve. You had us, if you didn't want to look after us . . .

MOTHER: Don't think I haven't regretted it. Time and time again.

ALAN: Nobody said you must have children. Nobody said . . .

MOTHER: I thought – children . . .

ALAN: You thought we'd look after you – in your old age.

MOTHER: I thought – love . . .

[*Silence.*]

I thought.

ALAN: Give love, you get love – maybe.

MOTHER: Terry . . .

[*Silence.*]

ALAN: If you talk to her – listen – try to understand . . .

[*The door opens and* FATHER *walks into the room.*]

MOTHER: Does she try to understand? Does anyone?

[FATHER *puts the package down on the table.*]

FATHER: Terry's present.

MOTHER: Oh, for – oh!

ALAN: Present? What present's that? [ALAN *walks across to the table.*]

FATHER: Terry's birthday present.

ALAN: Terry's birthday was – when was it?

MOTHER [*calmly*]: Last month.

FATHER: We've been keeping it for her.

TERRY: You don't have to . . . [TERRY *walks into the room.*]

FATHER: Go on, Terry. Open it.

[TERRY *looks at her* MOTHER, *who is standing by the fireplace, staring at her.*]

Can you guess what it is?

[TERRY *shrugs and walks across to the table.*]

TERRY: No. No, I've no idea. [TERRY *reaches for the ribbon and begins to untie it. She struggles with the paper.*]

MOTHER: I don't know what all the fuss is about. It's only . . .

FATHER: Oh, now – don't tell her. [FATHER *looks round angrily at* MOTHER.] Let her guess. Can you guess?

TERRY: Haven't the faintest idea.

[TERRY *struggles with the string round the box.* FATHER *turns back and puts his hand into his pocket.*]

FATHER: Here you are. [FATHER *takes out a penknife and hands it to* TERRY.] This'll help.

MOTHER: I don't know why you wrapped it up like – like – I don't know what!

[TERRY *takes the penknife.*]

FATHER: That's the fun, isn't it?

[TERRY *cuts the string and takes the lid off the box. Wrapped in tissue paper is a silk nightdress.* TERRY *takes it out of the box.*]

Your mother chose it.

TERRY: Yes.

FATHER: You like it, don't you?

TERRY: Oh, yes. Thank you. [TERRY *kisses her father.*]

FATHER: Couldn't think what else . . .

TERRY: It's super. Really. [TERRY *turns to face her* MOTHER.] Thank you.

FATHER: Happy birthday.

[TERRY *walks across and kisses her* MOTHER.]

ALAN: I've got nothing for you.

TERRY: I'll leave an address. You can send it on to me.

FATHER: Just like a brother.

[TERRY *puts the nightdress back into the box and shuts it.*]

MOTHER: If you don't like it, you can always go and change it. I asked them.

FATHER: Of course, she likes it.

TERRY: Yes. I like it.

[*Silence.*]

Well, then.

MOTHER: You're welcome to stay to supper.

TERRY: No, thanks. Oh, I'll – er – have you got something I can write with?

ALAN: A pen, maybe?

TERRY: I'll let you have my address.

[ALAN *gives* TERRY *a pencil and she tears a piece off the wrapping paper.*]

MOTHER: No, don't do that. I might find a use for it. [MOTHER *picks up the wrapping paper and begins to fold it.*]

TERRY: You'd better see how your friend's getting on. He was looking distinctly sorry for himself a couple of minutes ago.

ALAN: Oh, for goodness' sake!

[ALAN *goes out of the room, as* TERRY *finishes writing.*]

TERRY: There you are. Put it somewhere safe, so you can be sure and lose it.

[FATHER *takes the piece of paper and reads the address.*]

FATHER: 130A, Forsyth Street. [FATHER *lifts his head and looks at* TERRY.]

TERRY [*brightly*]: You'll never find it on your own. When you come and see me, give me plenty of warning. I'll make signs in chalk all along the pavements. It's really quite – well, it was – quite a smart neighbourhood just – difficult for the stranger to find his way. They sell survival kits at all the chemists.

FATHER: We'll find it.

[MOTHER *watches* TERRY *as she walks round the room, inspecting it as if she is placing it finally in her memory.*]

TERRY: Don't speak too soon. Better men than you have perished! The white man's grave – or is it burden? Anyway, if you are white, you need a passport.

MOTHER: You should be happy enough there.

[TERRY *looks at her* MOTHER.]

TERRY: Yes, I'm very happy. Thank you.

FATHER: We'll come and see you, Terry. Soon – very soon.

TERRY: Yes, Dad. Please. [TERRY *pushes an arm through her*

FATHER's *arm*.] It would be nice. I'd like to show it off to you.

MOTHER: Have to be a weekend, I suppose?

TERRY: Unless you like to make it an evening.

FATHER: We don't get out much in the evening. Do we, Mother?

TERRY: Stuck watching the telly, I suppose?

MOTHER: We watch television. Yes.

TERRY: I've got a set.

FATHER: I think the weekend would be best.

TERRY: Suit yourself. Well, then!

> [*Silence.*]

'Bye, now.

> [TERRY *walks out of the front room with her* FATHER. MOTHER *rests her hands on the edge of the table and lowers her head.*]

FATHER'S VOICE: Keep in touch.

> [*The noise begins to push forward into the front of* MOTHER'S *mind.*]

TERRY'S VOICE: Nice to see you again.

GORDON'S VOICE: And you. Er – I hope it won't be – so long . . .

TERRY'S VOICE: I hope so, too.

> [MOTHER *forces her head up and stares across the room at the door, trying to empty her mind of the screaming noise.*]

FATHER'S VOICE [*irritably*]: D'you hear me, Terry?

TERRY'S VOICE: Yes, Dad. Yes, of course. Anyway, you – are coming to see my new flat.

> [MOTHER *opens her mouth wide.*]

FATHER'S VOICE: You write to us.

TERRY'S VOICE [*laughing*]: Oh, Dad. You know I can't write my own name – let alone . . .

ALAN'S VOICE: Terry. Look after yourself.

> [*The noise hammers its way between the words spoken outside in the hall and* MOTHER'S *ears.*]

TERRY'S VOICE: Fireproof! You know me. I'm the one – pulled up the ladder. [*Pause: coldly*] Lots of things to do, sweetie. Sorry.

[MOTHER *turns and stumbles away across to the window. She looks through the net curtains.*]

ALAN'S VOICE: The fate of nations?

TERRY'S VOICE: Something like that.

FATHER'S VOICE: Why can't you stay to supper?

TERRY'S VOICE: 'Cause there are people expecting me. Your daughter is a very popular girl.

FATHER'S VOICE: You come all this way . . .

TERRY'S VOICE: Just 'cause I love you.

[MOTHER *presses a hand against the net curtains and flattens them against the windows, as the front door opens.*]

FATHER'S VOICE: I haven't had a chance to talk to you.

TERRY'S VOICE: All the more reason to come and see me – settled in my new home.

[MOTHER *steps back from the window abruptly and turns towards the door.*]

FATHER'S VOICE [*abruptly*]: Don't rush off.

TERRY'S VOICE: There's nothing I'd like better . . .

[MOTHER *walks across the room to the door.*]

. . . Dad, you know that! A quiet evening with you. But – needs must . . .

[MOTHER *pulls the door open and steps into the doorway. She looks along the hall at* FATHER *and* TERRY *standing in the doorway.* ALAN *and* GORDON *are standing at the bottom of the stairs.*]

TERRY: 'Bye, now. [TERRY *turns away.*]

FATHER: Mind how you go.

[*Silence.*]

MOTHER: She's old enough. She can look after herself.

FATHER: I don't know what gets into her.

[MOTHER *launches herself forward suddenly, towards* GORDON *and* ALAN.]

MOTHER: Gordon! What must you think of us!

FATHER: Always rushing off somewhere.

GORDON [*embarrassed*]: Don't worry . . .

MOTHER: You haven't even had a cup of tea, have you?

FATHER: We never see her.

GORDON: Really, it doesn't matter.

ALAN: Terry was kind of a surprise. We weren't expecting her to drop in.

FATHER: Never get a chance to talk to her.

GORDON: She's changed, hasn't she? I hardly recognized her . . .

MOTHER: Oh yes.

GORDON: . . . as the same girl.

MOTHER: Terry's changed.

FATHER: Six months. [FATHER *shuts the front door.*]

GORDON: If I'd had any idea . . .

FATHER [*interrupting*]: Must be six months, since we last saw Terry.

MOTHER: More than that.

FATHER: Is it? Yes, I suppose it is.

GORDON: She's a very attractive young lady.

FATHER: I think we ought to go and see that – what is it? – new flat she's living in.

MOTHER: If there's time.

ALAN: D'you mind waiting a bit longer?

GORDON: Well, as a matter of fact, old son . . .

FATHER: You've got the address?

ALAN: Just have a word . . .

GORDON: . . . wouldn't it be better . . .

FATHER [*fiercely*]: You have got the address? She seemed to want us to go.

MOTHER: Let me make you a cup of tea, Gordon?

GORDON: Oh, no. Really, Mrs Stephens.

MOTHER: I hate to think . . .

ALAN: I'll talk to Dad . . .

FATHER: I'd like to see where she's living.

ALAN: Five minutes.

MOTHER [*laughing*]: Not even a cup of tea.

FATHER: I want to go, anyway.

MOTHER [*abruptly*]: Yes, Ted.
    [*Silence.*]

FATHER: Don't you?

MOTHER: If there's time.

ALAN: Dad ...

GORDON: I'll give you a call later.

ALAN: Can I talk to you, Dad?

FATHER: Who's the girl – what did Terry say ...

MOTHER: Jessica.

GORDON: When you're at home.

ALAN: Honestly, Gordon, if I'd any idea!

GORDON [grinning]: Not to worry.

FATHER: Do you know her?

MOTHER: No, I don't.

ALAN: Dad.

FATHER: Who is she? What sort of girl is she? What does she do?

GORDON: I'll slip away?

FATHER: How did Terry meet her? How does Terry come to be sharing ... [FATHER breaks off abruptly and shakes his head.]

ALAN: I'm sorry.

FATHER: We don't know any of her friends. [FATHER walks through the group, away, along the hall.]

GORDON: Forget it.

ALAN: Mum.

MOTHER: I'll look after Gordon.

GORDON: There's no need.

ALAN: Dad.

[ALAN follows his FATHER towards the back room. MOTHER watches him, as he walks away.]

FATHER'S VOICE: Treats this house like a hotel. Coming and going – just as she pleases.

ALAN'S VOICE: Dad.

[Close shot of MOTHER.]

FATHER'S VOICE: Your mother's right.

[Silence.]

CUT TO the front room.

[Close shot of MOTHER'S fingers, pulling and twisting at a thread on the arm of the chair she is sitting in. The sound *of a match striking. Lift quickly to* MOTHER'S *face, as she looks up.*

Cut to GORDON, *who is lighting a cigarette, sitting in an armchair, opposite* MOTHER.]

MOTHER: Oh. Er . . .

[*Cut to* MOTHER, *as she lets go of the thread and tries to pull herself out of the dark trance she has been in.*]

Whatever – er . . . [MOTHER *stands up and looks at the clock on the mantelpiece.*]

[*Mumbling*] I'd no idea . . .

GORDON: I'm afraid I called at an inconvenient moment.

MOTHER [*abruptly*]: What? No. Of course not. Wait there a moment. I'll . . . [MOTHER *pushes back from the mantelpiece and turns.*] I'll tell Alan.

GORDON: I'd rather – you know – just leave it. I can always talk to him later.

MOTHER: Alan would be furious – no – of course, you can't – I'll . . . [MOTHER *walks across to the door.*]

[*Hesitantly*] How long – er –

GORDON: I'm sorry, Mrs Stephens. What . . .

MOTHER [*abruptly*]: Nothing. [MOTHER *walks out into the hall, and pulls the door shut behind her. She brings her hand up to the sides of her head and presses them hard against her temples. She rocks very slightly on the balls of her feet and closes her eyes. Suddenly, she loses her balance and rocks forward against the banisters, clutching to steady herself. She turns slowly and walks to the door of the back room. She opens the door.*] Alan, poor Gordon's still waiting . . . [*She stops speaking abruptly, looks at* ALAN *and then looks past him at* FATHER.]

ALAN: Yes, I know. I'm just coming.

[MOTHER *steps into the doorway and stops* ALAN *getting out of the room.*]

MOTHER [*quietly*]: What've you been talking about?

ALAN: Hey, no! Look – I've kept Gordon . . .

MOTHER: What have you been saying to your father?

ALAN: Please! Mum.

MOTHER: Look at him.

[*Silence.*]

ALAN: I asked him, should I take the job?

FATHER: I think he should. Don't you, Mother?

MOTHER: I think he should make up his own mind.

ALAN: I have. I'm taking the job. 'Off to Tipperary in the morning . . .' [ALAN *reaches out to take hold of his* MOTHER'S *shoulder and move her out of the doorway*.] Now – if you'll just get out of the way!

MOTHER: I want to know what's been going on – between you and your father.

FATHER: Is Gordon still here, mother? Did you say he was still here?

MOTHER: Yes, I did.

ALAN: We talked about Terry – just a bit about Terry. That's all.

[FATHER *walks towards the door*.]

FATHER: He must be wondering what's happening. Kept hanging about . . .

ALAN: He's got a family of his own.

MOTHER: What do you know about Terry?

FATHER: Something I want to show him.

ALAN: That's the great thing, isn't it?

FATHER: Out of the way, you two! Blocking the traffic!

ALAN: Everyone's got one. Everyone understands – about families.

FATHER [*calling*]: Gordon.

[FATHER *walks briskly between* MOTHER *and* ALAN, *out of the room.* ALAN *starts to follow him and* MOTHER *stops him*.]

MOTHER: I want to talk to you.

FATHER'S VOICE: Something I want to show you.

ALAN: Not just at the moment.

MOTHER: Yes!

ALAN: And leave Gordon . . .

MOTHER: He's waited an hour already . . .

ALAN: Quite long enough.

MOTHER: He can wait five minutes more.

ALAN: You want to know what we talked about – ask Dad. Now . . . [ALAN *tries again to get out of the room*.]

MOTHER: What did you say to make your father – why – was he so upset?

ALAN: Was he? I didn't notice. Just like always, I thought. Excuse me?

MOTHER: Why can't you leave him alone?

ALAN [*laughing*]: I didn't touch him.

MOTHER: Don't take it out on him.

ALAN: What?

MOTHER: I don't know. Something. Just – don't use him – take it out on him – because you're frightened of Ellen.

ALAN: I'm – what? Frightened – when did you get hold of that . . .

MOTHER: You want to hurt someone . . .

ALAN: You – come top of the list. Not him – believe me! If I'm ever looking round for someone . . . [ALAN *stops and stares at his* MOTHER.] Like the first time I thought – maybe, if she was dead, I wouldn't have all these problems – I could just feel sorry for her.

[*Silence.*]

CUT TO *the hall.*

[*Looking between* ALAN *and* GORDON *at* MOTHER. *The noise begins to push forward in* MOTHER'S *mind.*]

MOTHER: I'm sorry we've wasted so much of your time.

GORDON: No. Oh, no.

[*The noise claws at her mind.*]

MOTHER: It isn't often we see Alan, these days.

GORDON: I didn't mean . . .

ALAN: About six?

GORDON: Mrs Stephens, please . . .

MOTHER: It's perfectly all right, Gordon. I quite understand. [MOTHER *presses her hands hard against her thighs, to keep from clutching the sides of her head.*]

GORDON: My wife will be expecting me back for tea.

MOTHER: Ellen will be wondering where you've got to, Alan.

ALAN: Tomorrow evening then?

GORDON: Can you make it seven?

[MOTHER *walks carefully towards the front room.*]
Six is a bit early.

ALAN'S VOICE: Seven it is!

[MOTHER *stands in the doorway of the front room.*
FATHER *is kneeling in front of the sideboard.*]

FATHER: I was sure – absolutely sure . . .

[*The sound of the front door being opened.*]

MOTHER: What're you looking for?

[*The screaming retreats to the back of* MOTHER'S *mind,
deepens and throbs, insistently.*]

FATHER: There's a photograph I want to show to
Gordon.

MOTHER: He's gone.

FATHER: Has he? Oh, well.

MOTHER: His wife's expecting him home for tea.

FATHER: Oh, yes. He did say – something . . . [FATHER
looks at the photographs on the floor in front of him.]

MOTHER: What photograph is it?

FATHER: The school team. D'you remember? It was
taken their last year. Gordon was captain and Alan
centre forward.

MOTHER: You won't find it there, will you?

FATHER: I thought I saw it.

MOTHER: Not with those photographs. They're as old as the
hills.

[FATHER *reaches down and rests his hand on the floor.
He pushes on it and lifts himself up on to his feet again,
slowly.*]

FATHER: Funny, because . . .

[FATHER *shakes his head.*]
    Silence.]

[*Suddenly*] He's gone?

MOTHER: He couldn't wait any longer.

FATHER: He's a nice boy, Gordon.

[*The sound of a car being started, outside the house.*]
I like him.

MOTHER: What were you and Alan talking about?

FATHER: Whether or not he should take this new job he's

been offered. [FATHER *walks across to the window and looks at the road outside.*]

MOTHER: That's all?

FATHER: I don't know why, exactly – but, he wanted to ask me, should he take it?

MOTHER: You were talking a long time.

[FATHER *waves and nods, as the car drives away.*]

FATHER: They were a nice lot of boys. I wish I could have found that photograph.

[*The sound in* MOTHER'S *mind drifts away into silence.*]

MOTHER: I thought you were a bit upset.

FATHER: Me? Upset? When?

MOTHER: When I walked in. I wondered what Alan could've said – to upset you?

FATHER: I wasn't upset. [FATHER *turns and stands with his back to the window.*]

MOTHER: I thought you looked upset.

[*The sound of the front door being shut.*]

FATHER [*calling*]: Alan?

ALAN'S VOICE: Just coming, Dad.

MOTHER: If he said something . . .

FATHER [*abruptly*]: He didn't.

[*Push in towards* MOTHER.]

ALAN [*brightly*]: You could go this summer.

MOTHER: Don't put ideas into his head.

FATHER: As a matter of fact, only last summer [*he walks across to the window*] I was walking in the park – and the trees . . .

MOTHER: Leave him alone!

FATHER: The trees looked so beautiful.

ALAN: You could stay there, couldn't you? There must be a hotel – of sorts?

FATHER: I went for a walk . . .

ALAN: Come on! When was the last time you two had a proper holiday?

FATHER: I was on my own . . .

MOTHER: When you were children. [MOTHER *shuts the double doors of the sideboard.*]

FATHER: ... walking on my own – and I thought ...
[FATHER *rests a hand on the window sill.*]

ALAN: It's good and time you had another.

FATHER: I thought then – it isn't a bit like it used to be –
at home . . . [FATHER *shakes his head and smiles to
himself.*]

ALAN: You know what I think?

FATHER: You could walk a mile and never meet another
soul.

ALAN: You and Mum – get yourselves packed – and soon
as the sun shines – off you go! That's what I think.

MOTHER: God knows there's little enough to keep us
here.

FATHER: Something about the sun – in the trees – over my
head, it made me think – breaking and moving – smiling –
like home, I thought. Why don't I go back and see the
old place?

ALAN: People do. Lots of people.

MOTHER: When they get to your father's age?

ALAN: Yes, that's right.

MOTHER: It's very likely changed. It's a long time.

ALAN: Go and see.

MOTHER: Your father won't know anybody living there
now.

ALAN: Does that matter?

MOTHER: And nobody – will know him. [MOTHER *takes the
photograph away from* ALAN.]

FATHER: I certainly would like to see the old place. Once –
before . . .
    [MOTHER *looks angrily at* ALAN.]

MOTHER: Think! Why don't you think? [MOTHER *turns
away and pulls one of the sideboard doors open.*]

FATHER: No. Don't put it away.
    [MOTHER *straightens up and turns to face* FATHER, *as
    he walks across the room towards her.*]
I'd like to have another look at it.

MOTHER: You never stop looking at it.
    [FATHER *takes the photograph.*]

313

MOTHER: I hope Ellen will find time, before you all leave for Australia – to bring the children over to see us?

ALAN: I'm sure she will.

MOTHER: I would like to see my grandchildren once more, before . . .

ALAN: She would have come with me this afternoon, and brought the kids . . .

FATHER [*suddenly*]: I know where it is. Yes. [FATHER *edges between* ALAN *and* MOTHER.] Yes, of course!

ALAN: Look, Dad – don't run away.

FATHER: What an idiot I am!

ALAN: I'll have to go in a couple of minutes.

FATHER: I've thought now. I know.

[FATHER *walks out into the hall and* ALAN *starts forward to follow him.*]

MOTHER: Alan. No.

ALAN: Dad.

MOTHER: Leave him alone.

[ALAN *walks out into the hall.*]

Leave . . .

[MOTHER *breaks off and turns her back to the door.*

CUT TO *black. Silence.*

CUT TO *the front room again.* MOTHER *is now standing by the window.*]

ALAN'S VOICE: I tried to talk about the job, he talked about Terry. I asked him to help me. . . .

[MOTHER *turns slowly and looks across the room at* ALAN, *who is crouched in front of the fire, putting more coal on to it.*]

. . . he talked about Terry. Anything – everything I said . . . [ALAN *turns his head and looks up at his* MOTHER.]

MOTHER: You're jealous of Terry.

ALAN: Yes. [ALAN *stands up and dusts coal dust off his hands.*]

MOTHER: What do you mean – help you? How can he help you?

ALAN: He could – I mean, we don't talk to each other. Right! But, just this once . . . [ALAN *walks across to his*

MOTHER.] This is important. This once – something about me – you know? – it's important!

MOTHER: You don't have to shout at me.

ALAN: He could tell me – really – what he wants me to do. Stay – or go.

MOTHER: You're going.

ALAN: One way or the other.

MOTHER: You've made up your mind.

ALAN [*abruptly*]: No, I haven't made up my mind.

MOTHER: You said . . .

ALAN: I was angry. You . . . [ALAN *stops speaking for a moment and then, clumsily, he puts an arm round his* MOTHER'S *shoulders.*] Sometimes – most times! – you make me angry. [*Grinning*] Then, I say things . . .

MOTHER: How can you be jealous of Terry?

ALAN: . . . I don't mean.

MOTHER: I don't understand that.

ALAN: Love.

MOTHER: I wouldn't have her – [*violently*] I don't want her in the house.

ALAN: Oh, now, come on!

MOTHER: If I had my way, I'd tell her . . .

ALAN: How many times . . .

MOTHER: 'Don't come and see us again. Ever – again!'

ALAN: If I had a shilling . . .

[MOTHER *moves away from* ALAN *and his arm drops to his side.*]

MOTHER: If it wasn't for your father . . .

ALAN: Half my life!

MOTHER: How can you be jealous?

ALAN: You think about Terry. Worry about her . . .

MOTHER: I wouldn't open the door . . .

ALAN: If she came back now – right now – came back and asked you . . .

MOTHER [*harshly*]: No!

ALAN: Yes.

MOTHER: You saw the way she behaved. You heard the things . . .

315

ALAN: What possible difference . . .

MOTHER: Why does she come and see us?

ALAN: Love.

MOTHER: If she has to behave . . . [MOTHER *stops speaking and stares silently at* ALAN.] Terry?

ALAN: It surely isn't hate!

MOTHER: She wouldn't say – she couldn't . . .

ALAN: You can. Every time you speak to Terry . . .

MOTHER: What?

ALAN: You hurt her.

MOTHER: Oh.

ALAN: Sometimes – cut her in two.

MOTHER: Oh, yes!

ALAN: How long is it since you said – oh, I don't know – 'Thank you for coming to see us'?

MOTHER: My fault. Everything – of course – it's all my fault.

ALAN: No.

MOTHER [*viciously*]: How long is it since she said – how long . . . [MOTHER *shakes her head and turns away.*]

ALAN: Is it so difficult – really? Couldn't you . . .

MOTHER: Why should I?

ALAN: 'Cause she's had about all – don't you think – more – than she can take.

MOTHER: What about me?

ALAN: She doesn't know how to say – how – to ask . . .

MOTHER: The only time I asked – once – and that was something [*she looks at* ALAN] important – I thought – at the time – it was important – and I asked . . .
   [*Silence.*]
I didn't . . . [MOTHER *rests her hands on the mantelpiece.*] I was Terry's age – younger – funny – I always think she's much younger than she is. He didn't listen – didn't even hear . . .

ALAN: You can't blame Terry . . .

MOTHER: Thirty. She's really quite old – old enough, I said . . .

ALAN: It isn't her fault.

MOTHER: I was right. She is. [MOTHER *pushes away from the mantelpiece.*] I don't blame Terry. Of course it isn't her fault. She wasn't even born.

ALAN: You could try and tell her.

MOTHER: You'll like it in Australia ... [MOTHER *turns to face* ALAN.] You won't have all these – what was it you said – problems? You can forget about us. Your father, Terry – me – forget all about us – and get on – thinking about yourself!

ALAN: Suddenly, you're a happy family – pow! – like Terry says – and it's me – on the outside. Me – running away – leaving you?

MOTHER: Yes.

ALAN: Why – all this time – all these years! – and now – off. Why?

MOTHER: Either you go – or she goes.

ALAN: Ellen?

MOTHER: She's put up with us ...

ALAN: Nothing to do with me – just – Ellen says – and I jump?

MOTHER: She hates us. Doesn't she hate us?

ALAN: No, she doesn't. I could understand – if she did – but, no – she doesn't hate you. Not even you! Dad – she's rather fond of.

MOTHER [*abruptly*]: You can't leave me – Alan – you can't just ...

[MOTHER *stops and* ALAN *walks across the room, towards her.*]

ALAN: What is it?

MOTHER: Alone – with him. You can't – it isn't fair – what ...

[ALAN *takes hold of his* MOTHER *by the arms.*]

I mean – what am I going to do?

ALAN: What's happened?

MOTHER: Hmm?

ALAN: To make you feel – I don't know – whatever it is ...

MOTHER: You're going away.

ALAN: Oh, yes. But you always say ...

MOTHER: You know – surely! – the things I say . . .

ALAN: You don't mean them. Yes, I know. All the same . . .

MOTHER: Terry's going away.

ALAN: Honestly, you think she won't be back? Couple of weeks – couple of months – she'll be back.

MOTHER: She was saying good-bye. Today. She came to say good-bye – to him. That's all. She won't come back.

ALAN: If you could ask her . . .

MOTHER [*harshly*]: And the sun – come up at night. If I could ask her! I can't.

ALAN: If you could try.

MOTHER: Ask Ellen to let you stay. Tell her you can't – go to Australia.

[*Silence.*]

ALAN: It isn't Ellen.

MOTHER: No, of course! You think I don't know that. You [*she pulls away from* ALAN] want to get away. As far away – oh, yes!

ALAN: If that's what you want to think.

[*The noise scrapes at the darkness in* MOTHER'S *mind.*]

MOTHER: I know! You've done your bit. 'All these years' – isn't that what you said? You've done nothing! 'Poor old things, I'll look in and cheer them up. I can't really spare the time . . .'

ALAN: Honestly, you think . . .

MOTHER [*harshly*]: Three hours every week – more or less. D'you write it in your diary? 'Call in at home. Talk to Mum and Dad.'

ALAN: No, I don't write . . .

MOTHER: If you walked in – once – with a smile – pleased to see us. As if you wanted to come here – wanted to talk to your father – talk . . . [MOTHER *rubs her hand across her mouth.*]

ALAN: There's no point . . .

MOTHER: Duty! Like some kind of – what? – prison visitor?

318

And now, you're going away. You won't have to think –
plan! Now, your time's your own.

ALAN: If you won't even listen . . .

MOTHER: Now – when I need you – now!

> [*The jagged edge of noise cuts* MOTHER'S *thoughts in
> pieces.*]

You could help me – now – really – help.

ALAN: How can I help you?

MOTHER: You think you know what it's like – living –
just living – here? Days – and he doesn't talk to me. I
don't think – more than half the time – he doesn't know
what day – what year – what . . . [MOTHER *brings a hand
up to the side of her head.*]

ALAN: He's always been – well – vague?

MOTHER: Things he didn't want to hear, he didn't hear
them! Things he didn't want to know . . . [MOTHER
shakes her head.]

ALAN: Times I've talked to him . . .

MOTHER: It's not the same. Now, it's not . . .

ALAN: How d'you mean? Not the same. I don't understand.

MOTHER: When he was working, the days – each day was
different – things that happened – things he had to do – I
mean, just the deliveries – Monday, South-west – Tues-
day, North – Wednesday . . .

> [MOTHER *flicks her hand away from her head, when she
> notices* ALAN *watching her carefully.*]

He had something he could hold on to. Thursday, he
always had lunch with Barry Hulton. Now . . .

ALAN: You make him sound . . . [ALAN *hesitates and then
shrugs.*]

MOTHER: Days are all the same. He can't tell one from
another – just – night and he sleeps – day – and he waits
for the night.

ALAN: It's not that bad. Surely it can't be.

MOTHER: You don't know. You're not here.

ALAN: I talk to him.

MOTHER [*quietly*]: Oh.

ALAN: All right. He doesn't listen, any more than usual –
still . . .

MOTHER [*violently*]: Oh!
[*Silence.*]
    MOTHER *looks directly at* ALAN.]

ALAN [*hesitantly*]: Is it your head? Is it – bad? What is it?

MOTHER: Nothing. No. [MOTHER *walks across to the table which still hasn't been cleared.*] It's nothing. I must get on.

ALAN: You make him sound – d'you know? – perhaps he's – mad.

MOTHER: He isn't mad.

ALAN: The way you talk about him . . .

MOTHER: He's old and he's tired. He doesn't think. [*Abruptly*] Why should he? He's got nothing to think about. Give me a hand with this, will you?

ALAN: No. [ALAN *walks across to the table and stands beside his* MOTHER.]

MOTHER: Do you see much of Gordon these days?

ALAN: No, I don't.

MOTHER: I never liked him. When he was quite little, I thought – I can remember thinking . . .

ALAN: What's it all about?

MOTHER: Things he did, always told you about them.

ALAN: You going to tell me?

MOTHER: Always made himself . . . [MOTHER *stops, turns her head and looks at* ALAN.] What good would it do? Telling you. You're going away. [MOTHER *turns and starts clearing the table.*] Anyway, you don't want to know.

ALAN: It'll be some time before I go.

MOTHER: Weeks. Yes, I know. It isn't weeks. Maybe years. If you can't see now, you won't see . . .

ALAN: What? See what! I don't know – honestly – I don't know what you're talking about.

MOTHER: Come back in a couple of years.

ALAN: You want to say something to me. Look, you want me to do . . .

MOTHER [*harshly*]: I want you here!

320

[MOTHER *bangs the jam dish down hard on the table and then stares at it, amazed at the sudden violence.*

Silence.

MOTHER *then looks up, suddenly, as she realizes the noise has gone.*]

ALAN: He doesn't want me. I can't ... [ALAN *touches his forehead very lightly with his finger-tips.*] You know I can't help – with him – it's always been Terry – I was talking to him ...

[*Silence.*

MOTHER *pulls herself out of her maze of discovery, violence and relief. She looks at* ALAN.]

He doesn't want me. You – and Terry – he wouldn't let anyone else – look after him. You know he wouldn't.

MOTHER: Someone – to look after – me? [MOTHER *shrugs, embarrassed, turns and starts to clear the table yet again.*]

ALAN: If you could – if only – Terry ...

MOTHER: The perfect answer. Hmm. Come home to have her baby. Another grandchild – here – in my own house. Night and day. She'd have to go out to work. Terry. She's not the girl to sit and ... [MOTHER *gathers the plates into a pile.*] Heaven-sent. You might almost call it. A baby I could look after ...

[MOTHER *picks up the plate of small cakes and offers it to* ALAN. *He shakes his head.*]

They'll only go to waste.

ALAN: No, thanks.

MOTHER: No quarrels with Ellen. 'Why can't she leave the child alone? If she gives Michael one more sweet ... If little Sarah's sick tonight ...' [MOTHER *takes one of the cakes off the plate and bites into it, as she walks across to the fireplace.*] Was she sick? Was she ever sick, after she'd been here to tea? Honestly? You're always saying – 'honestly' – was she?

ALAN: No, she wasn't.

MOTHER: I've brought up children of my own ...

ALAN: There was no talking to her the next day. No telling her – anything.

MOTHER: You worry too much.

ALAN: 'Nanna lets me. Nanna said I could.'

MOTHER: What?

ALAN: Stay up half the night. Change her pyjamas three times, because she doesn't like the colour.

MOTHER: Little madam!

ALAN: Tell Ellen, she doesn't like her. She doesn't want to live with her.

MOTHER: She's only a baby.

ALAN: She'd rather live with Nanna.

MOTHER: She doesn't know what she's saying.

ALAN: Nanna lets her do anything at all she wants to do.

MOTHER: Well, of course, it's nothing to do with me – but I think Ellen's too strict with the child. It does no harm . . .

ALAN: Ellen is some kind of fairy godmother, in Technicolor and Cinemascope – compared with the way you brought us up. [ALAN *takes the plate out of his* MOTHER'S *hand.*] If you could remember – I mean, really – the way I can remember – you wouldn't want me here, any more than . . . [ALAN *puts the plate down on the table and leaves the sentence unfinished.*] I'll go and say good-bye to Dad.

MOTHER: Any more than you want to be here. No, well, that's clear enough.

ALAN: Think of it like this . . . [ALAN *glances round at his* MOTHER.] You're not just losing a daughter. You're losing a son as well.

MOTHER: How did I bring you up? How was it – different?

ALAN: You didn't make special tea for me – hmm? Jellies and cakes, biscuits and ice cream? You didn't push packets of sweets into my sticky hands.

[MOTHER *laughs.*]

You didn't fetch and carry for me. You didn't put your arms round me. You didn't tell me – you never told me I was . . . [ALAN *half-laughs and stops for a moment.*] Poor old Alan. Nobody loves him! It's pathetic, isn't it?

MOTHER: Told you – what? I never told you . . .

ALAN: You never stop telling little Sarah how pretty she is.

MOTHER: You were a boy. You can't tell a boy – what? – pretty!

ALAN: There must be something else. Something you can tell a boy. So he doesn't grow up – sort of surprised, if anyone even notices him.

MOTHER: I loved you. I told you . . .

ALAN: Did you?

MOTHER: How could you say – how – Alan – could you want me to be dead?

[Silence.]

ALAN: Nothing particularly special about that. I want everyone to be dead – one time or another. It's my favourite solution. If only – he, she or it – was dead. [ALAN walks away, round the table, leaving his MOTHER.] The tragedy – concern – the bravery in time of trouble. The spot-light and the centre stage. Deep inside – relief – 'cause all the problems, all the bitterness – and beastliness – hard words and hatred – gone away.

MOTHER: Me?

ALAN: When I was eight – or nine.

[The noise throbs back into MOTHER'S mind.]

MOTHER: Don't go, Alan – please.

ALAN: I'm sorry, Mum. I wouldn't – only I've got to get the work done. If I start the week . . .

MOTHER [harshly]: Australia! Don't go . . . [MOTHER half-lifts a hand and gestures towards ALAN.]

ALAN: I don't want to.

[Silence.]

I don't have a lot of choice.

MOTHER: You said – you could make up your own mind.

ALAN: Yes.

MOTHER [viciously]: All right. Yes! Take the job! Go to Australia. I hope I never see any of you again.

[Silence.

ALAN turns and walks across to the door. He pulls it open, hesitates and glances back at his MOTHER.]

ALAN: I'll just say good-bye. I won't . . .

MOTHER: Bloody children!

> [ALAN *turns and walks out into the hall.*
>
> *The noise splits* MOTHER'S *mind in half and she lurches forward.*]

[*Calling*] Alan.

> [*The sound stops abruptly and she straightens up, as* ALAN *pushes the door open and looks back into the room.*]

[*Quietly*] There's a programme your father wants to see. On the television. If he stays up there all night . . .

ALAN: I'll tell him.

> [ALAN *turns and walks out of the doorway again.*
>
> *The high-pitched noise at the limit of endurance.*

CUT TO *black.*

CUT TO *the front room again.*

> *Looking across the room at* MOTHER, *now standing with her face to the wall, leaning forward, her arms limp at her side.*
>
> *The sound of the doorbell ringing.*
>
> *Slowly,* MOTHER *pushes herself away from the wall and turns. Her mind is clear and silent. She listens for the bell again and when it rings, walks firmly out of the room to the front door.*
>
> *She opens it and steps back, as* MRS HAYTER *walks into the hall.*]

MRS HAYTER: You've had a busy afternoon.

MOTHER: Oh, yes.

MRS HAYTER: Did I see Terry? I thought I saw her.

MOTHER: Yes, you did.

MRS HAYTER: You weren't expecting her, were you?

MOTHER: No.

MRS HAYTER: How is she? I thought she might look in and say hello.

MOTHER: She was in rather a hurry.

MRS HAYTER: She always is. Alan still here?

MOTHER: He's talking to his father.

MRS HAYTER: Must've seemed a bit strange. All of you – in the same house at the same time.

MOTHER: Well, yes . . .

MRS HAYTER: It's been a long time, hasn't it? Alan staying on, is he?

MOTHER: No, no. He should've gone long ago. I don't know what's keeping him.

MRS HAYTER: I thought perhaps – Dick's going out this evening – and I thought, if you're doing nothing and Mr Stephens is watching television . . .

MOTHER: That's very kind of you.

MRS HAYTER: For an hour. Over a cup of coffee.

MOTHER: I haven't cleared the tea things away, yet.

MRS HAYTER: Gets a bit lonely, with Dick out for the night. I thought – you know? – if you felt like a bit of a gossip?

[ALAN *starts to walk down the stairs towards his* MOTHER *and* MRS HAYTER.]

MOTHER: Are you off then, Alan?

ALAN: 'Fraid so. Hello, Mrs Hayter.

MRS HAYTER: Hello, Alan. How are you?

ALAN: I'm fine.

MRS HAYTER: Those lovely kiddies of yours. How are they?

ALAN: Flourishing.

MRS HAYTER: When are we going to see them again? It's weeks since . . .

ALAN: Next Sunday, very likely.

MRS HAYTER: That's good. They grow so quickly. You can hardly recognize them – one week to the next.

MOTHER: Is your father coming down?

ALAN: Not just yet.

MOTHER: What's he doing?

ALAN: Oh – well, he's still looking for that photograph. At least, I think . . .

MOTHER: Once he gets an idea into his head!

MRS HAYTER: Your mother misses the children, Alan.

ALAN: Yes.

MOTHER: Phone us – during the week?

ALAN: Yes, I will.

MRS HAYTER: She won't say it herself.

ALAN: See you on Sunday.

[MOTHER *nods her head, but she doesn't speak.*]

MRS HAYTER: It isn't much to ask, is it?

ALAN: Er – no, it isn't. Goodbye, Mrs Hayter. [ALAN *opens the door and steps into the doorway.*]

MOTHER [*abruptly*]: Mind how you go.

ALAN: I will.

[MOTHER *follows* ALAN *to the doorway and stands, watching him.*]

MOTHER: Mind how you go.

MRS HAYTER: They won't respect you, letting them walk all over you.

[*The sound of a car starting, in front of the house.*]

Stand up to them. Show them – just because you're their mother doesn't mean they can treat you like dirt. Tell them!

[MOTHER *turns to face* MRS HAYTER.]

MOTHER: Well, now – I really must get on. All the tea things to clear ... [MOTHER *doesn't shut the door. She stands in the doorway leaving ample room for* MRS HAYTER *to walk out of the house.*]

MRS HAYTER: If you feel like coming over – a bit later – you're always welcome. You know that, don't you?

MOTHER: Hmm. Thank you. Yes.

MRS HAYTER: Anyway, I'll be glad of the company.

MOTHER: If there's time.

[MRS HAYTER *walks through the doorway.*]

MRS HAYTER: You work too hard. Give yourself a bit of a rest. [MRS HAYTER *walks away towards her own house.*] 'Bye.

[MOTHER *shuts the door and turns away. She walks to the bottom of the stairs. She rests a hand against the banisters.*]

MOTHER [*calling*]: What are you doing up there?

[*Silence.*]

Ted! [MOTHER *walks away from the stairs, along the hall, and clasps her hands in front of her stomach. She turns violently.*] Ted – for goodness' sake!

CUT TO *the main bedroom.*

    [FATHER *is standing by the window, looking down into the street outside the house.*]

MOTHER'S VOICE: Still looking for that photograph.

    [FATHER *turns his head.*]

FATHER: I can't think where it's got to.

    [*Cut to* MOTHER, *who is standing in the doorway of the bedroom.*]

MOTHER: Let's have a bit of light on the subject.

    [FATHER *and* MOTHER *stand at the extremities of the bedroom, staring at each other, across the beds.*]

It's got quite dark. [MOTHER *switches on the centre light.*]

FATHER: It doesn't matter now.

MOTHER: I'll help you look for it.

FATHER: I don't know where to start. He doesn't look well, does he? Alan.

MOTHER: Well enough. Have you looked in these drawers?

FATHER: She leads him a bit of a dance, doesn't she?

MOTHER: She wants him to take that job.

FATHER: He's going to take it. He said so.

    [MOTHER *pulls one of the drawers open.*]

I've looked there. It isn't . . . [FATHER *shrugs and turns back to look out of the window again.*] I don't know where it is. Anyway, it doesn't matter now.

MOTHER: You wanted to look at it.

FATHER: I wanted to show it to Gordon.

    [*Silence.*]

If he does take the job – if he does go to Australia – I shan't see him gain.

MOTHER: Nonsense! You know, there's a case in the attic.

FATHER [*harshly*]: It doesn't matter!

    [*Silence.*]

[*Blurred*] . . . did she want? Alan says . . . won't come and see us . . . something Terry wanted to say. She isn't happy. When she said 'Good-bye' . . . She should come and see us.

MOTHER: Come on. You've been up here most of the evening already. [MOTHER *puts an arm through his and holds on tight.*]

FATHER: I was looking for that photograph.

MOTHER: You can look tomorrow.

FATHER: I'd like to find it.

MOTHER: We'll both look – tomorrow.

FATHER: I can give it to Alan. He can show it to Gordon.

MOTHER: Yes.

FATHER: It was talking to Gordon, I remembered I still had it.

MOTHER: Did you have a nice talk with Gordon?

FATHER: Yes I did. I like him. He's a nice boy.

MOTHER: You must've found a lot to talk about. He was in there with you . . .

FATHER: School, mostly – going to school with Alan. He said Alan was top boy at school.

MOTHER: So he was.

FATHER: They were all – jealous of him.

MOTHER: He did very well. He always did very well.

FATHER: Yes, he did.

MOTHER: His teachers always said . . .

FATHER: Oh – and he showed me some photos.

MOTHER: What photos?

FATHER: His children. He's got a fine-looking boy – and a girl.

MOTHER: I wish I'd seen them.

FATHER: The boy's about the age Alan – er – no . . .

MOTHER: Michael.

FATHER: The girl's younger.

MOTHER: A pigeon pair.

FATHER: Yes, that's what I said.

MOTHER: I thought they might stay to supper. Both of them – Alan and Gordon.

FATHER: He showed me a picture of his wife, too. She's very pretty.

MOTHER: Is she local?

FATHER: I didn't know her.

MOTHER: You could have shown him some pictures of Michael and little Sarah.

FATHER: Really, they don't like us at all, do they, Sarah?

MOTHER: Like us? Who?

FATHER: Terry, Alan. They come and see us – you're their mother and I'm – their father.

[MOTHER *rubs* FATHER'S *shoulder with her free hand.*]

MOTHER: They're very lucky.

FATHER: We live here. They come here.

MOTHER: Not very often, they don't.

FATHER: I suppose we should be thankful they come and see us at all.

MOTHER [*indignantly*]: No. No, I won't – be thankful!

[FATHER *presses his palm down, against the window sill.*]

FATHER: He wants me to ask him to stay. He wants me – to beg him to stay.

MOTHER: Oh, no. [MOTHER *steps close behind him and puts her hands on his arms.*] He's asking for help.

FATHER: He thinks I need him. He thinks I'll – miss him so much . . . [FATHER *breaks off abruptly.*] I will. Yes.

MOTHER [*gently*]: He wants you to tell him what he should do.

FATHER: He said . . . [FATHER *breaks away from* MOTHER, *turning to face her.*] Do you know what he said? He said, we didn't talk together. When he was home, when he was a boy – he said . . . [FATHER *slants his head slightly, looking at* MOTHER.] We did, didn't we? We used to sit and talk. I remember. Alan – and me – by the hour. Talk about everything under the sun.

MOTHER: That's right.

FATHER: Why did he say it?

MOTHER: I don't know.

FATHER: Denying . . . [FATHER *leaves the single word hanging in the air.*]

MOTHER: I lit the fire in the front room. Why don't we go

329

down and get a bit warm. It's cold. Don't you think it's cold in here?

FATHER: They had a good childhood.

MOTHER: It's still winter, really. You want it to be summer so much, you forget . . .

FATHER: Why does he have to pretend – now – as if . . . [FATHER *shakes his head.*]

MOTHER: They had a wonderful childhood.

FATHER: Yes.

MOTHER: If every child . . .

FATHER [*abruptly*]: I remember my father! [FATHER *takes his cigarette case out of his pocket.*]

MOTHER: Now, don't have another one. You're smoking too much. Wait till after supper.

FATHER: I remember . . . [FATHER *puts his cigarette case away again.*] They had a wonderful childhood.

MOTHER: Of course they did.

FATHER: D'you remember that picnic? I was only thinking about it today.

MOTHER: What picnic?

FATHER: On the side of a hill, looking down – I can't remember where.

MOTHER: Oh, yes.

FATHER: I can see it so clearly. Terry ran away and fell over. She cut her knee. [FATHER *stops suddenly and looks at* MOTHER, *sharply.*] You do remember?

MOTHER: Certainly, I remember. There was a path. A very narrow path. Yes!

FATHER: That's right.

MOTHER: The three of you left me to carry the food. All by myself.

FATHER: Terry said – I was talking about it to her – asking – did she remember?

[*Silence.*]

She said – 'Did it happen?'

MOTHER: I can remember carrying that basket.

FATHER: She said – 'I thought I made it up.'

MOTHER: I thought I was going to have a heart attack.

FATHER: I thought I made it up.

MOTHER: Naturally it began to rain. D'you remember that?

FATHER: After tea.

MOTHER: We just got to shelter.

FATHER: Running – across the grass – and Alan ...

MOTHER: Shouting with excitement.

FATHER: I was carrying Terry.

MOTHER [*simultaneously*]: I was carrying Terry.

FATHER: She couldn't walk, she said.

MOTHER: As a matter of fact ...

FATHER [*laughing*]: 'My knee hurts.'

MOTHER: ... I think it was you ...

FATHER: Some funny sort of shelter.

MOTHER: ... carrying Terry.

FATHER: It couldn't have been a bus shelter?

MOTHER [*laughing*]: We were a long way from buses!

FATHER: 'I'm too ill to walk,' she said. She had a scratch the size of my finger nail!

MOTHER [*laughing*]: Little madam!

FATHER: I don't even recognize her now.

MOTHER [*quietly*]: No.

FATHER: Perhaps we should go and see her?

MOTHER: If you want to.

FATHER: See this new place she's got?

MOTHER: Yes.

FATHER: I'd like to know where she's living. The sort of place it is.

MOTHER: We can talk about it later.

FATHER: You'll come with me?

MOTHER: If there's time.

FATHER: She wants us to go.

MOTHER: She wants you to go.

FATHER [*abruptly*]: I can't go on my own.

MOTHER: You can. Of course you can.

FATHER: I want to see her.

MOTHER: Yes. I know. Go – and see her.

FATHER: If you won't come with me, how can I go?

MOTHER: It won't – believe me! – it won't make a scrap of difference to Terry, whether I come with you or not.

FATHER: It makes a lot of difference to me.

[*Silence.*]

MOTHER: Tell me when you're thinking of going. I'll see if I can manage ...

FATHER: Sarah, the girl needs you!

MOTHER [*harshly*]: 'The girl' – told me today – precisely – what she needs – wants! – from me. She wants to be left alone. That ... [MOTHER *stops abruptly and takes in a deep, shuddering breath.*]

[*Quietly*] That is what she wants and I am only too happy to oblige her.

FATHER: Something's happening to Terry. I don't know what it is. She wouldn't tell me. She told Alan. Perhaps she told you.

MOTHER: She told me.

FATHER: Whatever it is ...

MOTHER: She's pregnant. It's a fairly normal condition for a woman Terry's age. It's a pity she hasn't got a father for it, of course, but I don't suppose it matters to her, one way or the other.

[*Silence.*]

Yes.

FATHER: Terry.

MOTHER: She's always told you the good things she did. The things she wanted you to know about. Other things – if she told anyone ... [MOTHER *takes a step towards* FATHER.]

[*Hesitantly*] Ted? I'm sorry I didn't mean ...

[*Silence.*]

[*Abruptly*] Ted!

[FATHER *stares blankly across the room, at* MOTHER *and through her, into the past.*]

I'm going downstairs. Are you coming with me, or ... [MOTHER *turns away sharply.*] All right. You stay up here. If you want any supper [*she pulls the door open*] you can come and get it. You can ...

[*She walks out of the bedroom to the top of the stairs and the door swings shut behind her. She stops and leans on the banisters. She rests for a moment and then she turns and walks back to the bedroom door. She starts to push it open, to walk back into the bedroom and then, suddenly, she stops, her head to the door, listening.*

The sound of FATHER *sobbing, quietly, into his hands.*]

CUT TO *the kitchen.*

[*Close shot of a frying pan and two eggs frying, surrounded by three rashers of bacon. Lift to look up into* MOTHER'S *face, staring down at the contents of the frying pan.*

The sound of the front room door opening. MOTHER *lifts the frying pan and turns with it.*]

CUT TO *the front room.*

[MOTHER *puts a plate down in front of* FATHER.]

MOTHER'S VOICE: Eat it. Now I've cooked it for you, at least eat it, before it gets cold.

[*Pull back to include* MOTHER *as she walks round the table and* FATHER, *sitting at the table, with the plate in front of him.*]

FATHER: I wanted to go. [FATHER *picks up the knife and fork.*]

MOTHER: What are you talking about? [MOTHER *sits on the chair facing* FATHER.]

FATHER: Terry's wedding. I would've gone.

[*Silence.*]

MOTHER: I didn't stop you.

FATHER: You wouldn't come with me.

MOTHER: If you'd wanted to go, you would've gone.

FATHER: That's easy to say.

MOTHER: That's true.

FATHER: I wanted to go. [FATHER *starts to eat his supper.*] For Terry – I wanted to do it for her.

MOTHER [*coldly*]: You'd do anything for Terry?

FATHER: Yes. Yes, I would.

MOTHER: Liar.

333

[FATHER *lifts his head sharply and looks across the table at* MOTHER.]

You ruined that girl.

FATHER: Terry. Ruined – Terry?

MOTHER: Letting her think . . . [MOTHER *pulls her lower lip back between her teeth and stops.*]

FATHER: Go on. Say it. Say what you mean.

MOTHER: All her life, you let her think you could do anything. All she had to do was ask.

[*The noise grates in* MOTHER'S *mind.*]

FATHER: Isn't that natural? Only natural?

MOTHER: If it's a lie?

FATHER: All right. I couldn't stop the sun in the sky.

MOTHER: You couldn't stop the girl at school, who used to bully her.

FATHER: At school? The girl . . .

MOTHER: You couldn't stop the man . . . [MOTHER *shakes her head.*] Ten thousand – little things. Things – that matter.

FATHER: Man? What man? What d'you mean?

MOTHER: A man stopped her. She was coming home from school. He . . .

[*The noise rises in pitch scrambling* MOTHER'S *thoughts.*]

. . . exposed . . .

FATHER: She didn't tell me about that.

MOTHER: It was ten years before she told me – and then [*she shrugs wearily*] she was angry – she used it – against me – attacking . . .

FATHER: Nobody can stop – I mean, accidents . . .

MOTHER [*vehemently*]: You – made her think you could. You told her . . .

FATHER: She was only a child.

MOTHER: 'Anything happens – anything you do' – I heard you!

FATHER: Is it wrong – is that what you're saying? Wrong to tell a child . . .

MOTHER: 'Come and talk to me, I'll understand. I'll help you.' How many times did she come to you?

FATHER: When she was a baby ...

MOTHER: When she was a woman!

FATHER: She needed you!

MOTHER: You wouldn't let her – need – me. You made her think – every time – you ... [MOTHER *reaches her hands across the table, palms down against the surface of the wood.*] You didn't tell her about pain, you said – 'Don't worry, baby – Daddy'll take it away.' You didn't tell her about death – you said – 'No one dies.'

[*For the first time, the noise assumes an almost human pitch in its rasping scream.*]

FATHER: What was I supposed to tell her?

MOTHER: 'They go to heaven.'

FATHER: How could I know ...

MOTHER: You didn't tell her about heaven, you sent her to Sunday School. Let them ...

FATHER: I said what my father – said ...

MOTHER: You love her.

FATHER: Yes.

MOTHER: I know you love her.

FATHER: More than – more – I love her.

MOTHER: The things she does – you blame me. She hurts you – and you blame me.

FATHER: I made her.

[*The noise is clearly human now.*]

MOTHER: It isn't my fault. When she hurts you, it isn't my fault.

FATHER [*harshly*]: It isn't mine.

MOTHER: No.

FATHER: Is that what you're saying?

MOTHER: No ... [MOTHER *slams her hands down on the surface of the table.*] ... I'm not – Ted – I sat there – half my life – and let her ...

FATHER: It isn't my fault.

MOTHER: Everything that happened ...

FATHER: You can't blame me.

MOTHER: If I'd talked to her – if I could have talked to her...

[FATHER *pushes his plate away.*]

FATHER: What's the point! [FATHER *stands up.*] There's no point!

MOTHER: She won't come back.

[*The chaos of sound tumbles through her mind.*]

FATHER: You want to blame me.

MOTHER: She's gone.

FATHER: I tried – and tried – with the girl.

MOTHER: You can't have her.

FATHER: I wanted to help her.

MOTHER: You can't – live – with her.

FATHER: I can't expect you to believe – to understand ...

MOTHER: Even in memories, you can't ... [MOTHER *pushes her chair back and stands up, facing* FATHER.] She isn't coming back.

[*The noise stops sharply and* MOTHER'S *mind lurches, released from the tension.*]

FATHER [*quietly*]: She isn't coming back.

MOTHER [*simply*]: Me, Ted. You have to live with me.

FATHER: She told you.

MOTHER: All these years – pretending – now ...

FATHER [*simultaneously*]: And you – live with Alan? Is that the idea? You'd like that. He wouldn't ... [FATHER *stumbles over the words, chokes on them.*]

MOTHER: Alan's going away, too.

FATHER [*mumbling*]: ... hurt you.

MOTHER: We can't – either one of us.

[*Silence.*]

FATHER: I walked into the room and I saw my father hit – my mother – across the face. They were quarrelling. I don't know what it was all about. He hit her and she started to cry. I picked up a knife and pushed it into his stomach, deep into his stomach – low.

[*Silence.*]

No, I didn't. Of course, I didn't. Children don't murder their parents. [FATHER *takes his cigarette case out of his pocket.*] You don't mind if I have a cigarette now, do you?

[MOTHER *shakes her head.*]

She was so frightened of him, she used to hide me away, when he was in the house. He never saw me, unless he sent for me, of course. Twice a year. Once – on my birthday. Once – at Christmas. [FATHER *selects a cigarette from his case, carefully,*]

[*Smiling*] It was a long time ago. Things have changed since then. Changed for the better. I used to see my children almost every day. We used to go – on picnics together. [FATHER *puts the cigarette into his mouth and turns it slightly, wetting it. He puts the case away, carefully.*]

MOTHER: You do blame me.

FATHER: One day I was crying. It was nothing important. I think I must've cut myself – it was something quite trivial. But I was crying. [FATHER *takes his cigarette lighter out of his pocket.*] My mother put her hand over my mouth, so he wouldn't hear me. So he wouldn't be angry. Children shouldn't cry – shouldn't be heard – crying. I almost suffocated. [FATHER *lights his cigarette.*] I loved my father.

MOTHER: You blame me for everything.

[FATHER *drops his lighter back into his pocket.*]

FATHER: I respected him. He was a man you could respect.

MOTHER: I'm sorry.

FATHER: You don't mind if Alan goes to Australia. Why should you? [*Suddenly,* FATHER *shrugs his shoulders, as if feeling cold.*] I think I'll go to bed. There's nothing I want to watch on telly tonight, is there?

[MOTHER *shakes her head.*]

Alan – Ellen – the children – let them go to Australia. Let them stay there – two years – three – five – ten! You're still young. You'll be here when they come back. You'll be alive. [FATHER *walks slowly across the room towards the door.*] I won't. I'll be dead. [*At the door,* FATHER *turns and looks at* MOTHER.] I hate you, d'you know that? Not for anything you've done – just for being younger – for having – more years to live. You will be alive, when I'm dead.

[*Silence.*]

I don't want to die. [FATHER *pulls the door open and turns to walk out into the hall.*]

MOTHER: Ted.

FATHER [*quietly*]: I don't go out any more. You don't know why. You think . . . [FATHER *glances back at her.*]

'He's getting old. Stupid. Can't take things in, any more.' I hate – everyone – yes – almost everyone I see, Sarah. I hate them. They'll be here. They'll be alive – and I'll be dead – in the earth – rotting.

[*Silence.*]

'Till death us do part.' I always thought – if I thought about it – [*violently*] and I thought about it! Everyone will die, before I die. I'll live for ever. I've got to. 'Cause I'm so – frightened – hmm? – of dying. Isn't that silly? An old man like me – why should I want to stay alive? What is there left? What can I do?

MOTHER: I didn't know.

FATHER: You didn't think. I've got nothing left, Sarah – just – living – and you'll still be living – when I'm dead. [FATHER *shrugs and turns away. He walks slowly into the hall.*] Don't stay down here all night. You've had a tiring day.

MOTHER [*automatically*]: I've got a few things to do. I'll potter down here.

[*Silence.*]

CUT TO *the kitchen.*

[*High shot looking down at* MOTHER, *who is standing in the centre of the kitchen, on a carpet of broken china. Every piece of china in every cupboard lies in fragments on the floor, jumbled together with most of the cutlery.*

The sound of the front doorbell ringing.

MOTHER *lifts her head and the last cup falls from her hand. It smashes on the floor.*

Cut to a close-up of MOTHER *as she turns towards the door. Her feet crunch on the crockery and she looks down. Her eyes open wide with surprise seeing all the shattered cups and saucers, plates and serving dishes.*

The sound of the front doorbell ringing.

She picks her way carefully out of the kitchen, steps into the hall and pulls the kitchen door shut behind her. She turns and walks along the hall to the front door.

She opens the door, and MRS HAYTER steps quickly into the hall.]

MRS HAYTER: Are you all right?

MOTHER: All right? Yes. What d'you mean?

MRS HAYTER: I heard – thought I heard – a terrible lot of – I don't know – things – being broken.

MOTHER: Oh? [MOTHER *shuts the door.*]

MRS HAYTER: It went on and on – I thought – well, it seemed . . .

MOTHER: I didn't hear anything.

MRS HAYTER: . . . to come . . . [MRS HAYTER *stops speaking suddenly.*] Didn't you?

MOTHER: No.

MRS HAYTER: I would've sworn it came – I mean, that's why I'm here. I thought . . .

MOTHER: What?

MRS HAYTER: Your house. All the smashing and crashing – I would've sworn . . .

MOTHER: Something on the television? I'm always thinking . . .

MRS HAYTER: No.

[*Silence.*]

MOTHER: I can't think what it was. Come and sit down.

MRS HAYTER [*hesitantly*]: You are – well, yes – I can see . . .

MOTHER: Sorry to disappoint you. [MOTHER *leads the way to the front room.*] It's nothing to do with me.

MRS HAYTER: I wonder what . . .

[MRS HAYTER *follows* MOTHER. MOTHER *opens the door to the front room and glances in apprehensively before entering. The room is undisturbed. She walks in, followed by* MRS HAYTER.]

If I'd stopped to think . . . [MRS HAYTER *laughs.*] I don't know what I thought I was going to find.

MOTHER: I'll make up the fire.

MRS HAYTER: I won't stop. As long as – there's no one –
breaking up the happy home! I'm sort of expecting Dick
any minute.

> [MOTHER *puts some lumps of coal on to the fire and
> generally stirs it up, vigorously.*]

MOTHER: He's not home yet?

MRS HAYTER: I'm expecting him.

MOTHER: Would you like a cup of tea?

> [*Close shot of* MOTHER *as she stares into the fire and
> remembers the kitchen.*]

MRS HAYTER'S VOICE: I don't want to put you to all that
trouble.

> [MOTHER *turns and starts to stand up again.*]

Unless you'd let me ...

MOTHER: Sit down.

MRS HAYTER: Would you?

MOTHER: What's that?

MRS HAYTER: I could put the kettle on?

MOTHER: I won't hear of it. If you want a cup of tea ...

MRS HAYTER: I thought – you look a bit tired ...

MOTHER: Never mind about me. Would you like ...

MRS HAYTER: No. Thanks.

> [*Silence.*]

MOTHER: Sit down. Sit down. You look like the children.
Forever on the move. 'Can't stop. Must rush.' Sometimes
wonder what they do with all the time they save.

MRS HAYTER: How are they? Terry – and Alan.

MOTHER: Much as usual.

MRS HAYTER: I thought Alan ... [MRS HAYTER *pulls
back one of the chairs at the table and sits on it.*]

MOTHER: Come and sit here. By the fire.

MRS HAYTER: Is he worried about something?

MOTHER: Alan? No.

MRS HAYTER: He looked – well, it's a look Dick gets
sometimes, when he's worried.

MOTHER: He's got a new job. Promotion. More money. I
don't know what he's got to worry about. You must be
cold ...

MRS HAYTER: No, I'm fine. Really? He didn't look like a man with a new job.

MOTHER: He has to go to Australia. [MOTHER *turns and looks into the fire. She is perched on a stool at the corner of the fire.*] The new job.

MRS HAYTER: Taking them all with him?

MOTHER: Yes.

MRS HAYTER: First you knew about it?

MOTHER: First he knew about it. Last Friday. Something like.

MRS HAYTER: Telling his father?

MOTHER: What?

MRS HAYTER: When I looked in – he was upstairs talking to his father . . .

MOTHER: He told us over tea.

MRS HAYTER: How soon is it? He's going?

MOTHER: He doesn't know yet. Month – two months.

MRS HAYTER: You'll miss him.

  [MOTHER *half-turns her head and looks at* MRS HAYTER.]

You'll miss the children, too.

MOTHER [*abruptly*]: I asked him – er . . . [MOTHER *stops abruptly.*] Of course, Terry thinks he should take it.

MRS HAYTER: What does Mr Stephens think?

MOTHER: He hasn't . . . [MOTHER *shrugs and looks away.*] He knows – part of him knows – but he hasn't taken it in. Not really.

MRS HAYTER: Sort of a hectic afternoon?

MOTHER: Hmm.

MRS HAYTER: Let me make you a cup of tea. [MRS HAYTER *stands up.*]

MOTHER [*sharply*]: No!

  [*Silence.*]

Thanks all the same.

  [MRS HAYTER *walks across to the fire.*]

MRS HAYTER: I wonder what it was? Silly, I shan't rest until I know.

MOTHER: Sounds at night – quite ordinary sounds – at night . . .

MRS HAYTER: Oh, yes. I know. But this was so clear. So – it was china being smashed – and someone shouting. Plain as plain.

MOTHER: You thought . . .

MRS HAYTER: I was absolutely certain! I came over as fast as I could.

[*The sound of* FATHER *moving across the bedroom, overhead.* MOTHER *glances up at the ceiling.*]

Fearless Jill – to the rescue!

MOTHER: I thought he was in bed.

[MRS HAYTER *glances up at the ceiling.*]

MRS HAYTER: I saw the light was on.

MOTHER: What's the time?

MRS HAYTER: Time? Oh. [MRS HAYTER *looks at her watch.*] Half-past eleven.

MOTHER: In bed – and asleep. Unless he's still looking for that photograph. Oh!

MRS HAYTER: Alan mentioned a photograph . . .

MOTHER: He won't be happy till he's found it.

MRS HAYTER: I remember my father was like that. If he once started looking for something – the house was in a turmoil . . .

MOTHER: My father – if he was still alive . . .

MRS HAYTER: And then – once he'd found it – he couldn't understand what all the fuss was about.

MOTHER: I loved my father.

MRS HAYTER: Girls do, don't they? As a rule?

MOTHER: He was killed in the War. I suppose – really – I hardly knew him. The First War. I was very young and . . .

[*Silence.*]

I suppose I hardly knew him.

MRS HAYTER: You must have been young.

MOTHER: Nine – when he was killed. I remember my mother telling me. Lots of other girls lost their fathers, of course – but – I can remember thinking . . .

[*Silence.*]

I don't care about them. What does it matter? They can

342

all die – just – I always thought he would come back. I never really believed he was dead. People you love don't – die. He went away. He didn't come back. I always thought he would.

[*Silence.*]

[*Harshly*] I was very young!

MRS HAYTER: It must have been a terrible shock. For your mother, too.

MOTHER: Hmm.

MRS HAYTER: Were there any other children?

MOTHER: No.

MRS HAYTER: You don't think – I mean, till someone tells you . . .

MOTHER: I always thought I knew him. I always had this – picture . . .

MRS HAYTER: . . . How lucky – really – how very lucky . . .

MOTHER: He was gentle.

MRS HAYTER: . . . you've been.

MOTHER: What?

MRS HAYTER: I was saying – till someone tells you . . .

MOTHER: I didn't – hear – what you were saying. As if . . .

MRS HAYTER: It wasn't important.

MOTHER: Ted – time and time again – I know he hasn't heard – doesn't listen . . .

MRS HAYTER: It's quite usual, isn't it? He's not a young man . . .

MOTHER [*abruptly*]: I'm not old. I'm not as old as he is – and times . . . [MOTHER *stands up and rests her hands on the mantelpiece.*] . . . blank emptiness – darkness – and silence. I don't hear – I don't know – what . . . [MOTHER *shakes her head.*] Things happen – I know things – I do – things – I don't remember doing them. Suppose . . .

MRS HAYTER: You ought to talk to someone.

MOTHER: You see, I don't know – I don't – can't control . . .

MRS HAYTER: Have you told Alan?

MOTHER: I might do – anything. [MOTHER *looks at* MRS HAYTER.] I might . . .

MRS HAYTER: I think you should tell Alan.

MOTHER: He's going to Australia.

MRS HAYTER: They can't make him. If he says he wants to stay in England . . .

MOTHER: I think he should go.

MRS HAYTER: All right. He loses the job.

MOTHER: I think it's right.

MRS HAYTER: He's clever. He'll get another. If it was Dick . . .

MOTHER: If he's going to get on.

MRS HAYTER: . . . you'd be right to worry.

MOTHER: She wants him to – get on. She wants him . . .

MRS HAYTER: You tell him. He can't go running off to Australia. He's got a duty to you. He belongs here.

MOTHER: I can't stop him.

MRS HAYTER: You talk to him. Tell him about – whatever it is – tell him . . .

MOTHER: I can't – ask . . .

MRS HAYTER: He won't go.

MOTHER: If I could talk – just – explain . . .

MRS HAYTER: Who's going to look after Mr Stephens, with you feeling poorly?

MOTHER: And somebody – understand.

MRS HAYTER: After all, it's not as if Terry's going to be any help to you.

MOTHER: I've always wanted to share . . . [MOTHER *stops speaking abruptly.*] Terry?

MRS HAYTER: Lucky to see her twice in a year. Even then . . .

MOTHER: That doesn't make any difference.

MRS HAYTER: She can't speak a civil word . . .

MOTHER: How many times you see someone doesn't make any difference.

MRS HAYTER: You're always telling me . . .

MOTHER: Terry's got her own life.

MRS HAYTER: I hope my children show a little more sign – when they're grown up – I hope I see them more than once in six months!

MOTHER: Why they come and see you . . .

MRS HAYTER: I wish I had sixpence for every time I've heard you say – 'Terry comes to see us when she wants something.'

MOTHER: Yes. [MOTHER *turns away from* MRS HAYTER *and walks across the room to the window.*] I've said that.

MRS HAYTER: She's a selfish little bitch.

[MOTHER *turns her head and looks at* MRS HAYTER.]

You've said that, too. You're right. She is.

[MRS HAYTER *walks towards* MOTHER, *who backs away along the window.*]

A more selfish girl . . .

MOTHER: Yes.

MRS HAYTER: She wouldn't walk across the road to stop you jumping off a bridge.

MOTHER: Did I say that?

MRS HAYTER: You can't depend on her. If you want help – tell Alan.

MOTHER: If she is – like that – if she is so – selfish . . .

MRS HAYTER: Put it to him. He'd no more dream of leaving you in the lurch – than fly. Talk to him.

MOTHER: I told her – always told her – 'You'll let us down one day.'

MRS HAYTER: Is that a car?

MOTHER: How could she help . . .

MRS HAYTER: Just a minute. [MRS HAYTER *puts a hand on* MOTHER'S *arm and* MOTHER *stops speaking.*]

Yes, I think it is.

MOTHER: What?

MRS HAYTER: It's a car. Dick's car, by the sound of it. Well, now . . . [MRS HAYTER *turns and walks away across the room.*]

MOTHER: You're not going?

MRS HAYTER: One or two things to say to him.

MOTHER: Mrs Hayter!

MRS HAYTER: What sort of time is this to be coming home?

MOTHER: I don't want – er . . .

[MRS HAYTER *turns, halfway across the room.*]

MRS HAYTER: What d'you say?

MOTHER: Are you going?

MRS HAYTER: Yes, love. I'll see you in the morning.

MOTHER: Oh.

MRS HAYTER: There. It's stopped. Leaving it in the road. Won't take the chance of trying to put it away tonight. That shows you.

MOTHER: If you could stay . . .

MRS HAYTER: I'd like to. 'Course, I would. Not tonight. Anyway [*she looks at her watch*] time you were in bed. Mr Stephens'll be wondering what's happened to you.

MOTHER: Oh, no.

MRS HAYTER: I wonder if he's got his key. Forgets it more times . . .

MOTHER: What?

MRS HAYTER: Lucky if he can get it into the lock. I'll find my own way. [MRS HAYTER *walks across to the door. She hesitates in the doorway for a moment.*] Go to bed. You look as if you could do with a rest.

> [*The rasping noise grates into* MOTHER's *mind. She nods her head and then looks at the fire.*]

MOTHER [*mumbling*]: Wait till the fire – er – dies . . .

MRS HAYTER: What d'you say?

MOTHER [*abruptly*]: No point in wasting a perfectly good fire. [MOTHER *walks across to the fire.*]

MRS HAYTER: Suit yourself.

> [*The sound of a car engine being revved violently.*]

He's going to put it away. Er – I'll see you in the morning – if you're feeling better?

> [MRS HAYTER *looks across the room at* MOTHER, *waiting for an answer.* MOTHER *is struggling with the violence of noise in her head and doesn't answer.* MRS HAYTER *shrugs, turns and walks out of the room. Through the noise* MOTHER *hears the front door open and shut. She lifts her head and stares up at the ceiling.*
>
> *The sound of* FATHER *walking across to the window. Distantly, through the foreground noise,* MOTHER *hears him draw back the curtain.*]

346

She brings her head down and looks at the room . . . at the plate, with the remains of FATHER'S supper and the glass of water . . . at the door. She walks to the door and pushes it shut. She turns and leans back. She looks at the facing wall, the mirror above the fireplace, the television set in the corner by the window.

She smiles quietly and walks forward to the sideboard. She crouches down and opens one of the doors. Her mind is silent, peaceful. She takes out a tumbler made of thin glass and straightens up. She turns it over in her hand. She looks at the row of photographs along the mantelpiece – mostly the children. She looks at the walls of the room, one by one.

CUT. The glass lies on the floor, broken in pieces, with slight traces of blood around the jagged edges.

CUT. MOTHER crawls on hands and knees past the fire towards the chair in the television corner.]

CUT TO Terry's bedroom in her basement flat.
[TERRY lies on her side in her bed, with the bedclothes pulled up under her chin. Her eyes are wide open and she is staring blankly at the wall beside the bed.]

CUT TO the front room.
[High shot, looking down into the room, almost indifferently, as MOTHER drags herself in behind the chair in the television corner.]

CUT TO FILM: The front of the house.
Alan, Terry and Father leave the house.
Zoom in to Father. His face explodes into a million little dots, as it is drawn forward into close-up.

CUT TO the front room.
[Looking across the room, through the confusion of table legs and chair legs to the huddled figure, almost hidden by the chair.]

347

CUT TO FATHER'S *face, as he kneels beside* MOTHER'S *body, looking down at it.*

CUT TO *a long shot of the house and the three people frozen on the doorstep, Alan, Father and Terry.*
   Zoom in to a close-up of Alan.

CUT TO *Terry's bedroom in her flat.*
   [*Close-up of* TERRY *lying on her side in her bed.*]

CUT TO *the front room.*
   [*Looking through the confusion of table legs and chair legs. Start a slow zoom in towards the huddled figure.*]

CUT TO *close shot of Alan's hands as he pulls the front door shut and turns the key in the mortice lock.*

CUT TO *the front room.*
   [*Continue the slow zoom in towards the huddled figure.*]

CUT TO FATHER'S *face as he kneels beside* MOTHER'S *body, looking down at it.*

CUT TO *the long shot of the house and the three people frozen on the doorstep, Alan, Father and Terry.*
   Zoom in to a close-up of Terry half hidden by her Father.

CUT TO *the front room.*
   [*Continue the slow zoom in towards the huddled figure.*]

CUT TO *the front of the house.*

CUT TO *the front room.*
   [*Complete the zoom, push through the gloom under the chair and find* MOTHER'S *face, sideways against the floor.*]
MOTHER: Somebody – hold me.
   [*Silence.*]

FADE OUT

348

MORE ABOUT PENGUINS

Penguin Book News, an attractively illustrated magazine which appears every month, contains details of all the new books issued by Penguins as they are published. Every four months it is supplemented by *Penguins in Print*, which is a complete list of all books published by Penguins which are still available. (There are well over two thousand of these.)

A specimen copy of *Penguin Book News* can be sent to you free on request, and you can become a regular subscriber at 3s. for twelve issues (with the complete lists). Just write to Dept EP, Penguin Books Ltd, Harmondsworth, Middlesex, enclosing a cheque or postal order, and your name will be added to the mailing list.

The other volumes of Penguin Modern Playwrights are described on the following pages.

Note: *Penguin Book News* and *Penguins in Print* are not available in the U.S.A. or Canada.

STAIRCASE

Charles Dyer

The first play to be published in the Penguin Modern Playwrights series. Publication coincided with the world premiere of the play by the Royal Shakespeare Company at the Aldwych Theatre, London, directed by Peter Hall and starring Paul Scofield and Patrick Magee. The play has only two characters on stage, one named Charles Dyer, the other Harry Leeds. Charles Dyer's earlier play, *Rattle of a Simple Man*, recently had a successful London run.

FANGHORN

David Pinner

Fanghorn introduces a highly idiosyncratic young English playwright. David Pinner, born in 1940, was awarded an Arts Council Drama Bursary in 1965. His ambition as a dramatist is to reintroduce poetry and all that implies into the theatre. He is concerned with the potential rather than the limitations of humanity. *Fanghorn* is a purple comedy which shows the necessity of trusting and believing other people, even if other people are untrustworthy and unbelievable.

LEE HARVEY OSWALD
A FAR MEAN STREAK OF INDEPENDENCE
BROUGHT ON BY NEGLECK

Michael Hastings

Michael Hastings in his new play *Lee Harvey Oswald: a far mean streak of independence brought on by negleck* is in search of Oswald, the alleged assassin of John F. Kennedy. The action takes place in the courtroom, and in the homes of Oswald, his wife Marina and of his mother. There is no attempt to speculate, but the case is brilliantly followed through its principal areas of doubt.

MACBIRD!

Barbara Garson

'MacBird! is one of the best and most-needed political parodies of the post-war period.' Robert Brustein

'I have nothing to say about the political truth of this play, but I am sure a kind of genius has gone into the writing.' Robert Lowell

'To the artists of the stage, who give us all mankind in all its disguises and so give us ourselves as we truly are, I pay tribute . . .' Lyndon B Johnson 27 March 1966 (a statement for World Theatre Day)

NOT FOR SALE IN THE U.S.A. OR CANADA

THE NIGEL BARTON PLAYS

Dennis Potter

Dennis Potter's award-winning television comedies are almost savage in the irony they extract from British politics. '*Stand Up, Nigel Barton*', the first play, shows his central character contemplating politics as a career – having been a misfit at home, at school and at Oxford. In the second play, *Vote Vote Vote for Nigel Barton*, against a background of intrigue he is a candidate in a rural election, fighting a losing battle in a 'safe' opposition seat. The play reads brilliantly and Dennis Potter has provided a hard-hitting introduction in which he assesses the situation of those writing seriously for television today.